Forced Marriage: A Special Bulletin

Forced Marriage: A Special Bulletin

Clive Heaton QC

Louise McCallum

Razia Jogi

Family Law

Published by Family Law
A publishing imprint of Jordan Publishing Limited
21 St Thomas Street
Bristol BS1 6JS

British Library Cataloguing-in-Publication Data

A catalogue record for this book is available from the British Library.

ISBN 978 1 84661 167 4

Typeset by Letterpart Ltd, Reigate, Surrey

Printed in Great Britain by Antony Rowe Limited

Foreword

In 1999 Alice Mahon, the then MP for Halifax, and I decided that the time had come to go public on our anxieties regarding the ever-growing number of young people we were helping to avoid the consequences of forced marriage. Little did we realise that it would take almost 10 years before measures would come into force to provide a legal redress for such victims.

On 10 February 1999 I was successful in obtaining an adjournment debate, the title of which was 'Women's Human Rights'. Alice and I had decided not to refer openly to forced marriages in the title, such were our worries about telling the story that we knew only too well.

The previous week we had gone along to see Jack Straw in his Commons Office to explain our plan of seeking changes by openly talking about and challenging this problem, which he, given his constituency, also knew well. We told Jack that we hoped it would not cause him too many problems, either as Home Secretary or as a Blackburn MP. He, in the kindest words, said we should not worry about him, but we may have a few difficulties as a result of taking on this, at the time, taboo subject.

Jack was quite right to warn us. We both were given a hard time by our Asian male constituents. The exercise, however, was worthwhile, in that Mike O'Brien, then Minister of State at the Home Office, was amazingly positive in his response to the debate. We were surprised that he was prepared not to dodge the issue as we expected, but agreed to set up a working group and clearly announced the Government meant business

The following are extracts from Mike O Brien's comments, *Hansard* 10 February 1999:

> 'I shall now deal with the issue of forced marriages. I wish to state clearly that forced marriages are wrong. It is distressing to hear of instances of young people entering marriages not with joy and expectation, but with trepidation and fear. That treatment of a woman within a marriage or a relationship is unacceptable. We cannot tolerate compulsion on individuals to marry. The Government have put human rights at the heart of their agenda, and incorporated the European convention in UK law. The United Nations universal declaration on human rights states that "marriage shall be entered into only with the free and full consent of the intending spouses".'

> 'The Government must respond sensitively on those issues, but multicultural sensitivity is no excuse for official silence or moral blindness. We long ago abolished laws that treated women as chattels. We cannot shelter or tolerate bad practices under the guise of sensitivity.'

> 'The Government are aware of the issue of forced marriages. We will not retreat into silence on these matters. The communities involved should not ignore the fate of these girls. The victims may be small in number, but their voice will not be ignored. The vast majority of members of their community condemn their ill treatment, and many of them have spoken out.'

In August 1999 the Working Group on Forced Marriage was set up. As a result of the advice of that Working Group, which included Baroness Pola Uddin and Lord Nazir Ahmed, we eventually saw the setting up of the Forced Marriage Unit (FMU), a joint venture by the Foreign and Commonwealth Office and the Home Office. A hotline was established to give advice to young people who had been, or were about to be, forced to marry someone that they all too often had never met, didn't want to marry and certainly didn't want to sponsor that person for entry clearance as a spouse.

The FMU and the guidelines that eventually went out to police forces, schools and health workers were a great help. However, it took until 2007 and a Private Members Bill introduced in the Lords by the Liberal Democrat Peer Lord Lester, helped by Baroness Cathy Ashton as Leader of the Lords, to ensure its passage through the upper house. I did a fair bit of pushing with ministers in the Commons, including Tony Blair the Prime Minister. Eventually and amazingly the Forced Marriage (Civil Protection) Act 2007 came into force on 25 November 2008.

Almost immediately a woman doctor was saved from a forced marriage by the use of this Act and was returned from Bangladesh. This of course is not the end of the story; the success or otherwise of this measure will depend on getting the information out to practitioners, which is why I willingly accepted the invitation of Louise McCallum, Clive Heaton QC and Razia Jogi to write a foreword for their Special Bulletin on the Act.

The influence of the Act will, of course, also depend on victims and potential victims knowing about it and I understand that previous guidelines to police forces, schools and health workers will now be updated to take into account this new development. Eventually I hope the Forced Marriage (Civil Protection) Act 2007 will become redundant, since I believe a silent majority of our ethnic community citizens already disapprove of parents, families and biraderies[1] forcing young people into marriage. Their views will eventually spread to the cruel minority and this Act will no longer be needed.

Meanwhile, and finally, may I give my heartfelt thanks to Louise, Clive and Razia for publishing this special and much-needed Bulletin.

Ann Cryer MP

---

[1]   Clan or tribal networks. 'Networks' being an extension of systems of allegiance.

Preface

The Forced Marriage (Civil Protection) Act 2007 came into force on 25 November 2008, introducing a new remedy to protect the actual or potential victims of forced marriage: the forced marriage protection order. The legislation inserted a new Part 4A into the existing Family Law Act 1996.

This Bulletin is intended to provide practical guidance to legal practitioners and other front line practitioners concerned in making, and responding to, applications for forced marriage protection orders.

Forced marriage is a complex issue, encompassing sociology, religion, politics and the law. We hope that Chapters 1 and 2 of this Bulletin provide a useful overview of some of the wider dynamics, and the political and social background to the legislation. Chapter 3 provides an overview of existing remedies.

Chapters 4 to 7 are concerned with the provisions of the Forced Marriage (Civil Protection) Act 2007. The legislation is novel from a number of key perspectives. A forced marriage protection order is capable of containing wide-ranging prohibitions and requirements, emulating orders previously only available on application to the Family Division. The orders can be directed to control the behaviour of both named respondents and unnamed persons. Powers of arrest can be attached to the order to enable swift enforcement. Finally, the legislation introduces the concept of the 'Relevant Third Party', who may apply on behalf of a victim without leave of the court.

This Bulletin is published shortly before a significant development relating to this last issue: on 1 November 2009 a local authority will have the status of a 'Relevant Third Party', and may apply for a forced marriage protection order on behalf of a victim without leave of the court. It is hoped that this will further increase the access to justice for victims of forced marriage: a victim may be physically prevented from bringing an application in their own right; they may be subjected to intolerable emotional pressure; they may have been taken out of the jurisdiction; the victim concerned might be a child.

Prior to the introduction of this legislation, a local county court was able to offer only limited assistance to a victim of forced marriage and cases were traditionally heard in the Principal Registry. Forced marriage protection orders may be sought not just in the High Court, but also in specialist forced marriage county courts across the country.

We hope that fellow practitioners across England and Wales will find this Bulletin of assistance.

The law is stated as at 31 August 2009.

Clive Heaton QC
Louise McCallum
Razia Jogi
August 2009

Acknowledgements

We would like to thank all those who have assisted us in the production of this Bulletin. In particular, we would like to thank Ann Cryer MP and her assistant Moira Saunders for the Foreword.

Sarah Russell (joint Head of the Forced Marriage Unit), Jodie Smith (Head of Domestic Violence and International Family Policy Branch, Ministry of Justice), Janice Stevenson (Family Law & Justice Division, Ministry of Justice) and Jane Worsey (Legal Services Commission) have all provided detailed advice which has been invaluable. As ever, although all credit and thanks go to them for their assistance, any errors are of course the authors.

Our thanks go to those who have patiently proofread this Bulletin, in particular Michael Kennedy and Stephanie Kemp.

We are extremely grateful to Greg Woodgate at Jordan Publishing for his help and guidance and to Elisabeth Doyle for dealing with the text and getting it into proper order.

Finally, we would like to thank our loved ones, who have shown remarkable tolerance whilst we have undertaken this task. Clive would like to thank David and Richard, his sons, and Angela. Louise thanks Anesh, her parents, John and Joan, and Savitri. Razia thanks her parents, Ali and Zulekha.

CONTENTS

Chapter 7

Enforcement of Forced Marriage Protection Orders

TABLE OF CASES

References are to paragraph numbers.

TABLE OF STATUTES

References are to paragraph numbers.

TABLE OF STATUTORY INSTRUMENTS

References are to paragraph numbers.

TABLE OF EUROPEAN MATERIAL

References are to paragraph numbers.

CHAPTER 1

FORCED MARRIAGE – AN INTRODUCTION

'Forced marriage is a gross abuse of human rights. It is a form of domestic violence that dehumanises people by denying them their right to choose how to live their lives ... No social or cultural imperative can extenuate and no pretended recourse to religious belief can possibly justify forced marriage.'

Munby J, *Re K, A Local Authority v N*[1]

1.1 This chapter looks at what is meant by the term 'forced marriage' and the key distinction between forced and arranged marriage and considers what is known about the motivations driving forced marriage, its impact and likely prevalence in the United Kingdom.

WHAT IS A FORCED MARRIAGE?

1.2 In 2000 the Working Group on Forced Marriage, established by the Government,[2] cited the words of an anonymous young woman from Leicester:

'A person knows when they are being forced into a marriage against their will – that must be the starting point.'

Whilst simple and obvious this is a sound basis on which practitioners can approach cases of this nature.

1.3 The Working Group sought to clarify the definition of forced marriage at the very outset of its report, acknowledging that forced marriage was an issue often misunderstood and misrepresented:[3]

'From the outset the Working Group has been very clear that it is a marriage conducted without the valid consent of both parties, where duress is a factor. It is a violation of internationally recognised human rights standards and cannot be justified on religious or cultural grounds.'

1.4 The Forced Marriage (Civil Protection) Act 2007 avoids narrow definition of 'forced marriage'. Under the Act a person is forced into marriage if another person (whether their intended spouse or otherwise) forces them to enter into a marriage without their free and full consent.[4] The coercion need not be directly against the victim of the forced marriage and can be against a third party. Force includes coercion by threats or other psychological means.[5]

1.5 This wide definition reflects the nature of forced marriage. It would be oversimplistic to focus on purely physical violence as a means used to force marriage. The dynamics and

---

[1] [2005] EWHC 2956 (Fam), [2007] 1 FLR 399.
[2] The Working Group was established in 1999 further to the debate referred to by Ann Cryer MP in the Foreword.
[3] *A Choice by Right: The Report of the Working Group on Forced Marriage* (Home Office Communications Directorate, June 2000), p 6.
[4] Section 63A(4) of the Family Law Act 1996 (inserted by Forced Marriage (Civil Protection) Act 2007).
[5] Section 63A(5) and (6) of the Family Law Act 1996 (inserted by Forced Marriage (Civil Protection) Act 2007). See Chapter 4 for detailed consideration of definitions within the legislation.

motivations behind forced marriage, and the means employed to secure such a marriage, can be highly complex. The 1999 Working Group observed:[6]

> 'There is a spectrum of behaviours behind the term forced marriage, ranging from emotional pressure, exerted by close family members and the extended family, to the more extreme cases, which can involved threatening behaviour, abduction, imprisonment, physical violence, rape and in some cases murder. People spoke to the group about "loving manipulation" in the majority of cases, where parents genuinely felt that they were acting in their children and family's best interests.'

1.6   Forced marriage is part of a larger picture of abuse of women, men and children in some communities. Forced marriage has been included within definitions of 'honour' crimes, for example, Welchman and Hossain state:[7]

> 'The term crimes of honour encompasses a variety of manifestations of violence against women; including murder termed "honour killings", assault, confinement or imprisonment and *interference with choice in marriage* where the publicly articulated justification is attributed to a social order claimed to require the preservation of a concept of honour vested in male family and or conjugal control over women and specifically women's sexual conduct – actual, suspected or potential' (emphasis added).

'FORCED' IS ALWAYS DIFFERENT FROM 'ARRANGED'

1.7   Forced marriage as opposed to arranged marriage is a key distinction for practitioners in this area of law. Running through court judgments, political commentary and the research on the subject of forced marriage is a common theme: an emphasis upon the distinction between a forced marriage and an arranged marriage.

1.8   The issue of forced marriage is politically and culturally sensitive. At the time of the 1999 Working Group on Forced Marriage, there was a concern that addressing the issue of forced marriage might be seen as interference in religious traditions or cultural norms.[8] Indeed there was concern that victims of forced marriage were often not receiving help because of misplaced cultural sensitivities.

1.9   Throughout the near 10 years of policy development from the establishment of the Working Group to the enactment of the Forced Marriage (Civil Protection) Act 2007, the Government has sought to give reassurance to communities that it is not its intention to denigrate or to interfere with the long-standing and well-respected custom of arranged marriage. The Working Group emphasised that arranged marriage had operated successfully within many communities and countries for a very long time.

1.10   The 1999 Working Group was clear that the distinction between arranged and forced lies in the right to choose. In the tradition of arranged marriages, the families of both spouses take a leading role in arranging the marriage, but the choice whether or not to enter into the proposed marriage arrangement remains with the prospective spouses and can be exercised by them at any time. In forced marriage there is no choice for one or both of the prospective spouses.[9]

1.11   As to the range of undue influence, in *Re SK (An Adult) (Forced Marriage: Appropriate Relief)* Singer J stated:[10]

---

[6]   *A Choice by Right*, n 3 above, at p 11.
[7]   Lynn Welchman and Sara Hossain (eds) *Honour: Crimes, Paradigms and Violence against Women* (Zed Books, 2005).
[8]   *A Choice by Right*, n 3 above, at p 10.
[9]   *A Choice by Right*, n 3 above, at p 10.
[10]   [2006] 1 WLR 81, at [7], [2005] 2 FLR 230, [2005] 3 All ER 421.

'I emphasise, as needs always to be emphasised, that there is a spectrum of forced marriage from physical force or fear of injury or death in their most literal form, through to the undue imposition of emotional pressure which is at the other end of the forced marriage range, and that a grey area then separates unacceptable forced marriage from marriages arranged traditionally which are in no way to be condemned, but rather supported as a conventional concept in many societies. Social expectations can of themselves impose emotional pressure and the grey area to which I have referred is where one may slip into the other: arranged may become forced *but forced is always different from arranged*' (emphasis added).

1.12 This key difference between 'arranged' and 'forced' is again articulated by the Government in paragraph 1 of the Multi-agency Statutory Guidance for dealing with forced marriage, published on 25 November 2008:[11]

'There is a clear distinction between a forced marriage and an arranged marriage. In arranged marriages, the families of both spouses take a leading role in arranging the marriage but the choice whether or not to accept the arrangement remains with the prospective spouses. In forced marriages, one or both spouses do not (or, in the case of some vulnerable adults, cannot) consent to the marriage and duress is involved. Duress can include physical, psychological, financial, sexual and emotional pressure.'

WHO FORCES MARRIAGE?

1.13 Victims are commonly forced to marry by parents and close relatives. However, members of the extended family and even the wider community may become involved in exerting pressure or perhaps assisting in arrangements.

1.14 Mr Justice Munby stated in *NS v MI*:[12]

'The court's protective jurisdiction is also particularly important in this context because, sadly, it is precisely from those who ought to be their natural protectors – parents and close relatives – that all too typically victims of forced marriages need to be protected. The law must always be astute to protect the weak and the helpless, *not least in circumstances where, as often happens in such cases, the very people they need to be protected from are their own relatives*' (emphasis added).

1.15 In 2006 Dr Nazia Khanum OBE undertook research on the issue of forced marriage, using Luton as a case study. The resultant report, published in March 2008, includes an interesting analysis of why support may be given for forced marriage, from beyond the extended family:[13]

'Because of the appeal to traditional values, attempts to force marriage often receive support from a wider circle of relatives, friends and acquaintances within the community. Again, this is not usually because they consciously support the use of force in marriage. Most people can sympathise with parents trying to persuade rebellious children to act in their own best interests and it can be difficult to draw the line between reasonable persuasion and unnecessary force. Moreover, people seldom know what goes on behind closed doors, even among their near relations. They do not see for themselves the beating and bullying. Consequently, it is the victims of forced marriage who tend to be blamed by the community at large rather than the perpetrators.'

---

[11] *The Right to Choose: Multi-agency Statutory Guidance for Dealing with Forced Marriage* (FCO and others, November 2008), reproduced at Appendix D.

[12] [2006] EWHC 1646 (Fam), [2007] 1 FLR 444.

[13] Dr Nazia Khanum OBE *Forced Marriage, Family Cohesion and Community Engagement: National Learning Through a Case Study of Luton* (Equality in Diversity, 2008), at para 17, p 10.

WHY DO FAMILIES FORCE MARRIAGE?

1.16 The Working Group on Forced Marriage was keen to dismiss generalisations and stereotypes, emphasising that no major world faith condones forced marriage and its concern that describing forced marriage as a religious issue feeds prejudice and intolerance of other faiths.[14]

1.17 The motivations for family members to seek to force marriage are complex and wide ranging. The Multi-agency Statutory Guidance summarises some of the key motives identified by professionals working with victims of forced marriage:[15]

'• Controlling unwanted sexuality (including perceived promiscuity, or being lesbian, gay, bisexual or transgender) – particularly the behaviour and sexuality of women
• Controlling unwanted behaviour, for example, alcohol and drug use, wearing make-up or behaving in a "westernised manner"
• Preventing "unsuitable" relationships, e.g. outside the ethnic, cultural, religious or caste group
• Protecting "family honour" (or "izzat")
• Responding to peer group or family pressure
• Attempting to strengthen family links
• Achieving financial gain
• Ensuring land, property and wealth remain within the family
• Protecting perceived cultural ideals
• Protecting perceived religious ideals which are misguided
• Ensuring care for a child or vulnerable adult with special needs when parents or existing carers are unable to fulfil that role
• Assisting claims for UK residence and citizenship
• Long-standing family commitments.'

1.18 Dr Nazia Khanum comments as follows:[16]

'Where force is used in marriage it is generally justified through an appeal to traditional values – the authority and wisdom of parents, children's duty of obedience, customary patterns of marriage within specific ethnic religious, clan, caste or class groupings, the honour of the family, etc. The use of force itself is seldom justified. Forced marriage is universally condemned, even by the perpetrators. Few people openly support force in marriage. When it happens, the perpetrators do not say – or for the most part even believe – that they are forcing their children into an unpleasant situation. They say and usually believe that their greater age, wisdom and experience give them a better understanding of their children's long term welfare than the children themselves, and that their right to assert their authority to give their children a good start in life is sanctioned by custom, religion and common sense. The children's resistance only corroborates their immaturity.'

Dr Khanum later noted that the perpetrators themselves may be caught up in a cycle of family bullying and community pressures from which they feel there is no escape with honour.[17]

WHAT METHODS ARE EMPLOYED?

1.19 A marriage may be forced by means more complex than only physical violence.

1.20 The use of emotional blackmail is commonly reported. A victim might be withdrawn from their education and told by their family that they can only continue that education if they

---

[14] *A Choice by Right*, n 3 above, at p 6.
[15] *The Right to Choose*, n 11 above, at para 36, p 9, reproduced at Appendix D.
[16] *Forced marriage, Family Cohesion and Community Engagement*, n 13 above, at para 13, pp 8–9.
[17] Ibid, at para 14, p 9.

partake in the intended marriage. A victim might be told by their mother that she will kill herself should they not co-operate; or that the father will seek a divorce. A victim may be told that a parent or elderly relative will become seriously ill if they do not co-operate. A victim may be imprisoned within a family home for a period of time and subjected to persistent emotional pressure.

1.21 Families often create a pretext for a trip abroad: it might be said that it is for a family holiday; or to see members of the extended family; or to see a sick relative. Once abroad a victim may be effectively incarcerated through the removal of their passport and airline tickets.[18]

1.22 Threats may be directed at the victim of the intended forced marriage or another person whom they care about. For example, a family may have discovered that the victim is in a relationship with someone of whom the family disapprove; the victim may be threatened that their boyfriend or girlfriend will be harmed if they do not co-operate.

1.23 Physical means may be employed: an intended victim of forced marriage might be drugged to facilitate travel abroad for the purpose of a marriage. They may be trapped within a property pending the date of marriage or travel pursuant to that marriage.[19]

1.24 Ultimately, physical violence may be employed to ensure the victim undergoes the intended ceremony. In the Crown Prosecution Service (CPS) research 'CPS Pilot on Forced Marriage and so called 'honour' crime – findings', it was found that the spread of offences committed in the name of 'honour' and in forced marriage situations was notable, including crimes of kidnap and false imprisonment.[20]

1.25 An intended victim of forced marriage may be simultaneously subject to a wide range of coercive behaviours, including threats of or actual physical violence against themselves or others, emotional blackmail and threats of ostracisation. It is difficult to underestimate the coercive pressure that victims of a prospective forced marriage might experience.

WHO ARE THE VICTIMS AND FAMILIES CONCERNED?

1.26 Most victims of forced marriage are girls and young women between the age of 13 and 30 years. It is important, however, to emphasise that there is no 'typical' victim of forced marriage. Boys and men are also found to be victims of forced marriage. The following information has been collated to highlight some of the patterns which have been identified.

Ethnicity

1.27 In December 2008 the CPS published a report further to a pilot study indicating that the majority of the defendants in the cases identified as 'honour'-related crime or forced marriage were of Asian ethnicity (Pakistani, Bangladeshi or Indian).[21]

---

[18] Page 57 of the report prepared for the Community Liaison Unit (the predecessor to the Forced Marriage Unit) – Yunas Samad and John Eade *Community Perceptions of Forced Marriage* (Foreign and Commonwealth Office, 2002) – noted that such pretexts often resulted from discovery that a victim was in, or might enter into, an 'unacceptable' relationship.

[19] For a description of the experiences of a victim of actual forced marriage and the methods employed by family members to achieve that marriage, see 'Statement from Humayra Abedin' (statement released by lawyers acting on her behalf following her return to the United Kingdom), *The Guardian*, 19 December 2008 (www.guardian.co.uk/world/2008/dec/19/statement-nhs-doctor-abedin-forced-marriage).

[20] *CPS Pilot on Forced Marriage and so called 'honour' crime – Findings* (CPS, December 2008), at p 36.

[21] Ibid, at p 21. Note, however, that only 35 cases were identified and in seven of those no ethnicity was specified.

1.28 The Multi-Agency Statutory Guidance notes that the majority of cases of forced marriage reported to date in the United Kingdom involve South Asian families.[22] Of reportings made to the Forced Marriage Unit (FMU) of possible forced marriage in 2008, 57% of all reportings involved Pakistan, 13% involved Bangladesh and 7% involved India.[23]

1.29 These statistics are, however, partly a reflection of the fact that there is a large, established South Asian population in the United Kingdom. Indeed the FMU reports rising numbers of reportings from non-South Asian minority ethnic communities. It is clear that forced marriage is not solely a South Asian problem, and there have been cases involving families from the Middle East, Europe and Africa.[24] The FMU has been concerned with forced marriage cases concerning families who originate from the United Kingdom itself.[25]

Age of victims

1.30 Most of the cases encountered by the Working Group in 1999–2000 involved young women, from teenagers to people in their early twenties. The Working Group heard of some cases where girls under the age of 16 were married abroad. Many women forced into marriage had not sought help at the time and had only sought assistance much later and after they had endured the relationship for several years.[26]

1.31 In 2005 the FMU reported that the number of minors involved in FMU cases had increased significantly over the preceding couple of years. It was reported that:[27]

> 'It appears that parents are taking their offspring overseas younger. This may be for a variety of reasons but may include the fact that younger children will be less aware of their rights and more vulnerable to being emotionally or physically bullied into marriage.'

1.32 Of all persons actively assisted by the FMU in 2008, 39% concerned children under the age of 18; 14% concerned children under the age of 16.[28] In the same year, within local organisations concerned with forced marriage, 41% of reported cases concerned victims under the age of 18.[29]

Gender of victims

1.33 The 1999 Working Group believed that forced marriage should be seen primarily as an issue of violence against women; however, it recognised that forced marriage did also affect men and considered that further work was needed in this regard.

---

[22] *The Right to Choose*, n 11 above, at para 4, p 4.
[23] Data provided to the authors by the FMU, April 2009. Note that figures available in July 2009 encompassing the period January 2009 to 26 June 2009 indicate that the majority of reportings to the FMU concerned families of Pakistani (70%) and Bangladeshi (11%) origin: Department of Children, Schools and Families, press release, 2 July 2009.
[24] *The Right to Choose*, n 11 above, at para 4 'Part 1 Context, Chapter 1'.
[25] For example, there have been cases concerning members of the travelling community.
[26] *A Choice by Right*, n 3 above, at p 11.
[27] *Forced Marriage. A Wrong Not a Right* (Foreign and Commonwealth Office and Home Office, 2005), at para 2.2.
[28] Data provided to the authors by the FMU, April 2009.
[29] Data contained within A Kazimirski, P Keogh, V Kumari et al *Forced Marriage: Prevalence and Service Response* Research report DCSF-RR128 (Department for Children, Schools and Families, July 2009), para 2.1, p 2. Practitioners are referred to this report for a detailed analysis of data concerning the profile and prevalence of forced marriage. The report was the product of a commission by the DCSF for the National Centre for Social Research to carry out research on the issue of forced marriage in England. The research had a particular focus on UK resident children and young people under 18 years of age. The aim of the research was to improve understanding of the prevalence of forced marriage and examine the way that services were currently responding to cases.

1.34 Of cases reported as possible forced marriage to the FMU in 2008, 85% of the victims were women and 15% men.[30] As stated, these statistics are based on reported cases. In reality there may be a higher proportion of male victims. Many practitioners feel that male victims are less likely to come forward for help, whether because it still carries a greater stigma for men or due to fewer support services being available for male victims.

THE IMPACT OF FORCED MARRIAGE?

1.35 It is difficult to overemphasise the impact of actual or threatened forced marriage on an individual victim. A feeling of isolation is commonly reported; victims are afraid to speak out and may be physically isolated by family members from the wider world. Where the forced marriage takes place, subsequently rape and domestic violence are regrettably common.

1.36 Should the victim take steps to remove themselves from the situation, they face isolation from family and often the wider community. They may be ostracised and face a continuing threat of physical harm from family members who consider them to have impeached the family honour in the eyes of the community.

WHAT IS THE PREVALENCE OF FORCED MARRIAGE?

1.37 The Working Group on Forced Marriage observed in 2000 that 'Forced marriage is a hidden problem'.[31]

1.38 It has been suggested that a number of factors make forced marriage difficult to detect. These include:

- varying perceptions of forced marriage: some considering it a relatively small issue with a high profile; some as a growing problem with inadequate resources;

- affected communities being hard to reach and mistrusting of statutory agencies;

- forced marriage detection not being a strategic priority for local authorities because of competing priorities;

- lack of professional understanding of forced marriage;

- language barrier and lack of access to appropriate interpretation services; and

- lack of reporting sites and local 24-hour contact points for young people with limited freedoms.[32]

1.39 The 1999 Working Group was concerned that there was a lack of reliable data on cases of forced marriage, and that this was a barrier to: recognition of the problem; commitment to tackling it; securing the right skills and resources to take action; and planning for the provision of services.

---

[30] Data provided to the authors by the FMU, April 2009. Note that in 2008 only 4% of forced marriage cases reported to *local* organisations related to male victims, a smaller proportion than those reported by both the FMU and Karma Nirvana (the largest national organisation providing support to victims of forced marriage). Karma Nirvana reported that 43% of cases or inquiries concerned male victims: Kazimirski et al *Forced Marriage: Prevalence and Service Response*, n 29 above, at para 2.1, p 2.

[31] *A Choice by Right*, n 3 above, at p 11.

[32] Kazimirski et al *Forced Marriage: Prevalence and Service Response*, n 29 above, at para 2.3.1, p 3.

1.40 The Community Liaison Unit in the Foreign and Commonwealth Office was set up in October 2000 to deal with the problem of forced marriage abroad. In 2005, the Forced Marriage Unit (a joint Home Office and Foreign and Commonwealth Office unit) was established to lead on policy, raise awareness and handle cases. Since this time the gathering of statistics has markedly improved.

1.41 In 2008 the FMU dealt with just over 1,600 reportings of possible forced marriage. The FMU was actively involved in over 400 cases: over 200 'assistance' cases (cases where the Unit was actively involved in providing assistance, usually overseas) and over 200 'reluctant sponsor' cases (cases where the victim has already been forced into marriage and is being forced to sponsor their spouse's visa to enter the United Kingdom).[33]

1.42 The volume of cases dealt with by the FMU has increased. The Unit has noted a 27% increase in assistance cases since 2007 and a marked increase of 118% in reluctant sponsor cases.[34] However, forced marriage inevitably remains covert, making it difficult to assess the full scale of the problem in the United Kingdom. Experts agree that the number of cases seen by the FMU is likely to be only a small proportion of the whole.

1.43 Cases also come to the attention of the police,[35] social care services and health, education and voluntary organisations.

1.44 In a research report published in July 2009 it was estimated, based on data on the number of forced marriage cases encountered by local organisations and key national organisations, that the national prevalence of *reported* cases of forced marriage in England in 2008 was between 5,000 and 8,000. This estimate did not include a potentially large number of victims who have not come to the attention of agencies or professionals. Of the cases reported to local organisations, 62% related to threats of marriage and 38% related to marriages that had taken place.[36]

1.45 The numbers of criminal prosecutions relating to forced marriages are limited.[37] On 1 July 2007 the CPS implemented a pilot project to identify and monitor forced marriage and so-called 'honour' crimes cases for the first time. The CPS published its findings in a report dated December 2008.[38] The pilot scheme operated in four CPS areas: Lancashire; London;[39] West Midlands and West Yorkshire. The pilot only reported on data relating to cases actually referred by the police to the CPS over a period of 9 months[40] in those aforementioned areas. Thirty-five cases were identified, of which only three concerned forced marriage, the remainder being concerned with 'honour'-related crimes.[41]

---

[33] Data provided to the authors by the FMU, April 2009.

[34] Data provided to the authors by the FMU, April 2009.

[35] By way of example, on 20 June 2008 the Cleveland Police reported that a hotline set up in November 2007 to give advice to people suffering from honour-based violence and forced marriage issues had exceeded all expectations, with more that 210 calls received in 6 months (www.cleveland.police.uk/news_resources/press_releases/080618_HonourBasedViolence.htm). Cambridgeshire Constabulary indicated in June 2008 that the force currently gets around eight 'honour'-based violence calls a month from all over the county (http://lcjb.cjsonline.gov.uk/Cambridgeshire/1881.html).

[36] Kazimirski et al *Forced Marriage: Prevalence and Service Response*, n 29 above, at para 2.1, p 2.

[37] Note, however, that on 21 May 2009 a mother who forced her daughters to marry their cousins in Pakistan was sentenced by HHJ Goldstone QC sitting at the Manchester Crown Court to a 3-year period of imprisonment for criminal offences relating to the forced marriages (child sex offences and an offence of attempting to pervert the course of justice). The girls had been led to believe that they would be travelling to Pakistan for the purposes of a family holiday.

[38] *CPS Pilot on Forced Marriage and so called 'honour' crime – Findings*, n 20 above.

[39] Only four participating boroughs: Newham, Brent, Tower Hamlets and Ealing.

[40] 1 July 2007 to 31 March 2008.

[41] One case was reported in the London area, the other two in West Yorkshire.

1.46 Having regard to the range of information from differing sources it is clear that so-called 'honour' crimes and forced marriage are significantly under-reported.[42] It is likely that with a greater awareness of the help available to potential victims, the number of reported cases of forced marriage will increase.

1.47 It is to be hoped that the Forced Marriage (Civil Protection) Act 2007, in particular the recourse for victims to seek remedies in local courts in areas of the country historically most affected, will increase access to justice.

The 'one chance' rule

1.48 Finally, it is crucial to have at the forefront of one's mind when dealing with an alleged forced marriage that these are high-risk cases. The FMU emphasises the 'one chance' rule. A practitioner working with a victim of forced marriage, and honour-based violence, may have only one chance to speak to a potential victim and consequently they may have only one chance to save a life.

---

[42] The Association of Chief Police Officers has said that up to 17,000 women in Britain are being subjected to 'honour'-related violence, including murder, every year and that official figures on forced marriages are the tip of the iceberg. In 2008 ACPO warned that the number of girls falling victim to forced marriages, kidnappings, sexual assaults, beatings and even murder by relatives intent on upholding the 'honour' of their family is up to 35 times higher than official figures suggest (see www.independent.co.uk/news/uk/home-news/a-question-of-honour-police-say-17000-women-are-victims-every-year-780522.html).

CHAPTER 2

THE DEVELOPMENT OF POLICY

'An Act to make provision for protecting individuals against being forced to enter into marriage without their free and full consent and for protecting individuals who have been forced to enter into marriage without such consent; and for connected purposes.'

Introduction to the Forced Marriage (Civil Protection) Act 2007

2.1 The chapter will consider the political background to the Forced Marriage (Civil Protection) Act 2007 and the decision by the Government to create a new civil remedy whilst discounting the creation of a specific criminal offence.

THE GROWTH OF CONCERN

2.2 By the late 1990s there was growing public awareness of the problems of forced marriage and sometimes associated 'honour' violence, extending on some occasions to so-called 'honour' killings.[1] The following are just some examples of cases which attracted publicity:

- The case of Rifat and Nazia Haq in 1996. Nazia Haq, then 13 years old, had allegedly been forced by her father to marry her 40-year-old cousin soon after she and her family flew to the Punjab. Her sister, Rifat, too said that she was married against her will but was reconciled to the marriage. Mr Mohammed Sawar, then a Glasgow councillor and later Labour MP for Glasgow, flew to Pakistan to help bring the girls back.[2]

- The tragic case of Rukshana Naz brought the issue into sharp focus in 1998. Rukshana was a 19-year-old Asian woman murdered in Derby. She was taken to Pakistan and had an arranged marriage at the age of 15 years (some reports allege it was not only an underage marriage but also forced). She spent two separate periods of time with her husband in Pakistan. In the United Kingdom she had a relationship outside marriage and became pregnant. She refused to terminate the pregnancy. When 7 months pregnant Rukshana was strangled by her elder brother whilst her mother held her feet. On 25 May 1999 her mother and brother were sentenced to life imprisonment at Nottingham Crown Court.[3]

- The case of Zena and Jack Briggs also attracted considerable publicity. They were a dual heritage couple originating from West Yorkshire, Zena being of Pakistani origin, Jack White British. Zena was betrothed at the age of 13 to a cousin in Pakistan. She and Jack fell in love

---

[1] A detailed discussion of 'honour' killings or wider 'honour' violence is outside the scope of this work. Note, however, the recent decision of *Re B-M (Children)*, sub nom *AM v (1) A local Authority (2) Children's Guardian* [2009] EWCA Civ 205, [2009] 2 FLR 20 and comments of Wall LJ: 'My second point is that the time has surely come to re-think the phrase "honour killings". It is one thing to mock the concept of honour – as, for example, Shakespeare does through Flastaff in Henry IV Act V Scene i. It is quite another matter to distort the word "honour" to describe what is, in reality, sordid criminal behaviour' (at [117]). Note the facts of that case, including the 'remorseless pursuit' by the family concerned of the estranged wife of one of their family members, a woman fleeing from domestic violence.

[2] Sandra Barwick 'Girl of 14 tells of "dreadful" forced marriage', *The Telegraph*, 2 April 1996.

[3] See Sarah Hall 'Life for "honour killing" of pregnant teenager by mother and brother', *The Guardian*, 26 May 1999 (www.guardian.co.uk/uk/1999/may/26/sarahhall).

and ran away, resulting in death threats and the instruction by Zena's family of bounty hunters. Ultimately Jack and Zena were given new identities for their own protection. They published a book in relation to their experiences.[4]

2.3   A discussion of the cultural and demographic reasons behind the emerging issue of forced marriage is outside the scope of this book. It is interesting, however, to consider one of the early reported decisions of the High Court in relation to forced marriage. In May 1999 Mr Justice Singer gave judgment in the case of *Re KR (Abduction: Forcible Removal by Parents)*.[5] The case articulated some of the problems and conflicts arising from the differences in expectations of the older generations as to how the younger generation should behave, as against the life choices desired by that younger generation.

2.4   Singer J gave a judgment and authorised its publication, the purpose of which was to raise awareness of issues concerning the difficulties faced by adolescents, particularly young girls, if and when they sought to depart from the traditional norms of their religious, cultural and ethnic group. The judgment commenced with the following striking paragraph:[6]

> 'Child abduction is still child abduction when both parents are the abductors and the child is very nearly an adult. The circumstances of this case may appear to be somewhat extreme and unusual, but in fact they highlight the extent to which courts and other agencies concerned need to be alert to safeguard the individual integrity of children from attack, even from their own parents and family. This case has also highlighted what I am sure is not an isolated instance of the risk which adolescents, and in particular young girls, face if and when they seek to depart from the traditional norms of their religious, cultural or ethnic group. In a wider context, this case also illustrates the sort of pressures to which young persons may be subject, driven by the desire of their parents and family that they should marry in the manner culturally expected of them. Similarly, there may be (though in this case there was no suggestion of it) an element of exploitation of young persons if in effect treated as goods for sale in a trade, whether that trade be the making of marriages or the improvement of immigration or nationality prospects.'

2.5   Singer J stated further:[7]

> 'Sensitivity to these traditional and/or religious influences is however likely, in English courts, usually to give way to the integrity of the individual child or young person concerned. In the courts of this country the voice of the young person will be heard and, in so personal a context as opposition to an arranged or enforced marriage, will prevail. The courts will not permit what is at best the exploitation of an individual and may in the worst case amount to outright trafficking for financial consideration.
>
> What is important is that the sort of problem which this case demonstrates should be brought to fuller public consciousness than presently exists … Clearly there is also a need to attempt to help parents of

---

4   Jack and Zena Briggs, introduced by John McCarthy *Runaways* (Orion, 1999). They have since reportedly separated.
5   [1999] 2 FLR 542. In brief the facts of the case were that KR, a young woman of nearly 17 years of age had left home to live with her elder sister who had, much to the disapproval of their Sikh parents, earlier left home to cohabit with a young man. Despite assertions by the elder sister that KR was at risk of forcible removal and detention by her parents, KR was returned to the care of their father, who had reported her as a missing person and who had complained that the elder sister had kidnapped her. The elder sister, later plaintiff in the wardship proceedings, attempted to enlist assistance from professionals, asserting that her parents would remove KR to India. Unfortunately, KR's parents were informed by police that they were aware of the family's flight details, such that the parents took steps to travel with KR to India via Paris. KR was then taken to a village in the Punjab and left by her parents in the custody of a relative. KR later managed to arrange for a letter to reach her elder sister, pleading for help. Her sister instituted wardship proceedings and steps were put in place ultimately resulting in KR's return to the jurisdiction.
6   [1999] 2 FLR 542, at 542.
7   Ibid, at 548. Singer J urged education authorities and local authorities to consider creating policies and procedures and for local authorities to consider instituting care proceedings.

such children understand that they may face considerable difficulties if they hope on one hand to bring them up in an English educational system and society but at the time to retain every aspect of their own traditions and expectations.'

February 1999 – forced marriage is raised in the House of Commons

2.6 On 10 February 1999 a House of Commons adjournment debate took place on the topic of human rights (women). The debate was sought by, and the opening speech given by, Ann Cryer, Member of Parliament for Keighley and Ilkley, West Yorkshire.

2.7 The debate concerned wider issues of women's human rights, including female genital mutilation, but primarily focused on concerns relating to forced marriage. Many MPs told anecdotal stories of experiences in their own constituencies.[8] In starting the debate Ann Cryer spoke of personal experience in speaking with potential and actual victims of forced marriage in her own constituency.[9]

2.8 Mike O'Brien MP, the then Parliamentary Under-Secretary of State for the Home Department, gave a lengthy final speech in the debate in which he said:[10]

> 'Individuals' human rights should be respected by everyone. All British citizens should have equal rights and responsibilities, and respect for women's rights is central to that. It is incumbent on men and women in every community in this country to respect their partners, sisters, daughters and wives, and support them in making choices that will lead to fulfilling lives. Respect for the choices of others is important.
>
> Different communities have different traditions, and we are proud that Britain is a multiracial society. We are the stronger for it. Our multiracial and diverse society should give due respect to different beliefs and traditions, but not at the price of conflict with the fundamental rights of individuals or the laws of this country.
>
> The Government must respond sensitively on those issues, but multicultural sensitivity is no excuse for official silence or moral blindness. We long ago abolished laws that treated women as chattels. We cannot shelter or tolerate bad practices under the guise of sensitivity …
>
> The Government are aware of the issue of forced marriages. We will not retreat into silence on these matters. The communities involved should not ignore the fate of these girls. The victims may be small in number, but their voice will not be ignored. The vast majority of members of their community condemn their ill treatment, and many of them have spoken out.'

Subsequent to this debate, the Working Group on Forced Marriage was established.

THE WORKING GROUP ON FORCED MARRIAGE (1999–2000)

2.9 In August 1999 Mike O'Brien MP (by this time Minister for Community Relations, Home Office) established the Working Group on Forced Marriage. The terms of reference of the Working Group were to:

- probe the extent of the problem;

---

8   *Hansard* HC Deb, col 256ff (10 February 1999), available at www.publications.parliament.uk/pa/cm199899/ cmhansrd/vo990210/debtext/90210-07.htm#90210-07_spnew4.

9   See *Hansard* HC Deb, col 256ff (10 February 1999) for full transcript of Mrs Cryer MP's speech opening the debate, particularly relating her experience of problems of forced marriage in the West Yorkshire area.

10   See *Hansard* HC Deb, col 256ff (10 February 1999).

- engage all of the relevant service delivery agencies, affected communities and relevant non-governmental organisations on this issue;

- stimulate a public debate to raise awareness of the issue of forced marriage; and

- develop a comprehensive strategy for tackling the issue of forced marriage effectively, including preventative measures.

2.10 The Working Group was chaired by Baroness Uddin of Bethnal Green and Lord Ahmed of Rotherham. The Working Group undertook consultation from August 1999 to April 2000. This included: written submissions and evidence; seminars; visits to women's organisations; and meetings with victims of forced marriage and their families.

2.11 The report of the Working Group on Forced Marriage is entitled *A Choice by Right*.[11] The introduction to the report, inter alia, stated:

> 'We should celebrate our multi-cultural, multi-faith society, but we also need to make clear that difference, diversity and cultural sensitivity are not excuses for moral blindness.
>
> Forced marriage, marriage without freely given consent, is wrong. The government is developing a broad strategy to ensure that all people can live without fear, whether from racist attacks on the street or from domestic violence. This issue must be seen as part of that wider strategy, particularly of the action being taken to tackle violence against women.'

2.12 The Working Group found that, in practice, victims of forced marriage rarely knew about the provisions enabling them to seek a decree of nullity on grounds of duress. Further, it observed that the requirement that a petition of nullity be sought within 3 years often meant that women were unable to rely on these provisions. Women, often married young, could lack the self-confidence to challenge their situation in those first years of marriage. Further, women who married abroad often faced insurmountable difficulties in: financing proceedings; providing instructions; remaining protected during the proceedings; and having a decree of nullity recognised and enforced in the country in which they lived.[12]

2.13 The Working Group noted that the criminal law provides protection from the crimes that can be committed when forcing a person into marriage; it did *not* support the creation of a specific offence of forcing a person to marry. It was considered that decisions whether to prosecute for criminal offences in any given case were for the police and the prosecuting authorities (but perpetrators had to be aware that in forcing someone into a marriage they were likely to commit serious criminal offences).[13]

2.14 The Working Group noted that some service providers were concerned that action to tackle forced marriage might be seen as meddling in religious traditions or cultural norms. Equally, the Group heard from some victims of forced marriage who had sought help but who felt that they had been denied services which would have been available to other women fleeing other forms of violence and abuse.[14]

2.15 The Working Group recommended that further work be undertaken to evaluate mediation in cases of forced marriage, with the aim of ensuring safety of victims. This was a controversial

---

[11] *A Choice by Right: The Report of the Working Group on Forced Marriage* (Home Office Communications Directorate, 2000), available to download at www.fco.gov.uk/resources/en/pdf/a-choice-by-right.
[12] Ibid, at p 7.
[13] Ibid, at p 9.
[14] Ibid, at p 10.

issue. Some women's groups opposed the provision of mediation in any case of actual or threatened forced marriage because of the risk of continuing coercion.[15]

2.16 The Working Group found that the key to preventing forced marriage was challenging and changing people's attitudes. It set out a summary of the guiding principles that should be adopted in developing a response to forced marriage within any organisation or area of service delivery:

- commitment;

- safety and protection;

- sensitivity;

- involving communities;

- multi-agency working;

- monitoring;

- training; and

- promoting awareness of rights and services.[16]

2.17 The Working Group also recommended that there be an investigation of wider issues, including: immigration issues; housing issues; and support for women's organisations. A further concern was access to legal advice. In particular there was concern as to the lack of availability of third parties to intervene to protect a person threatened with forced marriage. Women reported particular problems in the following areas: securing legal aid; giving instructions to lawyers; and providing evidence to courts.[17]

2000–2007

2.18 The Foreign and Commonwealth Office responded to the recommendations in *A Choice by Right* by setting up the Community Liaison Unit in 2000. Through this unit the Office provided consular assistance to British nationals facing forced marriage.

The Forced Marriage Unit

2.19 In January 2005, the Unit developed into a joint Home Office and Foreign and Commonwealth Office Unit known as the Forced Marriage Unit (FMU). The role of the FMU is to provide advice and assistance to the victims of forced marriage, their friends and relatives, and to provide advice to professionals handling such cases. The FMU regularly organises rescues and repatriation of victims in foreign jurisdictions. It has been referred to by the Government as a 'One Stop Shop' for developing government policy on forced marriage, coordinating outreach projects and providing support and information to those at risk.

---

[15] By way of example, the leading women's organisation Southall Black Sisters withdrew its input to the Working Group due to this issue.
[16] *A Choice by Right*, n 11 above, at p 21.
[17] Ibid, at p 24.

2.20 The FMU, together with relevant government departments and agencies, published separate practice guidelines for police officers, health professionals, social workers and education professionals on dealing with cases. These have since been replaced by multi-agency practice guidelines contained within a single document.[18]

Forced Marriage, A Wrong not a Right

2.21 A joint Foreign and Commonwealth Office and Home Office consultation paper, *Forced Marriage, A Wrong Not a Right*, was published in September 2005. The consultation paper sought views as to whether there should be a specific criminal offence of forced marriage. The paper articulated arguments for and against introducing such a specific offence.

2.22 A summary of responses was published on 7 June 2006. Whilst there was no clear majority amongst respondents about whether or not a specific criminal offence should be created, the majority felt that the disadvantages of creating new legislation would outweigh the advantages and potentially drive forced marriage underground by preventing victims from coming forward. The following was recommended:

- increasing the level of training to professionals who work in this field and engaging more with affected communities;

- increasing the work done with statutory agencies in sharing best practice and implementing guidelines; and

- ensuring that existing legislation is fully implemented, including making better use of civil remedies and the family courts.

It was recommended that the possibility of developing new legislation only be considered once there had been delivery in those three areas.[19]

The path towards legislation

2.23 Unusually the Forced Marriage (Civil Protection) Act 2007 started its life as a Private Members' Bill: the Forced Marriage (Civil Protection) Bill (HL) (the 'Lester Bill'). The Lester Bill was introduced into the House of Lords on 16 November 2006 by Lord Lester of Herne Hill QC, a Liberal Democrat peer.[20] Lord Lester held concerns that, whilst the Government had expressed an intention to address the problem of forced marriages, no commitment had been given to introducing legislation. He was anxious that there be an urgent legislative response.[21]

---

[18]   Multi-agency Practice Guidelines: Handling Cases of Forced Marriage (FMU and others, June 2009), available to download at www.fco.gov.uk/resources/en/pdf/3849543/forced-marriage-guidelines-09.pdf.

[18]   Subsequent to the implementation of the Forced Marriage (Civil Protection) Act 2007, the FMU consulted with stakeholders and published a revised set of multi-agency practice guidelines for frontline professionals (such as teachers, police officers, social and health care professionals, housing officers). The aim of such guidance is to help them to work more closely together and better to identify and protect children and adults at risk of forced marriage. The revised guidelines replace the original individual guidelines which were tailored for specific professionals.

[19]   Home Office press release 'A Wrong not a Right: Further measures to Combat Forced Marriage', 7 June 2006, available at http://press.homeoffice.gov.uk/press-releases/combat-forced-marriage.

[20]   Lord Lester is a human rights advocate who has campaigned for a Bill of Rights and for equality legislation in the United Kingdom for some 30 years.

[21]   *Hansard* HL Deb, col 1322 (26 January 2007).

2.24 The Lester Bill in its initial form provided an injunction as the primary remedy. As a secondary remedy the Lester Bill allowed civil proceedings to be brought to obtain financial compensation where an injunction could not provide an effective remedy.

2.25 The terminology of the Lester Bill was substantially different to that ultimately contained in the final legislation. By way of example, the Lester Bill, in addition to prohibiting a person from forcing or attempting to force another person from entering into marriage without their free and full consent, also prohibited a person from practising a deception for the purposes of causing another person to enter into a marriage without their free and full consent. The Lester Bill also provided that it was unlawful to induce or attempt to induce a person to do the same.[22]

2.26 The Lester Bill had its Second Reading in the House of Lords on 26 January 2007. Lord Lester said in his opening speech:[23]

> 'The serious social evil which the Bill seeks to combat and remedy is the forcing of children and young adults to marry against their will. It gives rise to gross abuses of human rights especially affecting children and young people of either sex within our British Asian communities and elsewhere. It involves inhuman and degrading treatment and punishment of those who resist coercion, even their murder. It is a form of domestic violence and there is a direct link between forced marriages and honour killings, as was noted in the important debate on honour killings initiated by my noble friend Lord Russell-Johnston on 15 December 2005.
>
> Forced marriage is, of course, an oxymoron. It is condemned across and within all communities, including their more religious and traditional sections. It is a form of sexual enslavement, sometimes amounting to domestic slavery. Dowry is often paid and women are bought and sold in the process of being forced into a so-called marriage. As we mark the bicentenary of the abolition of the slave trade, we should surely take effective measures to tackle this gross abuse.'

He further stated:[24]

> 'The time is over-ripe for effective measures now to be enacted giving enhanced legal protection. Law is not a panacea, but a well designed law can influence anti-social attitudes and behaviour derived from cultural practices, condemned by all religious faiths but embedded in traditions of community, family honour and identity.'

2.27 During its second reading, the Lester Bill received widespread support from all sides of the House.[25] Universal concern was expressed by peers as to the inequity of forced marriage. Further, there was considerable support for the Lester Bill outside the House which was evidenced at a meeting prior to the reading of the Bill hosted by Lord Lester and the Southall Black Sisters. Several organisations distributed briefings in support of the Lester Bill, including: Liberty; the Children's Rights Alliance for England; and the National Society for the Prevention of Cruelty to Children (NSPCC).

2.28 At the time of the Second Reading the Lester Bill did not, however, have the support of the Government. Baroness Ashton of Upholland, the then Parliamentary Under-Secretary of State, Ministry of Justice, acknowledged the 'huge support' for the Lester Bill but that at that stage she could not commit the Government to the Bill.[26]

---

[22] For consideration of a mock draft of the Bill see www.odysseustrust.org/forcedmarriage/mockredraft/mockredraft.pdf.

[23] *Hansard* HL Deb, col 1319 (26 January 2007).

[24] Ibid, col 1322.

[25] Practitioners are referred to ibid, cols 1319–1367 for full consideration of the lengthy debates.

[26] Ibid, col 1364.

2.29   The Odysseus Trust[27] held a public consultation about various proposals to amend the Lester Bill. A consultation paper was published on 7 February 2007, seeking responses as to how the Lester Bill could be amended and improved.[28] The consultation period ended on 9 March 2007. During the consultation process it was evident that there was widespread support for the Lester Bill.

2.30   In early March 2007 a significant development took place: the then Prime Minister Tony Blair gave an interview indicating his view that the Lester Bill should be supported by the Government:[29]

> '… we listened to what people were saying … I was told we were in the wrong place on this, that the Bill should be supported and that we should think again. I reflected and realised that, if you approach the problem through civil law, it's very sensible. It [forced marriage] is a terrible thing.'

2.31   Thereafter there followed a process whereby the Lester Bill was rewritten; substantial amendments were made with the support of Lord Lester and the Government. Senior members of the judiciary were also consulted. The amendments included the incorporation of the Bill as a new Part 4A of the Family Law Act 1996. New ss 63A and 63B were drafted. The references to deception and inducement were removed. Section 63Q provided for the issuing of statutory guidance. The statutory claim for damages was removed. The Forced Marriage (Civil Protection) Bill ('the Bill') was considered in Grand Committee on 10 May 2007.[30]

2.32   The report stage took place on 13 June 2007. Further amendments were made at this stage. Some of those amendments were of a minor nature; however, at this stage the Bill was amended to include a provision that the terms of the forced marriage protection order could relate to 'other persons who are or may become involved in other respects as well as respondents of any kind'. It was considered that in the circumstances of forced marriage cases, enabling orders to be directed only to named respondents might be too restrictive. This was a significant amendment empowering the courts to direct orders against unnamed persons.

2.33   On 21 June 2007 the third reading of the Bill took place and the Bill was sent to the House of Commons on the same date for its first reading. The second reading took place on 10 July 2007, during which there was universal support for the principle of the Bill.[31] The Public Bill Committee convened on 17 July 2007.

2.34   The Forced Marriage (Civil Protection) Act received Royal assent on 26 July 2007. Thereafter there followed further consultation on the following issues:

- amendments to court rules;

- who should come within the definition of the 'relevant third party';[32] and

- statutory guidance.

2.35   Meanwhile tragic cases continued and the issues of forced marriage and wider 'honour' crimes attracted public attention. The following are examples:

---

[27]   The Odysseus Trust supports the activities of Lord Lester of Herne Hill QC in his work as a member of the House of Lords. The Trust 'seeks to promote good governance in the interests of the governed, based upon plural democratic values, public accountability and the effective protection of human rights and fundamental freedoms. It seeks legislative, political and social reforms to achieve these objectives'. See www.odysseustrust.org/.

[28]   See www.odysseustrust.org/forcedmarriage/consult/consult.pdf for a copy of the consultation paper.

[29]   'Blair U-turn over forced marriages', *The Observer*, 4 March 2007.

[30]   *Hansard* HL Deb, cols GC231–GC284 (10 May 2007).

[31]   There was however some dissent in relation to the issue of whether forced marriage should be criminalised.

[32]   Those third parties who would be permitted to apply for an order without needing the permission of the court.

- In September 2003 Shafilea Ahmed, a 17-year-old Warrington schoolgirl, vanished from her home in Great Sankey after telling friends of her fears of being forced into marriage. Five months later her body was found in the Lake District. That same year she had returned from a trip to Pakistan, during which she had drunk bleach. The coroner said that he saw that self-harm as a 'desperate measure' to avoid a forced marriage. The coroner concluded she had been the victim of a 'vile murder'. To date no one has ever been charged with an offence arising from these circumstances.[33]

- In 2006 Banaz Mahmod was murdered on instructions from her family following their learning of her relationship with a man of whom they disapproved.[34]

- In January 2007 Jasvinder Sanghera's[35] autobiographical story *Shame*[36] was published, recounting her personal experiences of fleeing a forced marriage.

- In July 2007 Bachan Athwal and Sukhdave Athwal were convicted of the murder of Surjit Kaur Athwal. The defendants were the victim's mother-in-law and husband respectively. Surjit Athwal had been murdered in India in 1998 following her husband's family learning of her plans to divorce him.[37]

Home Affairs Select Committee

2.36 The issue of whether forced marriage should be made a specific criminal offence remained live. In May 2008 the Home Affairs Select Committee published the report of its inquiry into domestic violence, including so-called 'honour' killings and forced marriage. Whilst the Committee did not recommend that forced marriage be made a specific criminal offence, it found there to be strong arguments in favour of this. The Committee recommended that if the implementation of the Forced Marriage (Civil Protection) Act 2007 did not have the effect of reducing forced marriage, the Government must reconsider criminalisation. The members considered it imperative that the implementation and effect of the Forced Marriage (Civil Protection) Act 2007 was monitored with 'extreme care'.[38]

25 November 2008 and beyond

2.37 The Forced Marriage (Civil Protection) Act 2007 came into force on 25 November 2008 and received widespread media attention. On the same day the statutory guidance[39] was implemented under s 63Q(1) of the Family Law Act 1996, inserted by the Forced Marriage (Civil Protection) Act 2007.

---

[33] See www.independent.co.uk/news/uk/home-news/a-question-of-honour-police-say-17000-women-are-victims-every-year-780522.html.

[34] James Sturcke 'Father guilty of daughter's "honour' murder"', *The Guardian*, 11 June 2007.

[35] Founder and Director of the Karma Nirvana refuge for Asian women, the largest national organisation providing support to victims of forced marriage; political campaigner on the issue of forced marriage; advocates creation of a specific criminal offence.

[36] Hodder, 2007.

[37] Terri Judd and Jerome Taylor 'Woman ordered honour killing of son's wife', *The Independent*, 27 July 2007 (www.independent.co.uk/news/uk/crime/woman-ordered-honour-killing-of-sons-wife-459194.html).

[38] Select Committee on Home Affairs *Sixth Report* (Home Affairs Committee Publications, May 2008). The Committee recommended that the Government produce an initial progress report one year after implementation of the Act, with fuller reports in subsequent years.

[39] *The Right to Choose: Multi-agency Statutory Guidance for Dealing with Forced Marriage* (FCO and others, November 2008), reproduced at Appendix D. Part 2 contains the statutory guidance.

2.38   As part of a joint approach the Home Office also announced a change to immigration rules, increasing the minimum age for both a spouse entering the United Kingdom and a spouse sponsoring entry to the United Kingdom from 18 years to 21 years.[40]

2.39   One of the first reported cases concerning an application brought under the new legislation attracted considerable press attention. An application was made under the Forced Marriage (Civil Protection) Act 2007 on behalf of a British doctor and Bengali national, Dr Humayra Abedin, who had previously expressed fears that she was to be forced to marry and was believed to be being held captive by family members in Bangladesh. The High Court issued an order on 5 December 2008 under the Act. Subsequently the High Court in Dhaka, Bangladesh also made an order requiring Dr Abedin's parents to release her and allow her to return to the United Kingdom. Regrettably a marriage ceremony did take place in Bangladesh; however, her return to the United Kingdom was secured, whereupon nullity proceedings were issued.[41]

2.40   Prior to the legislation coming into force it was anticipated by the Ministry of Justice that there would be approximately 50 applications for forced marriage protection orders each year. At the date of publication of this Bulletin, and having reviewed the number of applications made thus far, the Ministry of Justice still considers this to be a realistic figure.

2.41   It seems likely that the number of applications will increase during the first few years post implementation following publicity as to the availability of the new legislation, and therefore greater awareness amongst potential victims, and with increased familiarity amongst family practitioners.

---

[40]   See Home Office and UK Border Agency Website for sponsorship rules: www.ukvisas.gov.uk.
[41]   See 'Parents drugged, bound and gagged doctor in forced marriage bid', *The Times*, 19 December 2008 (www.timesonline.co.uk/tol/news/uk/article5370592.ece); 'Statement from Humayra Abedin' (statement released by lawyers acting on her behalf following her return to the United Kingdom), *The Guardian*, 19 December 2008 (www.guardian.co.uk/world/2008/dec/19/statement-nhs-doctor-abedin-forced-marriage).

CHAPTER 3

EXISTING REMEDIES FOR FORCED MARRIAGE

'Forced marriage is intolerable. It is an abomination ... the court must bend all its powers to preventing it happening. The court must not hesitate to use every weapon in its protective arsenal if faced with what is, or appears to be, a case of forced marriage.'

Munby J, *NS v MI*[1]

3.1 This Bulletin focuses on the Forced Marriage (Civil Protection) Act 2007 and the remedy created by that legislation: the forced marriage protection order (FMPO).

3.2 The remit of this Bulletin is not to explore in detail possible alternative remedies under existing legislation or under the inherent jurisdiction. It is, however, crucial that practitioners bear in mind the full range of remedies for victims of actual or threatened forced marriage. These can be used in conjunction with, or as an alternative to, an application for a FMPO.

OTHER PROTECTION AND ASSISTANCE AVAILABLE TO VICTIMS

The Forced Marriage Unit

3.3 Practitioners must always carefully consider, dependent on the facts of each case, whether an application for a FMPO is in fact the best means by which to secure the victim's safety.

3.4 The Forced Marriage Unit (FMU) provides advice not only to victims and concerned persons, but also to legal practitioners. Practitioners should always consider, particularly when it is feared that a victim has already been removed from the jurisdiction, contacting the FMU and seeking practical advice as to the best remedies to seek.[2]

3.5 There is a range of considerations to weigh in the balance before deciding which would be the most advantageous approach in a particular case. There may be legitimate concerns that the seeking of a FMPO would be counterproductive by serving to alert family members in advance of action being taken by the FMU. It may be that the FMU could take urgent steps to remove a victim from a location outside the jurisdiction. On the other hand, a FMPO may be helpful to professionals seeking mirror remedies in a court outside the jurisdiction: whilst not of course binding on another court, it may be persuasive.

---

[1] [2007] 1 FLR 444, at 447.

[2] The FMU runs a public helpline that provides advice and support both to practitioners handling cases of forced marriage and to victims themselves. Telephone number for the FMU: 020 7008 0151 (9am to 5pm Monday–Friday) or e-mail fmu@fco.gov.uk. For out of hours emergency advice, call 020 7008 1500 and ask for the FCO Global Response Centre. Further information can be found by visiting www.fco.gov.uk/forcedmarriage.

Other legal protection and assistance

3.6 The remedies available pursuant to the Forced Marriage (Civil Protection) Act 2007 do not affect any other protection or assistance available to a victim of threatened or actual forced marriage.[3]

3.7 Section 63R(2) of the Family Law Act 1996 provides that the new Part 4A of that Act, inserted by the Forced Marriage (Civil Protection) Act 2007, in particular does not affect:

- the inherent jurisdiction of the High Court;

- any criminal liability;

- any civil remedies under the Protection from Harassment Act 1997;[4]

- any right to an occupation order or a non-molestation order under Part 4 of the Family Law Act 1996;

- any protection or assistance under the Children Act 1989;

- any claim in tort; or

- the law of marriage.

3.8 A short discussion follows below in relation to the primary remedies.

INHERENT JURISDICTION

3.9 Where the victim is a child the High Court can have recourse to the *wardship jurisdiction*. For examples of its use prior to the enactment of the Forced Marriage (Civil Protection) Act 2007, see *Re KR (Abduction: Forcible Removal by Parents)*[5] and *Re B (A Child)*, sub nom *RB v FB v MA*.[6] Also see *Re K; A Local Authority v N and Others*[7] for a discussion by Munby J as to the circumstances in which invocation of the wardship jurisdiction is justified.

3.10 If the victim is a vulnerable adult the court can have recourse to the *adult inherent jurisdiction*.[8]

3.11 Practitioners will also note the assistance which can be obtained from tipstaff orders made in the High Court (eg 'seek and locate' orders backed by a bench warrant ordering any person with knowledge of a child or young person to give information to the Tipstaff, orders requiring surrender of a passport or travel documents to the Tipstaff[9] and the Tipstaff to take a child and deliver a child to a designated place on order of the court). The Tipstaff can execute a port alert,

---

[3] Family Law Act 1996, s 63R, inserted by the Forced Marriage (Civil Protection) Act 2007.

[4] An injunction can be sought. Note also that a claim for damages could potentially be founded on this legislation.

[5] [1999] 2 FLR 542.

[6] [2008] EWHC 1436 (Fam), [2008] 2 FLR 1624 (wardship order made in exceptional circumstances in respect of 15-year-old British and Pakistani national at risk of forced marriage in Pakistan; victim had always lived in Pakistan but her deceased father was British and she had a half-brother in Scotland offering her assistance).

[7] [2005] EWHC 2956 (Fam), [2007] 1 FLR 399, at [90]–[92].

[8] For examples of its use pre enactment of the Forced Marriage (Civil Protection) Act 2007 see *Re SK (an Adult) (Forced Marriage: Appropriate Relief)* (note the useful citation of preamble and order within the judgment); *M v B, A and S (By the Official Solicitor)* [2005] EWHC 1681 (Fam), [2006] 1 FLR 117; *Re SA (Vulnerable Adult with Capacity: Marriage)* [2005] EWHC 2942 (Fam), [2006] 1 FLR 867; and *X City Council v MB* [2006] EWHC 168 (Fam), [2006] 2 FLR 968.

[9] Orders for surrender of foreign passports must be made in the High Court.

potentially an invaluable tool if it is feared that a child or young person is imminently to be taken out of the jurisdiction for the purposes of forced marriage.

3.12 An application can be made for a sequestration order, subject to the offending party having assets within the jurisdiction.

CRIMINAL LIABILITY

3.13 Detailed consideration of *criminal offences* associated with forced marriage is outside the scope of this publication. Offences associated with forced marriage include: conspiracy; threatening behaviour; assault; kidnap; abduction; theft (of passport); threats to kill; imprisonment rape; and, even, murder.[10]

PROTECTION OR ASSISTANCE UNDER THE CHILDREN ACT 1989

3.14 *Police protection orders* can be made under s 46 of the Children Act 1989 (CA 1989) if the police have reasonable grounds to believe that a child is at risk of suffering significant harm, and appropriate steps can be taken to:

(1)   remove the child to suitable accommodation and keep him or her there; or

(2)   take such steps as are reasonable to ensure that the child's removal from any hospital, or other place, in which he or she is then being accommodated is prevented.

3.15   Children should only be taken into police protection in cases of immediate emergency, where the delay of applying for an emergency protection order (see below) would pose significant harm to a child. This method should not be used where a local authority can apply for an emergency protection order and has sufficient time to do so. The maximum duration a child can be taken into police protection is 72 hours.

3.16   Police stationed at airports have successfully used the police protection provision to prevent children from being removed from the United Kingdom for the purposes of forced marriage.

3.17   An application can be made for an emergency protection order (EPO) under CA 1989, s 44. Any person may apply to the court for an EPO to be made with respect to a child. A court must be satisfied that there is reasonable cause to believe that the child is likely to suffer significant harm if the child is not removed to accommodation provided by or on behalf of the applicant; or the child does not remain in the place in which he or she is then being accommodated. An EPO enables the applicant to have parental responsibility for the child, exercised 'as is reasonably required to safeguard or promote the welfare of the child (having regard in particular to the duration of the order)'. The maximum duration for an EPO is 8 days.

3.18   An EPO can also be made when a local authority has been directed to make inquiries by virtue of CA 1989, s 47(1)(b) and those inquiries are being frustrated by access to the child being unreasonably refused to a person authorised to seek access and the applicant has reasonable cause to believe that access to the child is required as a matter of urgency.

---

[10]   Note that police officers have power under s 17(1)(e) of the Police and Criminal Evidence Act 1984 to enter by force if necessary to protect life and limb. Also see police protection orders, discussed later in this chapter.

3.19 An EPO can include an exclusion requirement to ensure the child's safety at home. Like an exclusion requirement to an interim care order (discussed below), the court must be satisfied that another person in the dwelling house is able and willing to give the child care which it would be reasonable to expect a parent to give the child, and consents to the exclusion requirement.

3.20 *Care or supervision orders* may be made under CA 1989, s 31. If a child is at risk of forced marriage, or has already undergone such marriage, it must be incumbent on a local authority to consider issuing proceedings for a care or supervision order in relation to that child, under s 31. In circumstances of actual or threatened forced marriage, a court is likely to find the criterion of s 31 satisfied, namely that the child is suffering, or likely to suffer, significant harm attributable to the care given, or likely to be given, to them not being what it would be reasonable to expect a parent to give.

3.21 On a child being placed in the care of a local authority, that authority would share parental responsibility with the child's parents, with the additional implication (of key importance to many forced marriage cases) that whilst such order is in force, no person may remove the child from the United Kingdom without the authority's consent, being a person with parental responsibility. An exclusion requirement can also be attached to an interim care order, relevant, for example, if a particular individual in a household was considered responsible for attempts to force a marriage. If the risk of forced marriage remains live, a local authority is likely to be also assisted by the wide-ranging terms of a FMPO.

3.22 An application for a *prohibited steps order* (PSO) could be made under CA 1989, s 8. Such an application can be made by parents, guardians, those with a residence order and any other person with the court's permission (CA 1989, s 10(8)). A child concerned may apply for leave to make an application for a s 8 order, but the court may only grant leave if satisfied that that the child has sufficient understanding. The order can provide that a parent shall not act in a specified way in meeting his or her parental responsibility for a child without consent of the court. It should be noted that where there are no court orders in force, those who have parental responsibility have the right to remove a minor from the jurisdiction. A PSO can include a term prohibiting a parent from removing a child from the jurisdiction. This would assist a parent in requesting that the Passport Agency does not issue a passport for the child on the basis that there is a PSO in place, confirming that the child's removal from the jurisdiction is against the courts wishes.[11] However, it is the view of the authors that in few situations would a PSO suffice to address the risks posed in cases of forced marriage. Such an order could be directed only against a parent and would not address wider involvement of other family members or associates.

3.23 An application for a PSO is a precautionary measure to prevent the removal of a child from the jurisdiction, therefore if there is sufficient evidence to substantiate the potential removal of a child from the jurisdiction but insufficient evidence to support the risk of forced marriage, further to the believed trip taking place, then a PSO might provide an appropriate way forward to prevent the child from being removed in the first instance.

3.24 An application can be made for a *specific issue order* (SPO) under CA 1989, s 8. Such an order could require return of the child. As stated above in relation to PSOs, this is highly unlikely to offer sufficient protection in a case of forced marriage. If a child has been removed from the jurisdiction for the purposes of forced marriage, practitioners will be looking to an application to the High Court to invoke its inherent jurisdiction, together with an application for a FMPO.

---

[11]　An order can also be made by the court prohibiting applications for a passport for a child.

LAW OF MARRIAGE

3.25 A decree of *nullity* can be sought under s 12(c) of the Matrimonial Causes Act 1973, on the basis that the marriage is voidable for duress.[12]

FMPO OF COURT'S OWN MOTION WHEN SEIZED OF OTHER FAMILY PROCEEDINGS

3.26 A FMPO can be made by the court of its own motion when other family proceedings are before the court, the court considers that a FMPO should be made to protect a person (a party or otherwise) and a person who would be a respondent to the FMPO is a party to those existing family proceedings.[13] Practitioners are referred to Chapter 4, at **4.29** in respect of matters proceeding in courts not designated to hear FMPO applications.

VENUE OF APPLICATION

3.27 Consideration of venue is also important. The Forced Marriage (Civil Protection) Act 2007 was designed to make access to justice for forced marriage more readily available at relevant local county courts. Practitioners must also consider whether an application for a FMPO should be issued in the county court or the High Court and indeed whether an application for a FMPO suffices alone. Where, for example, the victim is an adult under a disability, or a child, the use of the inherent jurisdiction may also be preferred. Should the victim already be outside the jurisdiction, the persuasive power of a High Court order, and detailed requests to legal and administrative bodies in another jurisdiction, contained within the preamble to such an order, is likely to be helpful.

3.28 In cases of forced marriage concerning child victims feared to be imminently at risk of removal from the jurisdiction, the additional assistance offered by a Tipstaff order may indicate an application in the High Court.[14]

---

[12] See *Hirani v Hirani* (1983) 4 FLR 232, CA; *P v R (Forced Marriage: Annulment: Procedure)* [2003] 1 FLR 661; and *NS v MI* [2007] 1 FLR 444. Also of relevance in this area, a marriage may be voidable under s 12(c) on the basis that one or other party lacks capacity to marry; see, for example, *Re E (An Alleged Patient); Sheffield City Council v E and S* [2004] EWHC 2808 (Fam), [2005] 1 FLR 965; and *X City Council v MB* [2006] EWHC 168 (Fam), [2006] 2 FLR 968.Practitioners interested in this wider area may wish to consult Hutchinson, Hayward and Gupta 'Forced Marriage Nullity Procedure in England and Wales' [2006] IFL 20.

[13] Family Law Act 1996, s 63C(6). See s 63C(7) for assistance as to the definition of 'family proceedings'. By way of example, if the court made an EPO which included an exclusion requirement, the court would also be empowered to make a FMPO provided this was needed to protect a person and a respondent to the EPO would also be a respondent to the FMPO.

[14] Note also the possible correlation with legal remedies concerning child abduction. Note Child Abduction and Custody Act 1985. Note Hague Convention. Note also UK-Pakistan Protocol for Child Abduction (January 2003) [2003] Fam Law 199 which would become relevant in cases of abduction of a child to Pakistan for the purposes of forced marriage. Where a child has been abducted to a non-Convention country then it may be necessary to obtain legal advice as to the law and practice which exists in the country concerned. The Consular Department of the Foreign and Commonwealth Office will, upon request, provide practical advice. In cases of forced marriage, practitioners should first contact the FMU.

CONCLUSION

3.29 In conclusion, whilst the focus of this Bulletin must be on the new legislation specific to forced marriage, it is crucial that practitioners bear in mind the need to consider whether a FMPO offers the best remedy and whether it offers sufficient protection to a victim in isolation to additional applications.

CHAPTER 4

APPLICATIONS FOR FORCED MARRIAGE PROTECTION ORDERS

4.1   This chapter will consider in detail the legal framework for applications under the Forced Marriage (Civil Protection) Act 2007.

THE LEGISLATION CREATES A NEW PART 4A OF THE FAMILY LAW ACT 1996

4.2   The Forced Marriage (Civil Protection) Act 2007 inserts a new Part 4A into the Family Law Act 1996 (FLA 1996), adding new ss 63A–63S. Save as is otherwise stated, any references hereafter are references to sections within Part 4A of FLA 1996.

IN WHAT CIRCUMSTANCES IS AN APPLICATION FOR A FMPO LIKELY TO BE MADE?

4.3   There are four situations in which it is likely that a forced marriage protection order (FMPO) will be sought, namely where:

- there is a threat of forced marriage taking place within the United Kingdom;

- there is a threat of forced marriage taking place outside the jurisdiction, but the person to be protected remains within the jurisdiction at the time of the application;

- the person to be protected is outside the jurisdiction and it is believed that a forced marriage has taken place, or is at risk of taking place; and

- the person to be protected is within the United Kingdom, following a forced marriage having taken place within or outside the jurisdiction.

WHO MAY APPLY FOR A FMPO?

4.4   The application can be made by:

- the victim, defined in the legislation as 'the person who is to be protected by the order'.[1] For the remainder of this Bulletin the victim will be referred to as 'the person to be protected';

- a relevant third party;[2] or

---

[1]   FLA 1996, s 63C(2)(a).
[2]   FLA 1996, s 63C(2)(b).

- any other person with leave of the court.[3]

There is no lower age restriction for applicants applying for a FMPO, enabling both adults and children to make an application.

4.5   The court may make a FMPO on an application by those persons listed above or on its own motion if there are existing family proceedings before the court.[4]

Person to be protected

4.6   The person who is to be protected by the order may of course make an application for a FMPO.

4.7   The legislation, however, allows others to make an application on their behalf (see below). This recognises the reality that in cases of actual or threatened forced marriage, the person to be protected will commonly be unable to bring an application personally. By way of example:

- they may be being prevented from taking steps – they may be imprisoned or held against their will; they may be being watched or monitored by their family; they may not be allowed to receive mail; they may be residing in a tightly knit community where their actions would be reported on to others who may wish to force or coerce them;

- they may be intimidated, frightened or coerced;

- they may be outside the jurisdiction;

- they may suffer from a physical or mental disability; or

- they may have a communication or language difficulty.[5]

4.8   There may also be more subtle situations whereby a person to be protected wishes another person to make the application. The person to be protected may be anxious to distance themselves from the court process. These are highly sensitive cases where individuals may not wish to instigate proceedings against their own family.[6]

4.9   Whilst a child can make an application for a FMPO, it is more likely that a person will make an application on the child's behalf.[7]

A 'relevant third party'

4.10   There is a key distinction between 'relevant third parties' who may apply without leave of the court and other third parties who require leave of the court.

---

[3]   FLA 1996, s 63C(3).

[4]   FLA 1996, s 63C(1)(b), (6). See **4.27–4.29** for consideration of the other conditions which must be fulfilled for the court to make an order of its own motion and the definition of 'family proceedings'.

[5]   Illustrated using some of the examples given by respondents to the Government Consultation on who should be designated as a 'relevant third party'. See *Forced Marriage (Civil Protection) Act 2007 – Relevant Third Party – Summary of Responses* (Ministry of Justice, 13 November 2008), at p 11. Available at www.justice.gov.uk/consultations/docs/forced-marriage-third-party-response.pdf.

[6]   Ibid.

[7]   See Chapter 5 for practical guidance in relation to applications by or on behalf of a child.

4.11 A relevant third party is a person specified, or falling within a description of persons specified, by order of the Lord Chancellor.[8]

4.12 A 'relevant third party' can apply on behalf of the person to be protected without the need to obtain the court's permission to do so.

4.13 There is no requirement of a close connection between the relevant third party and the person to be protected. A relevant third party is able to apply for an order without the consent or knowledge of the person to be protected. Any relevant third party bears a responsibility to make only appropriate applications in these sensitive cases. The Government therefore conducted a consultation as to what need there was for relevant third parties, who should act and what safeguards might be required.[9]

4.14 The response to the consultation was published on 13 November 2008.[10] The Government decided that local authorities should be able to act as relevant third parties for adults and children. The consultation, however, identified the need to ensure that appropriate safeguards were in place, to ensure adequate protection is offered to victims before the relevant third party provisions come into force.

4.15 As of 1 November 2009 a *local authority* is specified as a 'relevant third party' for the purposes of applying for a FMPO under s 63C(2) of the FLA 1996.[11]

4.16 In time, other relevant third parties may be specified. The response to the Government Consultation explained that there would be a pilot scheme to determine whether Independent Domestic Violence Advisers (IDVAs) should also be allowed to act as relevant third parties. This would concern IDVAs who have experience in relation to issues such as forced marriage, are experienced multi-agency workers and work under an accredited scheme. From the Autumn of 2009 it is hoped that specialist IDVAs will be in place in a small number of areas, but based in some of the court areas where FMPO applications can be made. It is intended, at the time of publication of this Bulletin, that guidance will be produced which will look at the role they should play in working with victims before, during and after an application for a FMPO. The effectiveness of this role is to be reviewed and a decision will then be taken as to whether an order is needed also designating IDVAs as relevant third parties, or whether it is sufficient for them to apply for the leave of the court to make such an application, they having worked with the victim prior to the making of the application.

4.17 The Lord Chancellor may specify the Secretary of State as a relevant third party.[12] The Explanatory Notes to the legislation suggest that the Secretary of State would have to be designated a relevant third party to permit the FMU to operate as a relevant third party because the FMU has no legal identity or status of its own.[13] In the relevant third party consultation it was not, however, considered appropriate for the FMU to act in such a capacity.

---

[8] FLA 1996, s 63C(7).

[9] *Forced Marriage (Civil Protection) Act 2007 – Relevant Third Party Consultation Paper* (Ministry of Justice, December 2007). Available at www.justice.gov.uk/publications/cp3107.htm.

[10] See *Forced Marriage (Civil Protection) Act 2007 – Relevant Third Party –Summary of Responses* (Ministry of Justice, 13 November 2008). Available at www.justice.gov.uk/consultations/docs/forced-marriage-third-party-response.pdf.

[11] The Family Law Act 1996 (Forced Marriage) (Relevant Third Party) Order 2009, SI 2009/2023. This Order will come into force on 1 November 2009. In this Order 'local authority' means (a) a county council in England; (b) a metropolitan district council; (c) a non-metropolitan district council for an area for which there is no county council; (d) the council of a county or county borough in Wales; (e) a London borough council; (f) the Common Council of the City of London; (g) the Council of the Isles of Scilly.

[12] FLA 1996, s 63C(8).

[13] Paragraph 29, Explanatory Notes to the legislation.

4.18   Any organisation or a person who is a relevant third party must be capable of taking on the responsibility of making applications on behalf of others. Relevant third parties will have to be able to complete the paperwork, court forms, gather and provide evidence to the court, attend court for any hearings and apply for warrants of arrest. A relevant third party will also be expected to have access to appropriate legal expertise in order to proceed with and then conduct the application even in cases where the application is opposed. In addition to this relevant third parties will have to ensure that procedure is followed so that the correct documentation is served and sufficient evidence is collated to support and prove the case.[14]

4.19   The existing court forms, included within the Appendices, include provision for applications by relevant third parties in anticipation of the order of the Lord Chancellor. However, a revised application form for a FMPO (FL401A) will be in place from 1 November 2009 in consequence of the specification by the Lord Chancellor of local authorities as relevant third parties.[15]

4.20   In the absence of specification as a relevant third party it will nevertheless be possible for an organisation to apply on behalf of a victim, but such an applicant will need the court's permission.

Applications with leave of the court

4.21   FLA 1996 allows any person to apply for a FMPO, on behalf of the person to be protected, subject to the permission of the court.[16]

4.22   Likely applicants may include friends, boyfriends, girlfriends, siblings and other relatives of the person to be protected, in addition to the police and other voluntary organisations.

4.23   When determining whether a third party should be granted leave the court must give consideration to the criteria set out in the Act:[17]

> 'In deciding whether to grant leave, the court must have regard to all the circumstances including—
>
> (a)   the applicant's connection with the person to be protected;
> (b)   the applicant's knowledge of the circumstances of the person to be protected; and
> (c)   the wishes and feelings of the person to be protected so far as they are reasonably ascertainable and so far as the court considers it appropriate, in the light of the person's age and understanding, to have regard to them.'

4.24   The above criteria are intended to ensure that any application made is a responsible one. Any application for a FMPO, whether or not the order is ultimately made, is likely to have long-lasting repercussions upon the relationship between the person to be protected and other family members. Before allowing another person to make the substantive application, of which the person to be protected may have no knowledge, the court will wish to be satisfied that the applicant is acting in the person to be protected's best interests.

4.25   If the court grants the relevant permission for a person to apply on behalf of the person to be protected then that person becomes the applicant for the purposes of the proceedings.

---

[14]   *Forced Marriage (Civil Protection) Act 2007 – Relevant Third Party Consultation Paper*, n 9 above.
[15]   Family Proceedings (Amendment) (No 3) Rules 2009, SI 2009/2028, r 19. Rule 19, in force on 1 November 2009, replaces the existing Form FL401A (substantive form for an application for a FMPO) within the Schedules to the Family Proceedings Rules 1991, SI 1991/1247. See Chapter 5 for discussion as to the procedure for applications.
[16]   FLA 1996, s 63C(3).
[17]   FLA 1996, s 63C(4)(a)–(c).

4.26 If the court refuses permission to apply then the person cannot proceed with the application on behalf of the person to be protected, unless the circumstances change so that a fresh application can be made or the decision is reversed on appeal.

Orders of the court's own motion

4.27 The court may make a FMPO of its own motion in the following circumstances:

(1) when any other family proceedings are before the court;

(2) the court considers that a FMPO should be made to protect a person, whether or not they are a party to those existing family proceedings; and

(3) a person who would be a respondent to proceedings for a FMPO is a party to the existing proceedings.[18]

4.28 By FLA 1996, s 63C(7), 'family proceedings' has the same meaning as in Part 4 of the Family Law Act 1996[19] but also includes:

• proceedings under the inherent jurisdiction of the High Court in relation to adults;

• proceedings in which the court has made an emergency protection order under the Children Act 1989, s 44, which includes an exclusion requirement; and

• proceedings in which the court has made an order under the Children Act 1989, s 50 relating to the recovery of abducted children.

4.29 Only those courts that are designated to deal with forced marriage protection applications will be able to make orders of their own motion in existing family proceedings.[20] If those existing family proceedings are ongoing in a non-designated court a solution might be to transfer those family proceedings sideways to one of the designated courts or for the case to be transferred to the High Court.

IN WHAT CIRCUMSTANCES CAN A FMPO BE MADE?

4.30 A FMPO may be made to protect a person from being forced into marriage, or from any attempt to force them into marriage, or to protect a person who has already been forced into marriage.[21] An order may therefore be anticipatory, intended to prevent such a marriage taking place, or protective following an actual forced marriage.

---

[18] FLA 1996, s 63C (6)(a)–(c).
[19] FLA 1996, s 63(1) and (2) defines family proceedings as any proceedings under the inherent jurisdiction of the High Court in relation to children, or under FLA 1996, Part 2; FLA 1996, Part 4; the Matrimonial Causes Act 1973; the Adoption Act 1976; the Domestic Proceedings and Magistrates' Courts Act 1978; the Matrimonial and Family Proceedings Act 1984; the Children Act 1989, Parts 1, 2 and 4; and the Human Fertilisation and Embryology Act 1990, s 30.
[20] See **4.72** for a list of the designated courts.
[21] FLA 1996, s 63A(1).

What is a 'marriage' under the legislation?

4.31 Marriage is defined as 'any religious or civil ceremony of marriage (whether or not legally binding)'.[22] Thus the marriage need not be a marriage recognised in law. The marriage concerned might, for example, be a religious ceremony to be conducted in this jurisdiction in the absence of a civil ceremony.

4.32 The 'marriage' concerned can be within or outside this jurisdiction.

What is a forced marriage?

4.33 The legislation defines that a person ('A') is forced into marriage if another person ('B') forces A to enter into a marriage (whether with B or another person) without A's free and full consent.[23]

What is 'force'?

4.34 Under the legislation, force includes coerce by threats or other psychological means.[24] This reflects a feature of forced marriage, namely that the coercion may not be actual or threatened violence but more subtle psychological pressure to induce a person to marry.[25] By way of example, a person to be protected may be told that they will no longer be allowed to partake in education should they not proceed with the marriage; they may be told (in circumstances where they have already been removed from the jurisdiction) that they will not be allowed to return to the United Kingdom unless the marriage proceeds; they might be told by their mother that she is at risk of divorce from their father should the marriage not proceed. These are but a few examples of the sort of psychological pressure which might be applied.

Where might the relevant force emanate from?

4.35 The force need not emanate from the intended or actual spouse of the person to be protected, but could be from another person or persons.[26] This reflects the reality of forced marriage, namely that the person to be protected may be experiencing force from members of their own family. Indeed in cases where a person is removed from the jurisdiction to marry, or threatened with such removal, they may never have met their intended spouse.

To whom need the force be directed?

4.36 It does not matter whether the conduct of person 'B' which forces the person to be protected (person 'A') to enter into a marriage is directed against A, B or another person.[27] The wide ambit of this subsection is designed to encompass the many varied and complex circumstances in which a person may be forced to marry. The conduct which forces a person into marriage does not have to be directed against the person to be protected. The force can be directed against the perpetrator themselves ('B') or another person entirely. The Explanatory

---

[22] FLA 1996, s 63S.
[23] FLA 1996, s 63A(4).
[24] FLA 1996, s 63A(6).
[25] See Chapter 1 at **1.19**ff for further discussion.
[26] FLA 1996, s 63A(4).
[27] FLA 1996, s 63A(5).

Notes to the legislation give the example of this covering circumstances in which the perpetrator threatened to commit suicide if the person did not submit to the marriage.[28]

4.37 The wording of this subsection would also encompass a situation whereby physical harm was threatened against another person were the marriage not to proceed, for example, a boyfriend or girlfriend of the person to be protected.

What is free and full consent?

4.38 The outcome of the force must be that the person has married, or would marry if the attempt were completed, 'without [their] free and full consent'.[29] The Act does not define 'free and full consent'. The inclusion of this term reflects the wording of Art 16(2) of the Universal Declaration of Human Rights:

> 'Marriage shall be entered into only with the *free and full consent* of the intending spouses.'

4.39 The person to be protected's consent must be given freely and fully and must not to any degree be undermined by coercion, whether physical or psychological.

RANGE OF ORDERS AVAILABLE UNDER A FMPO?

4.40 The range of orders available under Part 4A of the FLA 1996 is wide. This ensures that the court has available to it sufficient flexibility to cover the extensive and varied circumstances in which a marriage might be 'forced'.

4.41 A FMPO may contain:

- such prohibitions, restrictions or requirements; and

- such other terms as the court considers appropriate for the purposes of the order.[30]

Some examples are given within this chapter and readers are invited to consider the sample orders given at Appendix F.

4.42 The provisions of the order can contain measures considered appropriate to control behaviour in order to prevent a person being forced into marriage and/or measures to protect a person who has already been forced into a marriage.[31]

4.43 An important feature of the legislation is that the terms of any orders made can regulate or control conduct inside and/or *outside* England and Wales.[32] Thus the court can by way of example require that the person to be protected be taken to, and allowed to be seen and interviewed by a member of the British High Commission or Embassy overseas.

---

[28] Explanatory Notes, para 21.
[29] FLA 1996, s 63A(4).
[30] FLA 1996, s 63B(1).
[31] FLA 1996, s 63A(1).
[32] FLA 1996, s 63B(2)(a).

4.44 Whilst a FMPO can seek to control conduct outside of England and Wales, it is not of course binding on another jurisdiction. A FMPO is likely to be persuasive upon authorities in another jurisdiction.[33]

4.45 The orders may 'prohibit'[34] or 'restrict'[35] certain activity. By way of example the court can order that:

- X be forbidden from removing Y from the jurisdiction;

- X be forbidden from applying for a passport or other travel documents for Y;

- X be forbidden from entering into any arrangements in relation to the engagement or marriage whether by civil or religious ceremony of Y whether inside or outside the jurisdiction of England and Wales;

- X be forbidden whether by him or herself or by instructing or encouraging another person within this jurisdiction or elsewhere from threatening, intimidating or harassing Y; or

- X be forbidden from using or threatening force against Y, whether directly or indirectly.

4.46 The order may impose a 'requirement'[36] upon a person to do something, for example:

- X hand in the passport of Y to the court by a certain time on a specified date;

- X disclose to the court or to a particular person the whereabouts of Y;

- Y to be returned to the jurisdiction of England and Wales; or

- X to allow Y to be interviewed by a member of the British High Commission in a specified country.

4.47 The court is given a wide discretion to include 'such other terms'[37] as may be appropriate.

TO WHOM MAY A FMPO BE DIRECTED?

4.48 The terms of such orders may relate to:

- respondents who are, or may become, involved in other respects as well as (or instead of) respondents who force or attempt to force, or may force or attempt to force, a person to enter into a marriage;[38] and

- other persons who are, or may become, involved in other respects as well as respondents of any kind.[39]

---

[33] For example in the case of Humeyra Abedin, the existence of a FMPO was persuasive upon authorities in Bangladesh.
[34] FLA 1996, s 63B(1)(a).
[35] Ibid.
[36] Ibid.
[37] FLA 1996, s 63B(1)(b).
[38] FLA 1996, s 63B(2)(b).
[39] FLA 1996, s 63B(2)(c).

Respondents who force, or attempt to force, a person into marriage, or who may do so

4.49 The terms of the order can be directed to respondents who force or attempt to force a person into marriage, or may do so. This targets respondents, most commonly relatives, who are directly concerned in the coercion designed to bring about the marriage. This would include the more obvious category of respondent, such as the father who threatens his daughter with harm should she not enter into the marriage.

Respondents who are, or who may become, involved 'in other respects'

4.50 More unusually, the terms of the order may relate to respondents who may be or may become involved in 'other respects'.

4.51 The legislation provides examples of involvement in 'other respects':

- aiding, abetting, counselling, procuring, encouraging, or assisting another person to force, or to attempt to force, a person to enter into a marriage;[40] or

- conspiring to force, or to attempt to force, a person to enter into a marriage.[41]

4.52 The effect of this subsection is that a FMPO can be directed against a wide range of respondents. The order can be directed to respondents who are aiding or abetting (et al) the primary perpetrator(s). This could, by way of example, include:

- the brother who assists in confining his sister within the family home;

- the family member who is to purchase the travel tickets; and/or

- the family member or member of the community who is making the wedding arrangements abroad.

4.53 Further, the inclusion of respondents who are *conspiring* to force the marriage enables the order to be directed at a number of respondents where a single perpetrator of a particular act or series of acts is not readily identifiable. This would encompass the common situation where a number of family members are acting together in order to force a person into marriage.

'Other persons' who are or may become involved in other respects

4.54 A highly significant, and unusual, feature of the forced marriage legislation is the ability to direct an order not just to respondents, but also to 'other persons' who are or may become involved in 'other respects'.[42] This means that the order(s) may be directed against unnamed persons.

---

[40]   FLA 1996, s 63B(3)(a).
[41]   FLA 1996, s 63B(3)(b).
[42]   For the definition of 'other respects' see again the discussion at **4.51**. Section 63B(3) provides for examples of involvement in 'other respects'.

4.55 It is helpful to consider the comments of Bridget Prentice, Parliamentary Under-Secretary of State at the Ministry of Justice, on this issue, made during the third reading of the Bill in the House of Commons on 23 July 2007:[43]

> 'In Committee, the issue of the Bill's application to people other than named respondents was raised. New section 63B(2)(c) of the Family Law Act 1996, which is inserted by the Bill, provides that a forced marriage protection order can be directed at unnamed persons who are, or may become, involved "in other respects", such as members of the family. However, an order can be so directed only if the court believes it appropriate to make such an order for the purposes of protecting the individual concerned. *That provision is necessary to reflect the real nature of forced marriage, which can come about following the involvement of a large group of people, possibly a whole family or even a community group. In many cases it simply is not feasible for the applicant to name all the potential respondents, especially if there is an urgency to the application, and it has been brought by a third party. The provision allows the court to make orders against people who appear to be involved in coercion, even if they cannot be readily identified.*
>
> It was suggested in Committee that those categories of people should be captured by the order only if they knowingly acted in a way that might force a person into marriage, but that would be extremely difficult for any applicant to prove, and it might in effect make the provision unworkable. For the most part, being involved "in other respects" will generally require some kind of knowledge of what the lead respondent is doing; for example, counselling, encouraging or conspiring all presuppose some sort of knowledge. *However, orders to protect the victim could still in theory be addressed to people who are not morally culpable in any way. An order could be addressed to any person prohibiting them from aiding, abetting or encouraging the victim to marry. To use the example mentioned in Committee, that would include the priest, if the court thought that the circumstances justified it.*
>
> However, it is necessary to distinguish between making an order and enforcing it. The Bill does not change the current law of contempt. Before a person can be committed for contempt, the court must be satisfied that that person had sufficient knowledge of the order to know that his actions would frustrate its intention. To continue with the example of the priest, the order could not be enforced against him unless he had knowledge of the order, and intended to interfere with the administration of justice by frustrating it' (emphasis added).

4.56 The ability to direct an order(s) towards unnamed persons ensures that protection is given in circumstances where it is not possible to readily identify all the possible perpetrators.

4.57 In circumstances where the applicant is not the person to be protected, they may have limited knowledge as to the family circumstances of the person to be protected or who within the family or wider community is instrumental in forcing the marriage. An order could, for example, be directed against all members of Y's family, or all persons residing at a particular address. A blanket order can be made providing that *no* person shall facilitate any arrangements in relation to the civil or religious ceremony of the person to be protected.

4.58 Whilst the terms of the order may be directed at other persons, not just named respondents, this raises questions in relation to enforcement of such an order should it be alleged that the 'other person' is in breach of it. This is an issue identified in the final paragraph of the extract of Bridget Prentice's remarks, set out at **4.55** (the issue is considered further in Chapter 7 concerning enforcement).

4.59 The issue of 'other persons' also raises potential pitfalls in relation to the imposition of a power of arrest to provision(s) of an order directed at unnamed persons (see commentary on powers of arrest at **4.100**ff).

---

43   *Hansard* HC Deb, col 642 (23 July 2007). Available at www.publications.parliament.uk/pa/cm200607/cmhansrd/cm070723/debtext/70723-0016.htm.

WHAT ISSUES MUST A COURT CONSIDER WHEN DECIDING WHETHER TO MAKE AN ORDER?

4.60 In deciding whether to make an order, and the nature of the order, the court must have regard to all the circumstances, including the need to secure the health, safety and well-being of the person to be protected.[44]

Wishes and feelings

4.61 In ascertaining the person's well-being, particular regard must be given to the wishes and feelings of the person to be protected (so far as they are reasonably ascertainable).[45] The proviso as to whether they are 'ascertainable' reflects the very common scenario in forced marriage cases, that it is not possible to ascertain the victim's wishes and feelings directly as he or she may be imprisoned within their own home, or may no longer be in the jurisdiction or may otherwise not be in a position to express their wishes and feelings freely.

4.62 The court is required to have regard to the wishes and feelings of the person to be protected so far as the court considers appropriate in the light of that person's 'age and understanding'.[46]

4.63 Clearly, in circumstances where the person to be protected is a minor, and that person contends that they wish to co-operate with the marriage arrangements, their wishes and feelings might be given little weight, both in view of the age and understanding of the protected person and the need for the court to safeguard their health and well-being.

4.64 Historically, a number of cases concerning forced marriage have involved adults who have a learning disability. The court may extend an invitation to the Official Solicitor to carry out investigations to ascertain the level of understanding of the protected person and their wishes and feelings.[47]

4.65 If the person to be protected is outside the jurisdiction, the court can direct that the person be taken to the Embassy or High Commission, in the relevant country, for the purpose of establishing his or her true wishes and feelings.[48]

4.66 It is likely that a court will be cautious in exercising its powers in circumstances where the wishes and feelings of the person to be protected are unclear or have not been ascertainable. Against this, however, a court's concern will be heightened should the person to be protected be outside the jurisdiction, and therefore at increased risk of forced marriage. In those circumstances the absence of cogent information as to wishes and feelings may have an impact on the duration of the order. The court may make short-term orders, the purpose of which is to protect the person pending clarification of their wishes and feelings.

---

[44] FLA 1996, s 63A(2).
[45] FLA 1996, s 63A(3).
[46] Ibid.
[47] *Re SA (Vulnerable adult with capacity: marriage)* [2005] EWHC 2942 (Fam), [2006] 1 FLR 867.
[48] Note that United Kingdom Embassies and High Commissions can only offer consular assistance to British nationals plus European Union or, in certain cases, Commonwealth nationals whose country does not have a local embassy or consulate in the country concerned. Assistance overseas cannot be provided to foreign nationals irrespective of their connection to the United Kingdom or to European Union or Commonwealth nationals in the country of their nationality.

THE APPLICATION

4.67　An application for a FMPO may be freestanding or within existing family proceedings.[49]

4.68　An application may be made on or without notice.

4.69　Readers are referred to Chapter 5 for the procedure for applications for FMPOs and Appendix G for funding information.

WHERE CAN AN APPLICATION BE MADE?

4.70　The legislation enables applicants to apply for FMPOs at a number of county courts across the country, in addition to the High Court. Prior to the commencement of the Forced Marriage (Civil Protection) Act 2007, applications by or on behalf of victims of forced marriage were commonly heard in the High Court, within wardship or under the inherent jurisdiction. Furthermore, applications were primarily heard in the Principal District Registry. It is hoped that easier access to local courts, and an increase in practitioners across the country with expertise in this area, will encourage more persons to seek protection.

4.71　The FMU has identified areas where cases most frequently arise and therefore a limited number of courts have been selected to deal with applications, due to their proximity to the communities identified as most likely to be affected by forced marriage.

4.72　The courts where applications can be issued, at the time of publication of this Special Bulletin, are:[50]

- High Court;

- Principal Registry of the Family Division;

- Birmingham Family Courts;

- Blackburn County Court;

- Bradford County Court;

- Bristol County Court;

- Cardiff Civil Justice Centre;

- Derby County Court;

- Leeds Combined Court;

- Leicester County Court;

- Luton County Court;

- Manchester County Court;

---

[49]　FLA 1996, s 63C(5). See s 63C(7) together with FLA 1996, s 63(1) and (2) for definition of 'family proceedings'. Previously discussed at **4.28**.

[50]　These courts were designated in the Allocation and Transfer of Proceedings Order 2008, SI 2008/2836, art 2.

- Middlesbrough County Court;

- Romford County Court; and

- Willesden County Court.

4.73 As well as High Court judges, district judges or county court judges who preside over public or private law family cases will be able to hear applications in the specified courts.

4.74 It is anticipated by the Government that following implementation of the Forced Marriage (Civil Protection) Act 2007 the initial volume of cases will be relatively low. Hence the small number of courts able to hear applications under the Act during the initial stage.

4.75 There is provision within the Act, yet to be taken up, to extend jurisdiction to the magistrates' courts.[51]

APPLICATIONS FOR EX PARTE ORDERS

4.76 A FMPO can be made in circumstances were the respondent has not been given notice of the proceedings.[52]

In what circumstances will an ex parte order be made?

4.77 The court may make a FMPO without notice where it considers it is 'just and convenient to do so'.[53]

4.78 Having given the courts a wide discretion to make without notice FMPOs, the Act sets out the criteria, modelled on s 45 of FLA 1996, which should be considered when deciding whether to make a FMPO without notice:[54]

> '... the court must have regard to all the circumstances including—
>
> (a) any risk of significant harm to the person to be protected or another person if the order is not made immediately;
> (b) whether it is likely that an applicant will be deterred or prevented from pursuing an application if an order is not made immediately; and
> (c) whether there is reason to believe that—
>   (i) the respondent is aware of the proceedings but is deliberately evading service; and
>   (ii) the delay in effecting substituted service will cause serious prejudice to the person to be protected or (if a different person) an applicant.

4.79 The above criteria are intended to ensure that orders without notice are only granted where the case is sufficiently grave and urgent to justify immediate intervention.

4.80 It is, however, likely that ex parte orders will be sought more frequently than not in applications for FMPOs. By way of example, in meritorious applications for FMPOs there will commonly be a risk of one or more of the following if family members/the wider community become aware of the proceedings in advance of a protective order being made:

---

[51] FLA 1996, s 63N.
[52] FLA 1996, s 63D(1).
[53] Ibid.
[54] FLA 1996, s 63D(2).

- there may be a violent response directed to the person to be protected and/or others;

- steps may be taken to hasten travel arrangements for the person to be protected;

- steps may be taken to conceal or move the whereabouts of the person to be protected, particularly if they are already outside the jurisdiction; and/or

- steps may be taken to place pressure upon the person to be protected or the applicant (if different) not to pursue the application.

Risk of 'significant harm'

4.81   The risk of significant harm, if the order is not made immediately, can be to the person to be protected or 'another person'.[55]

4.82   The new Part 4A of FLA 1996 does not provide assistance as to the interpretation of 'significant harm'.

4.83   It may assist to consider the interpretation of 'harm' in the context of the existing Part 4. There the word harm is to be interpreted as follows:[56]

> '(a)   in relation to a person who has reached the age of eighteen years, means ill treatment or the impairment of health; and
> (b)   in relation to a child, means ill-treatment or the impairment of health or development.'

Further definitions are provided within the same section: 'Health' is to be interpreted as including physical or mental health; 'Development' encompasses physical, intellectual, emotional, social or behavioural development. 'Ill-treatment' includes actions which are not physical. In relation to a child, ill-treatment includes sexual behaviour.

4.84   The word 'significant' is not defined within FLA 1996. The phrase 'significant harm' appears in the Children Act 1989. The guidance to that Act uses the dictionary meaning of the word 'significant', meaning 'considerable, noteworthy or important'.[57]

Risk of significant harm to 'another person' if the order is not made immediately

4.85   The terms of FLA 1996, s 63D(2)(a) are such that in deciding whether to make an order without notice, the court can consider not just risk of significant harm to the person to be protected themselves, if the order is not made immediately, but also to 'another person'.[58] The court can therefore take into account a risk of significant harm to:

- a person applying on behalf of the person to be protected; and/or

- any other person.

---

[55]   FLA 1996, s 63D(2)(a).
[56]   FLA 1996, s 63(1).
[57]   The Children Act 1989: Guidance and Regulations (HMSO, 1991), Vol 1, Court Orders, para 3.19. The definition was confirmed in the case of *Humberside CC v B* [1993] 1 FLR 257.
[58]   FLA 1996, s 63D(2)(a).

4.86 FLA 1996 reflects the reality of forced marriage whereby threats and intimidation are often directed towards third parties. It may be that another member of the family or boyfriend of the person to be protected is making the application and will attract opprobrium if the perpetrators are put on notice. It follows that it may be appropriate for ex parte injunctive protection to be also sought on behalf of such an applicant in anticipation of the respondents being served with notice of the order.

4.87 The 'another person' need not be an applicant. By way of example, the evidence in support of the application could make reference to a relationship between the person to be protected and another person, of which their family is unaware; the family being put on notice of the proceedings could put that person at risk of significant harm.[59]

4.88 It may also provide protection to such a person if their personal details are supplied to the court, either separately to the primary documents (they being referred to in an anonymised way in the primary documents) or alternatively for the court's permission to be sought to serve a redacted document.[60]

Deterred or prevented from pursuing an application if an order is not made immediately

4.89 This is a separate specific ground upon which a without notice application can be sought, encompassing the apprehended risk if notice is given that steps will be taken to deter the applicant (whether the person to be protected or a person applying on their behalf) by physical threats/force or by psychological means, not to pursue the application.

4.90 There may be a risk that an applicant will be prevented from pursuing the application, for example, by being physically constrained from leaving a household or by being taken out of the jurisdiction. There may even be a likelihood that the applicant would be subjected to physical harm such as to prevent their continued pursuit of the proceedings.

Deliberate evasion of service

4.91 The third category which a court will specifically consider in deciding whether to grant a without notice FMPO is where there is reason to be believe that the respondent is aware of the proceedings but is deliberately evading service, and that the delay in effecting substituted service would cause serious prejudice to the person to be protected or applicant.

4.92 In deciding whether to make an ex parte order, the court is not constrained by those categories specifically referred to above, but must have regard to 'all the circumstances'.

Procedure for ex parte orders

4.93 Readers are referred to Chapter 5 of this Bulletin for guidance on applications for ex parte orders.

---

[59] See Chapter 6 for steps which can be taken to limit disclosure of sensitive information contained within evidence filed in support of the application.

[60] Family Proceedings Rules 1991, SI 1991/1247, r 3.33(4) (as amended by the Family Proceedings (Amendment) Rules 2008, SI 2008/2446) provides that the court may direct the withholding of any submissions made or evidence adduced.

The need for an inter partes hearing following the making of an ex parte order

4.94 Having made a without notice order the court must give the respondent an opportunity to make representations about any order made.[61]

4.95 The court must ensure that the opportunity to make representations is:[62]

'(a) as soon as just and convenient; and
(b) at a hearing of which notice has been given to all the parties in accordance with rules of the court.'

4.96 This provision seeks to ensure, so far as is possible, that there is a proper balance between protecting a person who may be in need of immediate protection from the court and ensuring a fair hearing for the respondent(s) concerned.

4.97 On making an ex-parte order, the court must fix a return date for the inter partes hearing. An ex parte order will be made for short duration until an inter partes hearing, or for longer duration but with an inter partes hearing after a short period of time by way of review.

4.98 Chapter 6 considers issues concerning service of orders and safety considerations for on notice hearings.

DURATION OF A FMPO

4.99 There is no maximum period for which a final FMPO may be made. A FMPO may be made for a specified period or until varied or discharged.[63] It is implicit that variation includes extension of a FMPO. Readers are referred to Chapter 6 for guidance on variation (including extension) and discharge.

POWERS OF ARREST

When may a power of arrest be attached to a FMPO?

4.100 In providing for when a power of arrest may be attached, the legislation distinguishes between FMPOs made inter partes and those made ex parte.

4.101 A prerequisite to the attaching of a power of arrest, in either circumstance, is that the court must consider that the respondent has used or threatened violence against the person being protected or otherwise in connection with the matters being dealt with by the order.[64]

4.102 The phrase 'otherwise in connection with the matters being dealt with by the order' encompasses situations where the violence is not used or threatened against the person to be protected but, for example, a different applicant or another person entirely. The use or threat of violence could, for example, have been directed to an individual with whom the person to be protected is in a relationship.

---

[61] FLA 1996, s 63D(3).
[62] FLA 1996, s 63D(4).
[63] FLA 1996, s 63F.
[64] FLA 1996, s 63H(1)(b) and (3)(b).

Who is a 'respondent' for the purposes of the power of arrest provisions?

4.103 Interpretation of the power of arrest provisions of the legislation is complicated by a change in definition of the term 'respondent'. It is important to note that for the purposes of FLA 1996, s 63H, relating to attachment of powers of arrests to orders, 'respondent' includes any person who is not a respondent but to whom an order is directed.[65]

4.104 A power of arrest may therefore be attached in circumstances not just where the court is satisfied that a named respondent has used or threatened violence, but where the court is satisfied that another person to whom the order is directed has behaved in such a way. By way of example, the court may be satisfied that violence has been used or threatened within a family or household but be unable to identify the perpetrator from within a group of people.

4.105 The power of arrest can be attached to term(s) of an order directed against unnamed persons, for example, to a term that 'any member of X family by themselves, or by encouraging, assisting or agreeing with any other person whatsoever is forbidden from removing Y from the jurisdiction', or indeed even to a wider term forbidding any person from facilitating any arrangements in relation to the civil or religious ceremony of the person to be protected.

Powers of arrest attached to inter partes FMPOs

4.106 In the case of FMPOs made on notice, if the court considers that the respondent(s) has used or threatened violence, as defined above, the court must attach a power of arrest to one or more provisions of the order unless it considers that in all the circumstances of the case there will be adequate protection without the power.[66]

4.107 FLA 1996, s 63H(1) and (2) therefore creates a presumption that a power of arrest be attached to one or more parts of an inter partes FMPO where the respondent has used or threatened violence.

Ex parte FMPOs

4.108 The attaching of a power of arrest to one or more provisions of an ex parte FMPO is discretionary. In addition to the requirement that the court must consider whether violence has been used or threatened in the past, the court must, before attaching a power of arrest to one or more of the terms of the order, consider that there may be risk of significant harm in the future to a person, attributable to the conduct of the respondent, if the power of arrest is not attached to the provisions immediately.[67]

4.109 The risk of significant harm need only be to 'a person', not just the person to be protected. The risk could therefore be to a third party applicant or a separate person entirely. Readers are referred to the discussion earlier in this chapter as to the meaning of significant harm in the context of applications for ex parte FMPOs.

---

[65]   FLA 1996, s 63H(7).
[66]   FLA 1996, s 63H(1), (2).
[67]   FLA 1996, s 63H(3), (4).

Duration of a power of arrest attached to an ex parte FMPO

4.110 Where a court attaches a power of arrest to any provisions of an ex parte order, it may provide that the power of arrest is to have effect for a shorter period than the other provisions of the order.[68]

4.111 Where the power of arrest is to have such effect for a shorter period than other provisions of the order, it is possible for the court to extend the period on an application to vary or discharge the order. Such extensions may be made on one or more occasions.[69] As stated in the Explanatory Notes to the legislation, such an extension would be most likely to happen once the respondent has been given the opportunity to be heard in respect of the order.[70]

Who may be arrested under an attached power of arrest?

4.112 A police officer can arrest a person under an attached power of arrest in the following circumstances:[71]

- where he or she has reasonable cause to suspect that person to be in breach of a provision to which a power of arrest is attached; or

- where he or she has reasonable cause to suspect that person to be otherwise in contempt of court in relation to the order.

4.113 Therefore a power of arrest may be used to arrest not only the respondent(s) named in the proceedings but also unnamed persons alleged to be in breach of the order. For example, if there were a wide clause prohibiting any person from facilitating arrangements for Y to travel outside the jurisdiction, to which a power of arrest was attached, the driver of the car taking the protected person to the airport could be arrested.

4.114 Furthermore, even where the order does not have terms specifically directed to unnamed persons, individuals not named in the order could potentially be arrested under an attached power as being 'otherwise in contempt in relation to the order'. Thus any person who was reasonably believed to have aided and abetted breach of a FMPO could be arrested.

4.115 As orders against unnamed persons cannot be personally served, the court will have the responsibility of determining whether a person is aware of an order and is in contempt of the same. This issue will be considered further in Chapter 7, concerning enforcement.

WHEN MAY UNDERTAKINGS BE ACCEPTED?

4.116 If the court has power to make a forced marriage protection order it may (subject to **4.119**) accept an undertaking from a respondent to the proceedings.[72]

4.117 An undertaking is a solemn promise given by a party to the proceedings. A respondent may give an undertaking promising to perform an act or to abstain from performing an act.

---

[68]   FLA 1996, s 63H(5).
[69]   FLA 1996, s 63H(6).
[70]   Explanatory Notes, para 47.
[71]   FLA 1996, s 63I(2).
[72]   FLA 1996, s 63E(1).

4.118 No power of arrest can be attached to an undertaking given.[73] Undertakings therefore afford less protection than orders with powers of arrest.

4.119 The court may *not* accept an undertaking in those cases where a power of arrest would have been attached had an order been made.[74]

4.120 The legislation therefore seeks to prevent undertakings being inappropriately accepted where the circumstances of the case are sufficiently serious to warrant the attachment of a power of arrest to an order.

4.121 In all cases where a judge accepts an undertaking where otherwise an order might have been granted, Form N117 is to be completed.

4.122 An undertaking remains in force in accordance with the terms and time limits set out in it, unless and until it is varied or discharged by the court.[75]

4.123 The disadvantage to an applicant of not having a power of arrest and the limitation on the range of people against whom relief can be obtained means that careful consideration must be given in each case as to whether undertakings will suffice.

4.124 Breach of an undertaking is a contempt of court and is punishable in the same way as breach of court orders.[76]

STATUTORY GUIDANCE UNDER THE LEGISLATION

4.125 FLA 1996, s 63Q provides that the Secretary of State may, from time to time, prepare and publish guidance to such persons as the Secretary of State considers appropriate about the effect of FLA 1996, Part 4A or any provision of it, or other matters relating to forced marriages.

4.126 A person exercising public functions to whom such guidance is given must have regard to it in the exercise of those functions.[77]

4.127 Pursuant to this section, following consultation, Statutory Guidance was published in November 2008, entitled *The Right to Choose: Multi-agency Statutory Guidance for Dealing with Forced Marriage*, reproduced at Appendix D.

FORCED MARRIAGE UNIT PRACTICE GUIDELINES FOR PROFESSIONALS

4.128 To complement the new Statutory Guidance the FMU has updated its separate practice guidelines for police officers, health professionals, social workers and education professionals, and has issued revised practice guidelines in a multi-agency format. These Guidelines are entitled *Multi-agency practice guidelines: Handling cases of Forced Marriage*.[78]

---

[73] FLA 1996, s 63E(2).
[74] FLA 1996, s 63E(3).
[75] *Johnson v Walton* [1990] 1 FLR 350.
[76] FLA 1996, s 63E(4). See commentary in Chapter 7 regarding enforcement.
[77] FLA 1996, s 63Q(2). Section 63Q(3), however, specifies that nothing in the section permits the Secretary of State to give guidance to any court or tribunal.
[78] June 2009. Available to download at www.fco.gov.uk/resources/en/pdf/3849543/forced-marriage-guidelines09.pdf.

CHAPTER 5

PRACTICAL GUIDANCE: APPLICATIONS FOR FORCED MARRIAGE PROTECTION ORDERS

5.1 Having considered the law in relation to applications for forced marriage protection orders (FMPOs) in Chapter 4, this chapter will consider how such applications are made in practice. Copies of the relevant court forms may be found at Appendix E.

5.2 In the Family Proceedings Rules 1991[1] (FPR 1991), as amended by the Family Proceedings (Amendment) Rules 2008[2] (FP(A)R 2008), the person to be protected is referred to as 'the person who is the subject of the proceedings'.[3] Wherever possible, this chapter will continue to use the term 'person to be protected'.

SPECIAL CONSIDERATIONS

5.3 FMPOs will feature in highly sensitive cases and the issues arising are naturally more complex than practitioners will have experienced when issuing applications under the original Part 4 of the Family Law Act 1996.

5.4 Careful consideration needs to be given to the following:

- contacting the Forced Marriage Unit (FMU), which can provide assistance to victims of forced marriage within and outside the United Kingdom and can also provide practical advice to legal practitioners;

- whether and when the application should be issued;

- what other legal remedies should be sought, for instance, applications to invoke the inherent jurisdiction and nullity proceedings (see Chapter 3);

- venue of the application – if the person to be protected is outside the jurisdiction, this points to an application in the High Court;

- whether an application should be made by the person to be protected or by another person on their behalf;

- who are the relevant respondents;

- whether there are unnamed persons against whom the order should be directed;

- what terms of an order are to be sought, taking into account the wide ranging nature of orders envisaged by the legislation;

---

[1] SI 1991/1247.
[2] SI 2008/2446.
[3] FPR 1991, r 3.25(1), as amended by FP(A)R 2008.

- who is in possession of the passport(s) of the person to be protected. If the person to be protected is still in the jurisdiction but it is feared they could be taken abroad for the purposes of forced marriage, orders should be urgently sought for the surrender of passport(s) and retention by the court/applicant's solicitor;[4]

- whether the application should be issued in a court outside the locality in which the respondent family members and/or person to be protected reside;

- whether an application should be made without notice;

- what evidence should be filed and what applications should be made for non-disclosure (see **5.61** and further discussion in Chapter 6); and

- what protective measures should be sought for the person to be protected and/or the person applying on their behalf, including housing, applications for non-molestation orders, special provisions at court.[5]

Safety issues

5.5   Before issue, practitioners must be aware of the difficult situation in which an application for a FMPO is likely to place the person to be protected, with the risk of ostracisation within their family and/or community and actual physical harm.[6] If an ill-judged application is made or an application mishandled, there is a clear risk that the application of itself could increase the risk of harm to a victim.[7]

5.6   Practitioners must be aware of the risks to which a person exposes themselves when seeking legal advice on the issue of forced marriage. It may have been exceptionally difficult for the person to make the phone call or attend at the office for a first appointment. Consideration will have to be given to offering such clients out of hours appointments or appointments at a safe location.

5.7   Caution should be exercised in discussing the case with a client over the phone. Practitioners must be aware that a family member may make contact with a solicitors firm with a view to eliciting details as to a potential application or the victim's whereabouts. Support staff must be trained not to disclose any details as to whether a person is a client of the firm, nor under any circumstances disclose details of appointments to any third party.[8]

5.8   Whether making an application on instructions from the person to be protected or on instructions by another seeking to issue an application on that person's behalf, practitioners must consider what steps have been, or can be, put in place to ensure that the person to be

---

4   As discussed in Chapter 3, a request for an order to surrender/for collection/retention of a foreign passport must be made in the High Court.
5   Practitioners will need to consider local practices in individual designated courts. By way of example, Newcastle County Court has introduced a Protocol for Vulnerable Victims, covering forced marriage cases.
6   During consultation on the issue of the relevant third party, the Fawcett Society expressed concern that orders would only be appropriate and effective in safeguarding victims when immediately accompanied by provision of safe housing and appropriate support. If an application was brought and a victim remains in the family home they would be placed in significant danger: *Relevant Third Party Response to Consultation* (Ministry of Justice, 13 November 2008), at p 12.
7   In consultation on the issue of the relevant third party, concerns were raised as to the need to avoid making situations worse in potentially life or death situations. These concerns related to all possible relevant third parties: Fawcett Society *Relevant Third Party Response to Consultation* (Ministry of Justice, 13 November 2008), at p 21.
8   The authors are aware of cases where family members have contacted a fee earner's secretary and sought to obtain details of when X (estranged from their family and in fear of them) was next to attend a legal appointment.

protected has safe housing and appropriate support. Practitioners must ensure that they are knowledgeable about support agencies in their local area.[9]

5.9   Practitioners must also be aware that in circumstances where a friend or relative makes an application on behalf of a person to be protected, they too are likely to be placed in a difficult position and may also need to seek alternative accommodation/injunctive protection before the application is issued/served following a without notice hearing. Consideration must be given to whether a concurrent application should be made for a non-molestation order, or in circumstances where the person applying is not a relative, an application under the Protection from Harassment Act 1997.

Confidentiality

5.10   Confidentiality is of crucial significance in these cases. Practitioners must be ever vigilant to the risks to a person to be protected or a person seeking protection on their behalf should a family member, or even person within the wider community, discover that an application is being considered. There will be a high proportion of cases where the person to be protected or the person acting on their behalf does not wish their address to be disclosed.

5.11   Practitioners must be vigilant to the risks should such an address be inadvertently disclosed. The following is a relevant extract from the Multi-Agency Statutory Guidance:[10]

> 'Those who do leave often live in fear of their own families, who will go to considerable lengths to find them and ensure their return. Families may solicit the help of others to find their runaways, or involve the police by reporting them missing or falsely accusing the young person of a crime (for example theft). Some families have traced individuals through medical or dental records, bounty hunters, private investigators, local taxi drivers, members of the community and shopkeepers or through National Insurance numbers, benefit records, school and college records. Sometimes having traced them, the family may murder them (so called "honour killing").'

5.12   Practitioners will need to consider whether the application itself should be issued out of the area in which the respondent family and/or the person to be protected reside:

- the person to be protected may feel their personal safety is enhanced if the application is heard in a court away from the area in which the respondent family/wider community resides; and

- the person to be protected may have moved to a new area for safety reasons. It may be wise to issue the application out of area so as not to alert family members to the new area of residence.

5.13   Should the person to be protected have moved away from their old address for safety reasons, and then sought legal advice from a solicitors firm located in their new area of residence, consideration might be given to instructing solicitor agents to deal with the application. The very fact of the address of the applicant's solicitors could alert respondents to the area where the person to be protected now lives.

---

[9]   Practitioners are referred to the list of national and regional organisations which may provide support to victims, given in Appendix H.

[10]   *The Right to Choose: Multi-agency Statutory Guidance for Dealing with Forced Marriage* (FCO and others, November 2008), at para 43, Chapter 3 'Understanding the issues around forced marriage'. Contained in Appendix D.

Use of interpreters

5.14 In some cases the assistance of an interpreter will be required. Caution must be exercised in selecting an interpreter for cases of this nature. An interpreter who comes from the same local community as the person to be protected should not be used. A relative, friend, community leader or other member of the community should not be used as an interpreter even outside of the formal court arena. Practitioners must be mindful of the possibility of information getting back to the family of the person to be protected, directly or indirectly.

5.15 The Court Service will provide an interpreter if it is stated that this is required on the application form. It may, however, be that practitioners will wish to take their own steps to secure an interpreter in whom they have confidence.

Mediation should not be considered

5.16 Practitioners must be aware that the Statutory Guidance advises that attempts should not be made to resolve cases of actual or potential forced marriage by way of family counselling, mediation, arbitration or reconciliation.[11] This should not be suggested to a person to be protected, nor should a legal professional facilitate the same if requested. Mediation with family members prior to issue, thus making family members aware of the potential for proceedings to be brought, may lead to action being taken to pre-empt such an application. A person to be protected may be deprived of their liberty, taken overseas or even be subjected to grave physical harm. Should there be family counselling or mediation following issue, a person to be protected would be likely to be placed under enormous pressure from family members to discontinue proceedings.

Considerations for those acting for respondents

5.17 Judges will inevitably, on receipt of an application for a FMPO, be acutely aware of the potentially grave risks faced by a person to be protected were a court to refuse an application in circumstances in which the fears of forced marriage were in fact valid. The 'one chance rule' has not only been emphasised to professionals working in this field, but also to the judiciary.

5.18 There is no doubt that acting on behalf of a respondent to an application for a FMPO will be difficult. The court must be dissuaded from erring on the side of caution; from taking the view that on balance less harm would be caused by making an order which in retrospect was without foundation, as against refusing to make an order which did have foundation.

5.19 As a result practitioners acting on behalf of respondents are under a responsibility to subject the evidence produced in support of the application for an FMPO to rigorous scrutiny.

5.20 The following matters should be considered:

- The quality of the evidence that a forced marriage has taken place, or is at risk of taking place. Is there evidence to verify the concerns placed before the court? There is a risk that an innocent family holiday may be misconstrued, particularly if the application is made by a third party on behalf of the person to be protected.

---

[11] Part Two, Chapter 4 of the Statutory Guidance (*The Right to Choose*, n 8 above) warns agencies of the dangers of family counselling, mediation, arbitration and reconciliation. It is the authors' view that this warning applies equally to court proceedings.

- If the application has been made by a third party on behalf of the person to be protected, how much evidence is there of that applicant's contact with the person to be protected?

- What is the quality of the evidence put before the court as to the person to be protected's wishes and feelings?

- Is there a possibility that the application may arise as a result of a dispute within or between families?

- What other motivations could have led a person to be protected to make this application?

- Is there evidence to establish that this is a forced marriage, rather than an arranged marriage?

EVIDENCE

5.21 In many forced marriage cases, practitioners will be unable to obtain independent corroborative evidence of the allegations. These are cases rooted in secrecy.

5.22 Practitioners acting on behalf of applicants, however, must carefully explore opportunities for obtaining corroborative evidence. Each case depends on its own facts but the more common sources of evidence are discussed below.

5.23 There may be useful *police evidence*. There may have been reports of domestic abuse, harassment or breaches of the peace at the family home. The person to be protected may have sought police protection and then sought to withdraw their allegations under pressure from family members. Assistance may have been sought from the police prior to travel abroad. The person to be protected or other persons within the family may have been reported missing. There may well be a concurrent police investigation founded on the same allegations on which the FMPO application is based. Practitioners will be familiar with local protocols in force in relation to seeking disclosure from the police and will, where necessary, have to seek court orders for disclosure.

5.24 In the case of a child, evidence from the *child's school* may be crucial:

- Teachers may have noticed a change in behaviour.

- Has there been a sudden drop in performance?

- Is the school aware of a history of an older sibling marrying early?

- Have there been prolonged absences?

- Has a request been made for extended leave?

- Has there been a failure to return from a trip abroad?

- Has the child been withdrawn from school early?

5.25 There may be useful evidence within a victim's *medical records*. A victim may have been subjected to physical abuse. A victim may have confided in a GP of their fears concerning potential forced marriage. The family may be known to *social services*.

5.26   Practitioners are referred to FPR 1991, r 3.31 in relation to orders for disclosure against a person who is not a party to the proceedings.[12]

VENUE OF THE APPLICATION

5.27   At the time of publication of this Bulletin, a limited number of courts across the country have been selected to hear applications for FMPOs. The application must be made in:[13]

- High Court;

- Principal Registry of the Family Division;

- Birmingham Family Courts;

- Blackburn Family Courts;

- Bradford County Court;

- Bristol County Court;

- Cardiff Civil Justice Centre;

- Derby County Court;

- Leeds Combined Court;

- Leicester County Court;

- Luton County Court;

- Manchester County Court;

- Middlesbrough County Court at Teesside;

- Newcastle County Court;

- Romford County Court; or

- Willesden County Court.

---

[12]   FPR 1991, r 3.31 applies where an application is made to the court under *any Act* for disclosure by a person who is not a party to the proceedings. The application must be supported by evidence (r 3.31(2)). Rule 3.31(3) provides that the court may only make an order under this rule where the documents of which disclosure is sought are likely to support the case of the applicant or adversely affect the case of one of the other parties to the proceedings; and the disclosure is necessary in order to dispose fairly of the proceedings or to save costs. See full rule for requirement that the order specify classes of documents which the non-party must disclose and require the non-party to specify documents no longer in his or her control or in respect of which he or she asserts a right/duty to withhold inspection (r 3.31(4)). An order under this rule can require a non-party to indicate what has happened to any documents no longer under his or her control and specify time/place for disclosure/inspection (r 3.31(5)). See also r 3.32 as to procedure should a person apply without notice for an order permitting withholding of disclosure on the ground that disclosure would damage the public interest.
[13]   Allocation and Transfer of Proceedings Order 2008, SI 2008/2836, art 2.

APPLICATIONS BY OR ON BEHALF OF A CHILD/PROTECTED PARTY

5.28 A child may apply for a FMPO. If the child is the person to be protected, they do not need the leave of the court to apply for a FMPO.

5.29 Practitioners are referred to FPR 1991, r 9.2 in relation to the procedure for applications for FMPOs on behalf of a child or a protected party (a person who lacks capacity within the meaning of the Mental Capacity Act 2005[14]).

5.30 In specified circumstances a child may commence an application for a FMPO without a next friend or guardian ad litem. The circumstances are set out in FPR 1991, r 9.2A.

APPLICATIONS REQUIRING LEAVE OF THE COURT

5.31 Any designated 'relevant third party' may make an application for a FMPO, on behalf of the person to be protected, without requiring leave of the court.[15] As discussed in Chapter 4, as of 1 November 2009 a local authority is specified as such a 'relevant third party' (see further below).

5.32 This section considers the procedure which must be followed by all other third party applicants for a FMPO who have not been specified as a '*relevant* third party' and consequently require leave of the court.

5.33 A *non-designated* third party, seeking leave of the court to make an application on behalf of a person to be protected, must file a Form FL430 setting out:

- the reasons for the application;

- the applicant's connection with the person to be protected;

- the applicant's knowledge of the circumstances of the person to be protected; and

- the applicant's knowledge of the wishes and feelings of the person to be protected.[16]

5.34 In addition, the third party applicant must file a draft of the application for which leave is sought (Form FL401A see below), together with sufficient copies for one to be served on each respondent and the person to be protected.[17] The FL401A application form will be served (save if a without notice application for a FMPO is also sought) if the application for leave is successful.

5.35 Form FL430 consists of two pages requiring the third party applicant to provide the names of the third party applicant and the person to be protected and the reasons for application (see **5.33**).[18]

---

[14] FPR 1991, r 9.1(1), as amended.
[15] FLA 1996, s 63(2).
[16] FPR 1991, r 3.27(1)(a), as amended.
[17] FPR 1991, r 3.27(1)(b).
[18] See Chapter 4 at **4.21** onwards for discussion regarding applications requiring leave.

Procedure following receipt of application for leave

5.36 On receiving an application for leave, as soon as practicable the court will either grant the request or direct that a date is fixed for the hearing of the request and fix the date for the same.[19]

5.37 The court will inform the following persons of its determination:

- the person making the request for leave (the third party applicant);

- the respondent(s);

- (if different) the person to be protected; and

- any other person directed by the court.[20]

5.38 In many cases the application for leave will be made in conjunction with a substantive ex parte application for a FMPO. In the event of leave being granted and an ex parte FMPO thereafter being given, the respondent would only be informed of the determination on the leave issue after the ex parte FMPO.

5.39 If leave is granted, the application proceeds using the already completed Form FL401A.

LOCAL AUTHORITY APPLICANTS

5.40 From 1 November 2009 local authorities will be able to apply as relevant third parties for FMPOs on behalf of a person to be protected.[21] However, although local authorities will no longer need leave, a court will still carefully scrutinise whether the application is in the best interests of the person to be protected. The person to be protected may of course have no knowledge of the application. The application form (see below) has been amended to ensure that the court is still appraised as to what the local authority knows as to the circumstances of the person to be protected and their wishes and feelings.

5.41 Local authority applicants *must* of course have regard to the statutory guidance published in November 2008, entitled *The Right to Choose: Multi-agency Statutory Guidance for Dealing with Forced Marriage*, reproduced at Appendix D.[22]

5.42 In addition, local authority social workers should have regard to the publication *Multi-agency Practice Guidelines: Handling cases of Forced Marriage*.[23] This publication supplements the statutory guidance and provides advice and support to front-line practitioners who have responsibilities to safeguard children and protect adults from the abuses associated with forced marriage. Of particular relevance to social workers considering an application for a FMPO are Chapters 9 and 10, which give guidelines for Children's Social Care and Adult Social Care respectively.

---

[19] FPR 1991, r 3.27(2).
[20] FPR 1991, r 3.27(2).
[21] See discussion in Chapter 4 concerning the Government's intention to conduct a pilot scheme to consider whether Independent Domestic Violence Advisors (IDVAs) might also be designated as relevant third parties.
[22] FLA 1996, s 63Q(2) requires a local authority to have regard to the statutory guidance in exercising its public functions.
[23] June 2009. Written by Eleanor Stobart on behalf of the Forced Marriage Unit in collaboration with other government departments, including the Department for Children, Schools and Families.

5.43 Further, the Ministry of Justice is preparing some additional guidelines specifically for local authority applicants. It is anticipated that these will be published in October 2009.[24] In due course it is planned that the Ministry of Justice guidance will be incorporated into a second edition of the Multi-Disciplinary Practice Guidelines.

5.44 A Local Authority considering an application for a FMPO on behalf of a child will of course reflect on whether an application also needs to be made for a public law order under the Children Act 1989, whether an emergency protection order, care order or supervision order.

THE SUBSTANTIVE APPLICATION FOR A FMPO

5.45 The application for a FMPO (when made either by a person to be protected, relevant third party or other third party applicant) must be made in Form FL401A. The same form is used should the application be made within existing proceedings.[25] The commentary below concerns the revised Form FL401A, in use from 1 November 2009 following a local authority being specified as a relevant third party.[26]

Non-disclosure of the address of the applicant and/or person to be protected

5.46 In view of the sensitive nature of applications for FMPOs and safety concerns which arise, many applicants will commonly apply to withhold their address from the respondent(s).

5.47 Section 1 of the form invites applicants to state their address. Should an applicant seek that their address not be disclosed, this part of section 1 should be left blank and a Confidential Address Form C8 should be completed.

5.48 Where the applicant is a third party, section 2 requires the applicant to state the name of the person to be protected, their address and date of birth. However, should the applicant not wish to disclose the address of the person to be protected, this part of the section can be left blank and a Confidential Address Form C8 should be completed.

Completion of Form FL401A

5.49 This discussion will highlight particular aspects of Form FL401A, readers are referred to the form itself, reproduced in Appendix E.

5.50 Section 1 of the form is to be completed by the applicant, whether the application is made by the person to be protected, a relevant third party or any other person. Should the applicant not be the person to be protected, section 2 also requires completion. Details must be provided concerning the person to be protected.

---

[24] Practitioners are advised to consult the Courts Service and Ministry of Justice websites to obtain this document once published.

[25] FPR 1991, r 3.26(1).

[26] Rule 19 of the Family Proceedings (Amendment) (No 3) Rules 2009, SI 2009/2027, provides for the substitute revised Form FL401A. The form has been changed to include a new section 3 entitled 'Your reasons for applying on behalf of the person to be protected (for Relevant Third Party applications only, e.g. local authority applicants)'. In light of the fact that local authorities will no longer need to complete a leave Form FL430, this revision to the main application form is intended to ensure that local authorities applying for FMPOs are able to explain what they know about the background to the case, the circumstances of the person to be protected and the wishes and feelings of the person to be protected.

5.51 If the application for a FMPO is being made by an organisation (whether a relevant third party or otherwise), the application form must state:

- the name and address of the person submitting the application; and

- the position which that person holds in the organisation.[27]

5.52 Whilst FPR 1991 does not specifically address this issue, it is suggested in accordance with usual practice persons within an organisation need only provide their work address.

5.53 It may be that the organisation applying on behalf of the person to be protected does not wish its address to be disclosed, for example, in circumstances where the organisation is a refuge. In such circumstances a C8 form should be completed as outlined above.

5.54 Section 3 of Form FL401A is to be completed by relevant third party applicants only. Such relevant third parties should outline in brief their reasons for applying on behalf of the person to be protected, which must include:

- what they know of the circumstances of the person to be protected; and

- the wishes and feelings of the person to be protected, so far as they know them.

5.55 Section 4 requires the applicant to state the names and addresses of the respondent(s) to the application. A separate piece of paper should be annexed to the application should there be more than two respondents.

5.56 Section 7 of the form contains a box in which 'other information' can be inserted. It is said that this should include the name and address of any other person who may become involved as a respondent. However, practitioners are reminded that, particularly at the early stages of an application, it may be safer to include parties as formal respondents where there may be doubt.

5.57 Section 5 requires the applicant to state the orders which are sought. Readers are referred to sample orders given at Appendix F.

5.58 Section 5 also requires applicants to give full details in support of their application. This must include details of any violence that the respondent has used or threatened.

5.59 Section 5 contains a box in which details in support can be inserted. It is unlikely that this will provide sufficient space to outline the details in support of an application for a FMPO. A separate sheet can be annexed to the application. Practitioners are, however, likely to prefer to file a separate statement from the applicant. Readers are referred to the sample statements in support given at Appendix F.

5.60 Practitioners should consider whether there are matters within the statement which, even after a FMPO being made ex parte, the applicant/person to be protected would wish to be withheld. The evidence in support might, for example, make reference to the person to be protected being in a relationship, a fact which might be unknown to the respondent family. Practitioners may wish to consider providing to the court, in addition to the substantive statement, a redacted statement removing those matters which it is submitted should be withheld.

---

[27] FPR 1991, r 3.26(2), as amended.

5.61   The court can at the hearing of the FMPO direct that submissions made or evidence adduced should be withheld:

- in order to protect the person to be protected or any other person; or

- for any other good reason.[28]

FPR 1991, r 3.33(4) applies both to the information provided at ex parte hearings and also at substantive on notice hearings. It follows therefore that at substantive on notice hearings practitioners will need to give consideration to how such confidential information is to be managed within the context of the hearing.

5.62   Section 6 of the form requires applicants to state whether they will need an interpreter at court, should the applicant wish the court to arrange the same. As discussed earlier in this chapter, in view of the sensitivities concerning the instruction of an appropriate interpreter, many practitioners may wish themselves to make arrangements to instruct a particular interpreter in whom they have confidence.

5.63   Section 6 also allows the applicant to indicate whether they need any special assistance or facilities should they have a disability.

Request for special arrangements pertaining to security

5.64   Section 6 also contains a separate box in which applicants can state whether the court needs to make any special arrangements for their attendance at court, such as provision for a separate waiting room from the respondent or other security provisions.

5.65   Security is a key consideration in forced marriage cases. A person to be protected or other third party applicant, particularly if from the same community as the alleged perpetrators, is likely to be under significant pressure from family and even the wider community to bring an end to the proceedings. There is a risk that family may attend court seeking to exert physical or emotional pressure. As outlined earlier in this Bulletin, there may be a risk of physical harm.

5.66   Security provisions might be requested, protecting a person during their physical attendance at court and might include (dependant on availability in each individual court):

- a separate entrance and exit for the applicant and/or witnesses;

- a separate waiting room for the applicant and/or witnesses from that of the respondent; and/or

- parking on court premises to facilitate easy access to the court building.[29]

5.67   Consideration must also be given to arrangements to assist the applicant and/or witnesses in giving their evidence by way of special measures. This issue will be further discussed in Chapter 6, pertaining to the hearing of an application for a FMPO.

5.68   If unfamiliar with the facilities offered by a particular court, a practitioner could, time allowing, seek advice from the court manager prior to issue.

---

[28]   FPR 1991, r 3.33(4).
[29]   Leaflet FL701 containing guidance to making applications for FMPO cites this as a security measure that courts may be able to offer.

5.69 Should a request for special arrangements be mistakenly omitted from the application form, or such concerns arise subsequent to issue, a request should be made in writing to the court manager.

Applications for ex parte FMPOs

5.70 It is anticipated that the majority of applicants for FMPOs will seek initial hearings without notice to the respondent(s).

5.71 Should the applicant wish the court to hear the application without notice to the respondent(s), this must be indicated by ticking the box in section 5.

5.72 A sworn statement must be provided in support, outlining the reasons relied upon in support of the application being heard without notice.[30]

5.73 In drafting such statements, practitioners will focus on those matters referred to in the Act:

• all the circumstances of the case;

• any risk of significant harm to the person to be protected or another person if the order is not made immediately;

• whether it is likely that an applicant will be deterred or prevented from pursuing an application if an order is not made immediately; and

• whether there is reason to believe that the respondent is aware of the proceedings but is deliberately evading service; and the delay in effecting substituted service will cause serious prejudice to the person to be protected or (if a different person) an applicant.[31]

5.74 Practitioners are referred to the sample sworn statement in support of an application being heard without notice, given at Appendix F.

Procedure for applications on notice

5.75 Should the application be made on notice, a copy of the application, together with the notice of proceedings in Form FL402A must be personally served on the following persons not less than 2 days before the date on which the application is to be heard:[32]

(a)   the respondent;

(b)   the person who is the subject of the proceedings (if they are not the applicant); and

(c)   any other person directed by the court.

5.76 The period for service may, however, be abridged by the court.[33] The court may also order substituted service.[34]

---

[30]   FPR 1991, r 3.26(3).
[31]   Family Law Act 1996, s 63D(2).
[32]   FPR 1991, r 3.28(1).
[33]   FPR 1991, r 3.28(2).
[34]   FPR 1991, r 3.28(3).

5.77 If the applicant requests, service of the application shall be effected by the court.[35] This includes on the request of a third party applicant.[36]

5.78 A statement must be filed by the applicant in Form FL415 after the application has been served.[37]

TRANSFER OF PROCEEDINGS

5.79 Where proceedings under Part 4A of the Family Law Act 1996 are pending, the court may transfer the proceedings to another court of its own motion or on the application of a party or (if not a party) the person who is the subject of the proceedings.[38] The order for transfer is made on Form FL417.[39]

---

[35] FPR 1991, r 3.28(3).

[36] The original draft court rules provided for personal service of a court order by the court only where the applicant was acting in person; an organisation would not have such a facility and would be obliged to pay the costs of instructing a process server to serve the order on a respondent personally. In consultation there were concerns about the costs implications of the same in circumstances where there could be more than one respondent and the costs could be significant. Further, where the organisation was a charity, such as a women's refuge, it would have to pay such costs in the absence of public funding. In the response further to the consultation on the court rules, it was acknowledged that there may be circumstances in which an organisation would not be in a position to serve a respondent. The draft rules were therefore amended to provide that *any* applicant could ask to effect service of the application or the court order.

[37] FPR 1991, r 3.28(4).

[38] FPR 1991, r 3.29(1).

[39] FPR 1991, r 3.29(2).

CHAPTER 6

PROCEDURE POST APPLICATION

6.1 This chapter discusses the procedure following the issue of an application for a forced marriage protection order (FMPO), including joinder/discharge of parties, the hearing itself and the procedure post making of a FMPO. The chapter will also consider the procedure followed in circumstances where the court makes an order of its own motion. The chapter will then consider variation, extension and discharge of a FMPO and appeals.

JOINDER OF FURTHER PARTIES TO AN APPLICATION FOR A FMPO/DISCHARGE OF PARTIES

6.2 Once proceedings for a FMPO have commenced, the court may direct that a person who would not otherwise be a respondent under the rules be joined as a party.[1]

6.3 The court may also order that a person cease to be a party to the proceedings.[2]

6.4 The court may direct joinder/discharge of a party of its own motion, or alternatively on the request of a person (see below).[3]

6.5 By way of example, a practitioner may, having issued the application for a FMPO, learn of information suggesting that another person is involved in attempts to force a marriage and therefore wish to join that person as an additional respondent.

6.6 Alternatively, a practitioner may be instructed by a person who is a respondent to the application but asserts that they have no connection with the activities alleged and wishes to be discharged as a party.

6.7 It should be noted, however, that, even if a respondent is formally discharged as a party, that respondent could still be arrested under any power of arrest attached to a term of a FMPO if a police officer has reasonable cause to believe that person to be in breach of that term, or to be otherwise in contempt of court in relation to the order. In this respect they are placed in no better position than any other person simply by virtue of their discharge as a respondent.

6.8 Further, if it can be established that they acted in breach of a term(s) of the order and were aware of the existence of the order and its terms, they could be found in contempt of court and sentenced to prison. Practitioners are referred to Chapter 7 on enforcement for further discussion.

---

[1]   Rule 3.30(3)(a) of the Family Proceedings Rules 1991, SI 1991/1247 (FPR 1991), as amended by the Family Proceedings (Amendment) Rules 2008, SI 2008/2446.

[2]   FPR 1991, r 3.30(3)(b).

[3]   FPR 1991, r 3.30(3) and (1).

Procedure for application for joinder/discharge of a party

6.9 Following the issue of an application for a FMPO, a request may be made for a person to be joined as a party or cease to be a party.[4]

6.10 Such a request must be made on Form FL431 and filed with the court.[5]

Who may make such an application?

6.11 The application for a person to be joined as a party/cease to be a party may be made by the person themselves or by another person.[6]

Procedure on such a request being filed

6.12 As soon as practicable after receiving a request for joinder/removal of a party, the court will do one of the following:

- if it is a request for joinder *not* removal, the court can simply grant that request on paper without hearing oral or any further written representations;

- order that the request be considered at a hearing and fix a date for the same; or

- invite written representations as to whether the request should be granted, to be filed within a specified period. On expiry of that period the court may either grant the request for joinder/removal on paper or list a hearing.[7]

6.13 The court must inform the following specified persons of the court's action:

- the person making the request;

- the applicant and the respondent(s);

- the person to be protected (if different); and

- any other person directed by the court.[8]

THE HEARING OF AN APPLICATION FOR A FMPO

Presumption that the hearing will be in chambers

6.14 The hearing of an application for a FMPO will be in chambers unless the court otherwise directs.[9]

---

4   FPR 1991, r 3.30(1).
5   FPR 1991, r 3.30(1).
6   FPR 1991, r 3.30(1).
7   FPR 1991, r 3.30(2).
8   FPR 1991, r 3.30(2).
9   FPR 1991, r 3.33(1).

Media attendance

6.15 Practitioners will be mindful of the impact of the change implemented by FPR 1991, r 10.28, which took effect on 27 April 2009 and the consequent right of media representatives to attend at private hearings in family proceedings in the county courts and the High Court.[10] This is, however, subject to the discretion of the court to exclude such representatives from the whole or part of any hearing on specified grounds.[11]

6.16 The subject of forced marriage is one which has historically attracted considerable media interest. It is important that practitioners in this area are familiar with the reforms in relation to media attendance at hearings and the grounds on which exclusion can be founded. It seems likely that the majority of both applicants and respondents in these sensitive cases are unlikely to welcome media attendance. It also seems likely, for example, that the courts will be sympathetic in cases of this nature to arguments that media attendance could prejudice the safety of a party or witness in the proceedings.

6.17 On the other hand, in some cases the media may be used positively to assist, perhaps in the case of a third party applicant where the person to be protected has been taken abroad and publicity may help in locating them.

Outcomes

6.18 At the hearing the court may:

- make a FMPO;

- if necessary, direct that there be a further hearing to consider any representations made by the respondent(s), the person being protected by the order (if not the applicant) and any other person named in the order.[12] This course *must* be followed if a FMPO has been made at an ex parte hearing;[13]

- apply a power of arrest to some or all of those terms if the requisite circumstances are satisfied;

- accept an undertaking from the respondent, completed on Form N117 (an undertaking cannot be accepted in circumstances where a power of arrest would otherwise have been imposed);

- make any other directions or orders of its own motion. By way of example, the court could make orders for disclosure (eg from the police). The court could, where a child is the person to be protected, make the child a party to the proceedings and appoint a guardian ad litem.

---

[10] FPR 1991, r 10.28(3) enables duly accredited representatives of news-gathering and reporting organisations to be present during a private hearing in family proceedings (save hearings for the purposes of judicially assisted conciliation and negotiation).

[11] Under FPR 1991, r 10.28(4). At any stage in the proceedings the court may direct that media representatives shall not attend the proceedings or any part of them where satisfied that: this is necessary in the interests of any child concerned in, or connected with, the proceedings; for the safety and protection of a party, a witness in the proceedings, or a person connected with such a party or witness; or for the orderly conduct of the proceedings; or where justice will otherwise be impeded or prejudiced. A detailed discussion of the impact of this change is outside the scope of this Bulletin. However, practitioners are referred to r 10.28 itself, the Practice Direction: 'Attendance of Media Representatives at Hearings in Family Proceedings' (20 April 2009) and the President's Guidance in relation to applications consequent upon the attendance of the media in family proceedings (22 April 2009).

[12] FPR 1991, r 3.33(7).

[13] FLA 1996, s 63D(3).

The court could make a direction that a local authority undertake an investigation of the child's circumstances, under s 37 of the Children Act 1989. The court could, on making such a direction, also make an interim care order or interim supervision order with respect to the child concerned.[14] The court could appoint a guardian ad litem where the person to be protected is a vulnerable adult;

- dismiss the application.

Record of hearing and forms for orders

6.19 A record of the hearing of an application for a FMPO must be made in Form FL405.[15] This form records who attended the hearing and what evidence was used. A copy of the record of hearing is served with the order made at the hearing and a copy is kept on the court file.

6.20 Any FMPO made at the hearing is issued in Form FL404B.[16]

6.21 A power of arrest attached to a FMPO is issued in Form FL406A.[17]

6.22 Practitioners *must* ensure that the FMPO drawn up by the court is endorsed with, or incorporates, a penal notice warning the respondent of the consequences of breach. A penal notice is required in order to enforce the order.[18]

Requests for non-disclosure

6.23 The court has a wide discretion to direct the withholding of any submissions made or evidence adduced for or at the hearing. The court may make such a direction:[19]

- in order to protect the person who is the subject of the proceedings or any other person; or

- for any other good reason.

6.24 This is a *key* provision which must be considered in cases of this nature. Submissions made and evidence adduced may well be highly sensitive. By way of example, the application may be made on behalf of the person to be protected by a boyfriend of whom the family disapproves or is unaware, or evidence relied upon may refer to such a relationship. Careful thought must be given as to the potential impact of evidence and what should be served and if so at what stage.

6.25 Practitioners must be vigilant to the potential implications if sensitive evidence is disclosed whilst a person remains at risk of being harmed or forced into marriage. This is particularly so in circumstances where the person to be protected remains outside the jurisdiction.

6.26 Practitioners should attend hearings prepared to make submissions as to what evidence or submissions should be withheld. Practitioners may wish to attend court with suitably redacted versions of documents.

---

[14] Pursuant to s 38 of the Children Act 1989. The court must have reasonable grounds to believe that the child is suffering or is likely to suffer significant harm (see CA 1989, s 31(2)).

[15] FPR 1991, r 3.33(2).

[16] FPR 1991, r 3.33(3).

[17] FPR 1991, r 3.35(2)(b), modifying FPR 1991, r 3.9A.

[18] FPR 1991, r 3.35(7)(b).

[19] FPR 1991, r 3.33(4).

EX PARTE HEARINGS

6.27 In many cases the first hearing will be without notice to the respondent(s), following an application for an ex parte FMPO.

6.28 The court may make a FMPO at such an ex parte hearing, if it considers that it is just and convenient to do so.[20] Readers are referred to Chapter 4 at **4.76–4.92** for a more detailed discussion as to the circumstances when a court may exercise this power.

Need for an inter partes hearing after the making of any ex parte FMPO

6.29 An inter partes hearing must be listed after an ex parte FMPO is made. The court must give the respondent an opportunity to make representations about any ex parte order made.[21] This opportunity must be as soon as is just and convenient, and at a hearing at which notice has been given to all the parties in accordance with the rules of the court.[22]

6.30 The court may direct that a further hearing be held to consider not just representations made by the respondent but by the person to be protected by the order (if they are neither the applicant nor a respondent) and any other person named in the order.[23]

Service following the making of an ex parte FMPO

6.31 When an FMPO is made ex parte, the applicant must serve on the respondent, the person to be protected (if neither the applicant nor a respondent) and any other person named in the order, the following documents:[24]

- a copy of the order together with any power of arrest made;

- a copy of the record of the hearing; and

- a copy of the application together with any statement supporting it.

6.32 The above must be served personally, and as soon as reasonably practicable.[25] Practitioners should consider the timing of service of the FMPO. By way of example, it might be that a practitioner would wish to provide a copy of the FMPO to the Forced Marriage Unit, police and/or embassy officials to facilitate steps being taken to protect the victim, before any respondent is given notice of the order.

6.33 The applicant can request that the court effect service.[26]

6.34 The above must be served not less than 2 days before the date on which the inter partes hearing has been listed.[27] The court can, however, abridge time for service.[28]

---

[20] Family Law Act 1996 (FLA 1996), s 63D(1).
[21] FLA 1996, s 63D(3).
[22] FLA 1996, s 63D(4); see FPR 1991, r 3.28(1).
[23] FPR 1991, r 3.33(7).
[24] FPR 1991, r 3.33(5).
[25] FPR 1991, r 3.33(5).
[26] FPR 1991, r 3.33(6).
[27] FPR 1991, r 3.28(1).
[28] FPR 1991, r 3.28(2).

Procedure to follow if power of arrest is attached to an ex parte FMPO

6.35 In circumstances where a power of arrest has been attached to the order, specified documents must be delivered to the police.

6.36 The following must be delivered to the officer in charge of any police station for the address of the person being protected by the order, or of such other police station as the court may specify:[29]

- Form FL406A (the power of arrest itself);

- a statement showing that the respondents and any other persons directed by the court to be served have been served with the order or informed of its terms (whether by being present when the order was made or by telephone or otherwise); and

- details of the address of the person to be protected.

Further, it could be considered best practice to ensure that the following are also provided:

- an out of hours telephone number for the applicant's solicitors, which is not required under FPR 1991 but may be of assistance to the police. Similarly it may assist to provide the respondent's solicitors details where known.

6.37 In many cases the person to be protected will have moved away from their family home to an undisclosed address.[30] To ensure that the order has the greatest chance of being effectively policed, careful consideration should be given to the lodging of duplicate relevant documents at the closest police station to where the respondent still lives.

INTER PARTES HEARINGS

6.38 Practitioners are referred to Chapter 5 as to the procedure for making applications for FMPOs on notice. The inter partes hearing will take place following an application on notice, or will be a return date, following an ex parte order having been made. There may be a number of inter partes directions hearings prior to a contested substantive hearing.

Security arrangements and arrangements for giving of evidence

6.39 Clearly, it is at the inter partes hearing(s) that security issues are most acute. As outlined in Chapter 5, at **5.64–5.69**, the application form itself requires specific consideration to be given to special arrangements for attendance at court, including security measures.

6.40 At a directions hearing (but not a substantive hearing) the court may dispense with the attendance of the person to be protected or other third party applicant.

6.41 Where the person to be protected or other vulnerable applicant or witnesses are to attend court, practitioners should liaise with the court manager to ensure that appropriate security measures are in place. As discussed in Chapter 5, these may include: a separate entrance and exit

---

[29] FPR 1991, rr 3.35(3) and 3.9A(1A).
[30] In such circumstances practitioners should exercise caution in relation to disclosure of the statement of service proving service on the police station. This could inadvertently reveal the victim's new whereabouts.

for the applicant and/or witnesses; a separate waiting room for the applicant and/or witnesses; and parking on court premises to facilitate easy access to the court building.

6.42 If acting for the person to be protected or other applicant, consideration should be given to whether arrangements can be put in place for their participation in the hearing, even if a directions hearing only, by way of video link. Video link facilities may be available such that the applicant or person to be protected can remain in another room within a different part of the court building; alternatively video link facilities may be available such that they can participate via video link from an entirely different location.

6.43 Should the inter partes hearing be a substantive contested hearing, consideration must be given to whether any special measures should be put in place to assist the person to be protected or other applicant and/or witness to give evidence.[31] Consideration should be given to the following:

- evidence being given from behind screens;

- video recorded evidence. An interview with the person to be protected/other witness could be recorded before the hearing, to be shown as their evidence in chief. They would, however, still be required for cross examination;[32] and

- live TV/video links. This would allow an applicant and/or witness to give evidence from outside the courtroom. The TV link could enable the person giving evidence to do so via a link from another room in a court building, or from another building entirely. By way of example, one of the authors has experience of a 2-week hearing in family proceedings taking place in circumstances where one of the parties participated in the hearing throughout by way of video link from an undisclosed building in another part of the country. The mother in that case was at serious risk of an 'honour' killing.

6.44 In considering the use of special measures, the key issue is establishing arrangements which will permit the witness to give their evidence most effectively. For those witnesses who are able, and for whom it can be made safe, it will usually be best for them to give evidence before the judge, perhaps protected by screens.[33] Some applicants, persons to be protected or witnesses will not be able to be present in the courtroom or it will be not safe for them to be so. For those persons the giving of evidence by video link either from a different part of the building or an entirely different building might be the better option.

6.45 The issue of what special measures might be appropriate must be a matter considered on a case-by-case basis.

6.46 Cultural considerations may arise in relation to the giving of evidence, in particular the wish of a female witness to wear the full face veil. A female witness may be reluctant to remove the same when giving evidence in the presence of a male judge or other male persons within the court.

---

[31] Practitioners will note that FPR 1991, r 10.21(1A) provides that in proceedings under FLA 1996, Part 4A a party is not required to disclose the address of any witness unless the court directs otherwise.

[32] This, like the other bullet points in this section, is an example specifically given in Form FL701 (the leaflet published by the Ministry of Justice containing guidance on making applications for FMPOs).

[33] For further reading on the issue of special measures see, for example, Burton, Evans and Sanders 'Vulnerable and Intimidated Witnesses and the Adversarial Process in England and Wales' [2007] 11 Int J Evidence and Proof 1, February (research into effectiveness of special measures in criminal proceedings).

6.47 This issue was considered by Mrs Justice Macur in the authority *Re S (Practice: Muslim Women Giving Evidence)*.[34] Macur J stated (per curiam) that the ability to observe a witness' demeanour and deportment during the giving of evidence was important and essential to assess accuracy and credibility. It was a matter of extreme importance that witnesses in such sensitive cases should be permitted to present their case to the satisfaction of the court but also observe their religious observance of dress. It was Macur J's view that the facility of screens, and the ability if at all possible, to list such cases before a female judge, would obviate the objections of litigants or witnesses. This was subject to an assessment of the genuine nature of their unwillingness to appear before the court without a veil.

6.48 Each case must be looked at on its own circumstances and the court would be alert to any opportunistic attempt to derail proceedings (eg if the case was listed for final hearing and a late application for the above was made).[35]

6.49 There are not as yet procedural rules determining how applications for special measures for witnesses are to be made in FMPO cases. As noted above, whilst the application form requires an indication by the applicant as to whether special arrangements are required for their attendance at court, it does not specifically mention special measures for giving evidence. A prudent applicant would make a formal application before the day of the hearing if possible.

6.50 Whilst the timing of hearings may make long periods of notice impossible, applicants' solicitors would be well advised to make applications for special measures as soon as practicable. This is especially the case as many courts require notice to be able to accommodate parties' requests for such measures. It will be essential to apply in advance for a video link. One way in which this could conveniently be accomplished is for the application for special measures at the inter partes hearing to be filed with the ex parte application. The judge could then make the appropriate order and the respondent would have to apply to vary the order if reasonable objections are made.

Service of orders following an inter partes hearing

6.51 After the hearing the following must be served:

- a copy of the order together with any power of arrest made;[36] and

- a copy of the record of hearing.[37]

6.52 The above must be served personally on the respondent, the person being protected by the order (if not the applicant) and any other person named in the order.[38]

6.53 Service must be effected as soon as reasonably practicable.[39]

6.54 Service shall be effected by the court if the applicant so requests.[40]

---

[34] [2007] 2 FLR 461. A female petitioner in nullity proceedings was a practising Muslim, wearing a full face veil. Whilst the petitioner was willing to remove her veil in order that the female judge could observe her demeanour and expression during oral evidence, she wished to be screened from her male counsel. Guidance was sought in relation to this practical problem.

[35] [2007] 2 FLR 461, at 465.

[36] Forms FL404B and FL406A.

[37] Form FL405.

[38] FPR 1991, r 3.33(5).

[39] FPR 1991, r 3.33(5).

[40] FPR 1991, r 3.33(6).

Powers of arrest attached to inter partes FMPOs

6.55 When a power of arrest is attached, specified documents must be delivered to the police. The same procedure must be followed as when a power of arrest is attached to an ex parte FMPO. Readers are therefore referred to the earlier discussion in this regard at **6.35–6.37**.

FMPOS MADE BY THE COURT OF ITS OWN MOTION

6.56 A FMPO may be made by a court of its own motion, in circumstances where:[41]

- there are existing family proceedings before the court;[42]

- the court considers that a FMPO should be made to protect any person (party to those proceedings or otherwise); and

- the respondent to such a FMPO is a party to the existing family proceedings.

Procedure following the court making an order of its own motion

6.57 Where a court makes a FMPO of its own motion it must set out in the order:[43]

- a summary of its reasons for making the order; and

- the names of the persons who are to be served with the order.

6.58 The court may order service of the order on the following:[44]

- any of the parties to the already existing family proceedings;

- (if different) the person to be protected; and

- any other persons whom the court requires to be served.

6.59 The court will give directions as to how the order is to be served.[45]

6.60 Following its making of a FMPO the court may direct that a further hearing be held to consider any representations made by any of the persons named in the order.[46]

APPLICATION TO VARY, EXTEND OR DISCHARGE

6.61 An application can be made to vary, extend or discharge a FMPO or any term thereof.

---

[41] FLA 1996, s 63C(1)(b) and (6).
[42] 'Family proceedings' has the same meaning as in FLA 1996, Part 4 (see s 63(1) and (3)), but also includes proceedings under the inherent jurisdiction of the High Court in relation to adults; proceedings in which the court has made an emergency protection order under s 44 of the Children Act 1989 (CA 1989), which includes an exclusion requirement; and proceedings in which the court has made an order under CA 1989, s 50 (FLA 1996, s 63(7)).
[43] FPR 1991, r 3.34(1).
[44] FPR 1991, r 3.34(2).
[45] FPR 1991, r 3.34(3). Note, however, that r 3.33(6) indicates that service of a copy of the order and record of the hearing will be effected by the court where the court has made the FMPO of its own motion.
[46] FPR 1991, r 3.34(4).

6.62 FPR 1991 refers to applications to vary, extend or discharge[47] whilst FLA 1996 itself refers only to variation or discharge.[48] It is the view of the authors that 'variation' within the statute should be read so as to include 'extension' of the order. Section 63F makes it plain that an order shall last for a specified period or until varied or discharged. This means that any variation can affect the duration of the order, so must include variation of the period for which the order shall run.[49]

Who may make an application to vary, extend or discharge?

6.63 The court may vary or discharge a FMPO on an application by:[50]

• any party to the proceedings for the order;

• the person being protected by the order (if not a party to the proceedings for the order); or

• any person affected by the order.

6.64 In circumstances where the court has made an order of its own motion[51] the court can vary or discharge that order without an application.[52]

Procedure for applications to vary, extend or discharge

6.65 Applications to vary, extend or discharge a FMPO must be made on Form FL403A. The same form is used where an application is made to vary, extend or discharge a FMPO made of the courts own motion.[53]

6.66 Applications for variation of an order can be made on an ex parte basis, even if the order of which variation or extension is sought was made on an inter partes basis. In such circumstances the court will exercise its powers in accordance with the principles relevant to the making of ex parte orders.[54]

6.67 Upon an application to vary an order the court, if it deems it appropriate, may accept an undertaking and discharge all or part of an order.[55] Practitioners are referred to the particular circumstances in which undertakings can be accepted which will still apply.[56]

6.68 The court may vary or discharge a power of arrest attached to an order.[57] A power of arrest can be varied or discharged whether or not there is also a variation or discharge of any other provision of the FMPO.[58]

---

[47] FPR 1991, r 3.33(8).
[48] FLA 1996, s 63G.
[49] By way of further analogy, in the context of anti-social behaviour orders and even less clear statutory wording, the Divisional Court in *Leeds City Council v RG* [2007] EWHC 1612 (Admin), [2007] 4 All ER 652, [2007] 1 WLR 3025 held that variation included extension of the term of an Order.
[50] FLA 1996, s 63G(1).
[51] By virtue of FLA 1996, s 63C(1)(b).
[52] FLA 1996, s 63G(2).
[53] FPR 1991, rr 3.34(5) and 3.33(8).
[54] FLA 1996, ss 63G(3) and 63D.
[55] FLA 1996, ss 63G(4) and 63E.
[56] FLA 1996, s 63E.
[57] FLA 1996, s 63G(6) and (7).
[58] FLA 1996, s 63G(7).

6.69 FPR 1991, r 3.33(8) deems that r 3.33 shall apply to the hearing of any application for variation, extension or discharge. Thus the same rules apply in relation to:

- the hearing being in chambers unless the court otherwise directs;

- the requirements for the form of recording of hearing and order made;

- the power to withhold submissions made or evidence adduced;

- requirements for service by the applicant; and

- the power to order a further hearing to consider further representations.

Procedure following variation or extension of power of arrest

6.70 Where a power of arrest has been varied or extended, Form FL406A and a statement showing that the respondents and any other persons directed by the court have been served or informed of its terms, must be again delivered to the officer in charge of the police station for the address of the person to be protected or other police station as specified by the court.[59]

6.71 Best practice is that if a power of arrest is discharged, this should be communicated immediately to the police to prevent an arrest on the misapprehension that the power of arrest continues.

APPEALS

6.72 The following discussion focuses primarily on appeals from the decision or order of a district judge in FMPO proceedings.

Appeals from district judges

6.73 The procedure for appeals from an order or decision of a district judge in FMPO proceedings is governed by FPR 1991, rr 8.2–8.2H, as amended by the Family Proceedings (Amendment) Rules 2009[60] which came into force on 6 April 2009. The rules are supplemented by a Practice Direction made by the President of the Family Division of the same date. This statutory instrument is reproduced within the Appendices to this Bulletin.[61]

To which judge/court does the appeal lie?

6.74 An appeal from a decision of a district judge sitting in the county court in FMPO proceedings under FLA 1996, Part 4A lies to a judge of the county court. Similarly a decision of a district judge sitting in the Family Division of the High Court lies to a judge of that court.[62]

---

[59] See FPR 1991, r 3.35(3).
[60] SI 2009/636.
[61] Readers are advised to note that r 8.1B concerning appeals from orders made under FLA 1996, Part 4A, inserted by r 8 of the Family Proceedings (Amendment) Rules 2008, SI 2008/2446 (also reproduced in the Appendices) has been revoked, together with the original FPR 1991, r 8.1A.
[62] FPR 1991, r 8.2(1)(b), as amended by the Family Proceedings (Amendment) Rules 2009, SI 2009/636.

6.75 Any party may appeal from an order or decision made in FMPO proceedings on notice.[63] Such appeals will be heard in chambers unless the judge directs otherwise.[64]

6.76 The appellant must file and serve, on the parties to the proceedings at first instance and any children's guardian, the following documents:[65]

- notice in writing of the appeal, setting out the grounds of the appeal;

- a certified copy of the summons or application, the order appealed against and any order staying its execution;

- a copy of any notes of the evidence; and

- a copy of any reasons given for the decision.[66]

6.77 The notice of appeal must be filed and served in accordance with the following timetable:

- within 14 days after the determination against which the appeal is brought;[67] or

- with the leave of the court to which, or judge to whom, the appeal is brought, within such other time as that court or judge may direct.[68]

Readers are referred to rule FPR 1991, r 8.2D concerning the procedure for amendment of the appeal notice.

6.78 The other documents referred to at **6.76** above must be filed and served as soon as practicable after the filing and service of the notice of appeal, subject to any direction of the judge/court.[69]

6.79 A respondent must file and serve a notice in writing on all other parties, should that respondent wish to contend that:

- the decision of the court below should be varied, either in any event or in the event of the appeal being allowed in whole or in part;

- that the decision of the court below should be affirmed on grounds other than those relied upon by that court; or

- by way of cross-appeal that the decision of the court below was wrong in whole or in part.

Such notice must be filed and served within 14 days of receipt of notice of the appeal and must set out the grounds on which the respondent relies.[70]

6.80 Unless the court orders otherwise, an appeal under these provisions does *not* operate as a stay of the order or decision in the FMPO proceedings.[71]

---

[63]   FPR 1991, r 8.2(2).
[64]   FPR 1991, r 8.2(3).
[65]   FPR 1991, r 8.2A(1) and (2).
[66]   Practitioners are referred to the Practice Direction supplementing FPR 1991, rr 8.A1 and 8.2–8.2H for guidance as to what constitutes a suitable record of the judgment of the court below.
[67]   FPR 1991, r 8.2A(3)(a).
[68]   FPR 1991, r 8.2A(3)(d).
[69]   FPR 1991, r 8.2A(4).
[70]   FPR 1991, r 8.2B(1).
[71]   FPR 1991, r 8.2C.

Powers of the judge hearing the appeal

6.81 The appeal court has all the powers of the court below.[72] The appeal court has power to do the following:[73]

- affirm, set aside or vary any order or judgment made or given by the court below;

- refer any application or issue for determination by the court below;

- order a new hearing;

- make orders for the payment of interest;

- make a costs order.

The appeal court may exercise its powers in relation to the whole or part of any order made by the district judge.[74]

Format of the appeal hearing

6.82 Each appeal will be limited to a *review* of the decision of the district judge unless:[75]

- an enactment makes different provision for a particular category of appeal; or

- the court considers that in the circumstances of an individual appeal it would be in the interests of justice to hold a re-hearing.

6.83 The appeal court will not receive oral evidence or evidence which was not heard by the district judge unless it orders otherwise.[76]

6.84 The appeal court will allow an appeal where the decision of the district judge was:[77]

- wrong; or

- unjust because of a serious procedural or other irregularity in the proceedings in the court below.

The appeal court can draw any inference of fact which it considers justified on the evidence.[78]

---

[72] FPR 1991, r 8.2F(1).
[73] FPR 1991, r 8.2F(2).
[74] FPR 1991, r 8.2F(3). Note that once the appeal is lodged, a district judge may dismiss the appeal for want of prosecution, or with the consent of the parties, or give leave for the appeal to be withdrawn. The district judge may also deal with any costs issues arising out of such dismissal/withdrawal (FPR 1991, r 8.2E).
[75] FPR 1991, r 8.2G(1).
[76] FPR 1991, r 8.2G(2).
[77] FPR 1991, r 8.2G(3).
[78] FPR 1991, r 8.2G(4).

Appeals from the order or decision of a circuit judge or High Court judge

6.85 There is no special provision in relation to appeals in FMPO proceedings from the decision or order of a circuit judge, recorder of the county court or High Court judge. Appeals lie to the Court of Appeal and practitioners are referred to Part 52 of the Civil Procedure Rules 1998,[79] supplemented by Practice Direction 52, 'Practice Direction – Appeals'.[80]

---

[79] SI 1998/3132.

[80] Practitioners are referred to the latest edition of Family Court Practice, published by Jordans, for detailed procedural guides concerning the routes of appeal.

CHAPTER 7

ENFORCEMENT OF FORCED MARRIAGE PROTECTION ORDERS

7.1 This chapter outlines the various methods by which a court may enforce a forced marriage protection order (FMPO).

SUMMARY OF METHODS OF ENFORCEMENT

7.2 A person can be brought before the court for alleged breach of a FMPO by the following means:

- under a power of arrest attached to the FMPO;[1]

- under a warrant of arrest issued by the court;[2] or

- by application for a warrant of committal.[3]

7.3 A power of arrest cannot be attached to an undertaking. A person can therefore be brought before the court for alleged breach of an undertaking pursuant to only the latter two options listed above.

7.4 Section 63E(4) of the Family Law Act 1996 (FLA 1996) provides that an undertaking given by a respondent to FMPO proceedings is enforceable under the legislation as if the court had made the order in the same terms as the undertaking. The court's powers to enforce an *order* without a power of arrest include the issuing of a warrant of arrest. It seems therefore that s 63E(4) enables a court to issue a warrant of arrest further to alleged breach of an undertaking.

7.5 The court's powers to punish breach of a FMPO or undertaking given in response to such an application are contained in the Contempt of Court Act 1981.

ARREST UNDER A POWER OF ARREST

7.6 As discussed in Chapter 4,[4] powers of arrest may be attached to FMPOs in specified circumstances.[5]

---

[1] Family Law Act 1996 (FLA 1996), s 63I.
[2] FLA 1996, s 63J.
[3] Under CCR Ord 29.
[4] See Chapter 4 at **4.100–4.115**.
[5] Pursuant to FLA 1996, s 63H.

Procedure following the court attaching a power of arrest

7.7 When a power of arrest is attached to one or more of the provisions of a FMPO, a Form FL406A is completed by the court. This form sets out only those provisions of the order to which the power of arrest is attached.[6]

7.8 As discussed in Chapter 6, when a power of arrest is attached the following documents must be delivered to the officer in charge of the police station for the address of the person being protected by the order, or to such other police station as the court may specify:

- Form FL406A; and

- a statement showing that the respondents and any other persons directed by the court to be served with the order have been so served or informed of its terms (whether by being present when the order was made or by telephone or otherwise).[7]

7.9 The relevant documents must be delivered to the police by the applicant or a representative, unless the court is responsible for serving the FMPO:

- following a request by the applicant; or

- because the court has made the FMPO of its own motion.[8]

In what circumstances may a person be arrested under the power of arrest?

7.10 If a power of arrest is attached to the provisions of a FMPO a police officer may arrest without a warrant a person whom the officer has reasonable cause for suspecting to be in breach of any such provision or otherwise in contempt of court in relation to the order.[9]

Who could be subject to arrest?

7.11 The following persons could be subject to arrest:

- a named respondent;

- an unnamed person placed within a category of persons to whom the order is directed; and

- *any* third party who frustrates the terms of the order and is therefore 'otherwise in contempt'.

7.12 The Forced Marriage (Civil Protection) Act 2007 enters into novel legal territory. Not only can respondents who have been served with the order be arrested but a person can potentially be arrested for breach of an order, the terms of which they were unaware, if they are within a category of persons to whom the order is directed.

---

[6] Family Proceedings Rules 1991 (FPR 1991), SI 1991/1247, r 3.9A(1), modified by FPR 1991, r 3.35(2). FPR 1991, r 3.9A generally applies to a FMPO as it applies to an order under FLA 1996, Part 4, subject to the modifications set out in FPR 1991, r 3.35.
[7] FPR 1991, r 3.35(3), substituting FPR 1991, r 3.9A(1A).
[8] FPR 1991, r 3.35(4), modifying FPR 1991, r 3.9A(1B).
[9] FLA 1996, s 63I(2).

7.13 As discussed in Chapter 4, the terms of a FMPO may be directed not just against respondents, but also to persons who are, or may become, involved in other respects.[10] An order can therefore be directed against named respondents and other persons. This could include unnamed individuals.

7.14 An order could be directed to 'any person' or to a category of persons, for example, members of the 'Z family'.

7.15 A power of arrest may be attached to provisions which are directed to persons who are not named respondents, provided that the court considers that a person to whom the order is directed has used or threatened violence against the person to be protected or otherwise in connection with the matters being dealt with by the order.[11]

7.16 A FMPO could, for example, include a blanket provision that no person shall assist in arrangements in relation to the engagement or matrimony, whether by civil or religious ceremony, of the person to be protected. A power of arrest could be attached to such a provision provided the conditions in FLA 1996, s 63H were satisfied.[12]

7.17 If a power of arrest is attached to such a provision, the police officer may arrest any person whom he or she has reasonable cause to suspect is in breach of that provision of the order, even if they were not a respondent to the original proceedings.

7.18 A person can also be arrested if they are 'otherwise in contempt in relation to the order'. As discussed in Chapter 4, a person could be otherwise in contempt by having aided and abetted breach of a FMPO.[13] As a result a person could be arrested should they have frustrated a term of the order to which a power of arrest is attached.[14]

Procedure following arrest under an attached power

7.19 When an arrest is made under a power of arrest attached to the FMPO the person must be bought before the relevant judge within the period of 24 hours commencing from the time of the arrest.[15]

7.20 Sundays, Christmas Day and Good Friday are ignored when calculating the 24-hour rule.[16]

7.21 When an arrest is made under a power of arrest then the person arrested must be kept in custody whilst the police inform the court.

7.22 The provision that a person be brought to court within 24 hours of their arrest assumes particular importance in this context where it is possible that they have been arrested for being in breach of an order of which they were wholly unaware.

---

[10] FLA 1996, s 63B(2).
[11] FLA 1996, s 63H(7).
[12] See Chapter 4 at **4.100** onwards.
[13] This follows the long-established legal principle: see, for example, *Elliott v Clinger* [1967] 3 All ER 141; and *Seaward v Patterson* [1897] 1 Ch 545, CA.
[14] Similarly, a warrant of arrest may be issued on an application if the judge has reasonable grounds to believe that the person is otherwise in contempt of court in relation to the order.
[15] FLA 1996, s 63I(3).
[16] FLA 1996, s 63I(4).

Who is the 'relevant judge'?

7.23 A 'relevant judge' is as follows:

- where the order was made by the High Court, a judge of that court; and

- where the order was made by a county court, a judge or district judge of that or any other county court.[17]

7.24 Therefore, there is no requirement that the arrested person must be brought before a circuit judge or district judge of the county court in which the FMPO was made, or indeed one of the other courts designated to deal with FMPOs.

7.25 However, it is the authors' understanding that the police will be encouraged to bring the person arrested before the originating court or another forced marriage court in the first instance.

7.26 Further, if the person is brought before the relevant judge and the matter is not disposed of immediately, the matter may be transferred to be heard by the relevant judge or court which attached the power of arrest.[18]

WARRANTS OF ARREST

7.27 A warrant of arrest may be issued by the court in circumstances where a person has failed to comply with the FMPO or otherwise appears to be in contempt of court in relation to the FMPO.[19]

In what circumstances may an application be made for a warrant?

7.28 An application for a warrant of arrest can only be made if a FMPO has been made but:[20]

- no power of arrest has been attached to any provision of the order under FLA 1996, s 63H;

- a power of arrest is attached only to certain provisions of the order; or

- a power of arrest was attached for a period and that period has expired.

7.29 A warrant cannot be granted if the breach relates to a term of the order to which a power of arrest has been attached, unless the power of arrest has already lapsed in time.

7.30 An interested party (see below) may apply to the relevant judge for a warrant of arrest to be issued, if they consider that a person has breached the FMPO or is otherwise in contempt of court in relation to the FMPO.[21]

---

[17] FLA 1996, s 63S.
[18] Allocation and Transfer of Proceedings Order 2008, SI 2008/2836, art 24. Similarly, if a person is brought before the relevant judge or court pursuant to a warrant issued, and the matter is not disposed of immediately, the matter may be transferred to the judge or court which issued the warrant.
[19] FLA 1996, s 63J(3).
[20] FLA 1996, s 63J(1).
[21] FLA 1996, s 63J(2).

7.31 An application can also be made for a warrant of arrest in circumstances where a person has failed to comply with an undertaking given to the court further to an application for a FMPO.[22]

Who is an 'interested party'?

7.32 An 'interested party', who may make an application for a warrant, is:[23]

- the person being protected by the order;

- (if a different person) the person who applied for the order; or

- any other person.

7.33 An interested party was extended to include 'any other person' at the report stage of the Bill (13 June 2007). The Government had originally defined 'interested party' as being the person protected by the order or the person who had applied for the order on their behalf. Following further consideration it was decided that the definition should be extended to cover the situation where the third party applicant was not available to apply for the arrest warrant and the only person then being left to apply would be the victim. Had the victim not applied for the original order, whether because of fear or otherwise, they were extremely unlikely to apply for a warrant of arrest.

In what circumstances can a person other than the person to be protected/applicant apply?

7.34 'Any other person', namely a person other than the person to be protected or the applicant (if different), cannot make an application for the issue of a warrant unless the relevant judge has given leave.[24]

Against whom could a warrant of arrest be issued?

7.35 As with arrests under substantive attached powers of arrest, the warrant could be issued against not just a named respondent but any other person who the interested person asserts to have failed to comply with the order, or to be 'otherwise in contempt in relation to the order'.

Procedure for application of the issue of a warrant

7.36 An application for the issue of a warrant for the arrest of a person must be made in Form FL407A and must be accompanied by a sworn statement.[25] The sworn statement should particularise the alleged breaches.

---

[22] FLA 1996, s 63E(4) provides that an undertaking given to the court is enforceable as if the court had made the order in terms corresponding to those of the undertaking.
[23] FLA 1996, s 63J(4). See earlier discussion at **7.5**.
[24] FLA 1996, s 63J(4).
[25] FPR 1991, r 3.35(6), substituting a new para (3) for FPR 1991, r 3.9A(3).

Application by a person who is neither the person to be protected nor the applicant

7.37 If the application for the issue of a warrant of arrest is made by 'any other person', no separate leave application is necessary and the application will be treated in the first instance as an application for leave.[26]

7.38 The court will need to be satisfied that the person applying has sufficient interest in the case for the application for a warrant to proceed.

7.39 The court will either grant the application on paper or direct that a date be fixed for the hearing of the application and will fix a date for the same.

7.40 The court will in any event inform the following of its decision:[27]

- the person applying for the warrant;

- the person to be protected by the order; and

- any other person directed by the court.

In what circumstances may the relevant judge issue a warrant of arrest?

7.41 A relevant judge can only issue a warrant of arrest if the application is substantiated on oath.[28]

7.42 Further, the relevant judge must have reasonable grounds to believe that the person to be arrested has failed to comply with the order or is otherwise in contempt of court in relation to the order.[29]

7.43 A warrant of arrest application can only be heard ex parte. If granted, then a warrant of arrest is issued on existing FLA 1996 Form FL408.[30]

7.44 There is no equivalent rule to that relating to arrests under a power of arrest, requiring a person arrested under a warrant to be brought before the court within 24 hours of arrest.

PROCEDURE ON AN ARRESTED PERSON BEING BROUGHT BEFORE THE COURT

7.45 When a person is brought before the court following arrest, either under an attached power or a warrant, the court may do the following:

- determine whether the facts, and the circumstances which led to the arrest, amounted to disobedience of the order,[31] and determine the appropriate penalty, if any; or

---

[26] FPR, r 3.35(6), substituting a new para (3A) for FPR 1991, r 3.9A(3).
[27] FPR 1991, r 3.35(6), inserting a new para (3A) to FPR 1991, r 3.9A(3).
[28] FLA 1996, s 63J(3)(a).
[29] FLA 1996, s 63J(3)(b). See discussion above as to the meaning of this phrase.
[30] FPR 1991, r 3.35(6), inserting a new para (3B) to FPR 1991, r 3.9A(3).
[31] FPR 1991, r 3.9A(4)(a).

- adjourn the proceedings. Where an order for adjournment is made, the arrested person may be released and, unless the court directs otherwise, should be dealt with within 14 days of the day on which he or she was arrested. The arrested person must be given not less than 2 days' notice of the adjourned hearing;[32]

- release the person without remand (additional terms may be added to the existing FMPO);

- remand the person on bail; or

- remand the person in custody.

IMMEDIATE DISPOSAL

7.46 On the arrested person first being brought before the court, the judge can determine whether on the facts of the case the person is in breach of the terms of the FMPO.

7.47 Adjournments will, however, be common. The person who has been arrested will be encouraged to seek legal advice. Further, evidence may have to be obtained either by the applicant or the respondent, for example, police disclosure. Witnesses may have to attend court to give oral evidence.

7.48 Readers are referred to the commentary below on penalties for contempt of court should a breach be proved.

ADJOURNMENTS

7.49 In circumstances where the case cannot be disposed of immediately, the court is faced with the alternative of a simple adjournment or remanding the person who is arrested either in custody or on bail.

7.50 In circumstances where the proceedings are adjourned and the person arrested is released, the arrested person should be dealt with within 14 days of the day of arrest unless the court directs otherwise.[33]

7.51 Should the person not be dealt with within those 14 days, an application to commit (see below) can still be issued.[34]

REMAND

7.52 When an arrested person is brought before the court, either under a power of arrest or a warrant of arrest, and the matter is not disposed of immediately, the court may remand the person concerned.[35]

7.53 An order for the remand of the arrested person shall be in Form FL409.[36]

---

[32] FPR 1991, r 3.9A(4)(b).
[33] FPR 1991, r 3.9A(4)(b).
[34] FPR 1991, r 3.9A(4).
[35] FLA 1996, s 63K(1).
[36] FPR 1991, r 3.9A(9), modified by FPR 1991, r 3.35(10).

7.54   The power to remand is governed by FLA 1996, Sch 5.[37]

7.55   A person may be remanded:

- in custody;

- on bail; or

- for the purposes of enabling a medical examination and report to be made.

For how long may an arrested person be remanded in custody?

7.56   An arrested person may not be remanded in custody for a period exceeding 8 clear days.[38]

7.57   If the remand is for a period not exceeding 3 clear days, the court can commit the arrested person to the custody of a constable.[39]

7.58   The arrested person must be brought before the court on the expiry of the remand. At this time the person may be the subject of a further remand in custody.[40]

7.59   The legislation does not provide for a maximum number of remands, nor for a maximum total period of remand. A court will always be mindful of the need to deal with committal applications urgently given that they deal with liberty of the subject. A period of remand in custody must be taken into account on sentence.

Bail

7.60   The court may remand the arrested person on bail. The court can remand an arrested person on bail on his or her own recognizance, with or without sureties, to appear before the court at the end of his or her remand period or at every subsequent hearing.[41]

7.61   Under the Forced Marriage (Civil Protection) Act 2007 the relevant judge can impose further requirements on the arrested person to ensure that whilst on bail the person does not interfere with witnesses or otherwise obstruct the course of justice.[42] The need for this will have to be assessed against the merits of extending/varying the FMPO or making a non-molestation order. Unlike breach for provisions of a FMPO, no specific action can be taken for breach of bail conditions.

7.62   The court will consider what conditional bail would add over and above a simple adjournment with the FMPO continuing/being varied in the interim to reflect additional concerns which may have arisen.

---

[37]   FLA 1996, s 63K(2), subject to modifications made by s 63K(3). The most pertinent sections are summarised here but readers are directed to the full Schedule.

[38]   FLA 1996, Sch 5, para 2(1)(a) and (5). Note that if the person is unable by reason or accident to appear/be brought before the court at the end of the period for which he or she was remanded, the court may in his or her absence, remand him or her for a further time and para 2(5) will not apply (para 3(1)).

[39]   FLA 1996, Sch 5, para 2(6).

[40]   FLA 1996, Sch 5, para 2(5).

[41]   FLA 1996, Sch 5, para 2(1)(b)(i) and (3). See Forms FL410 (form for taking recognizance), FL411 (form for taking surety) and FL412 (bail notice). Note that a person may be remanded in custody, to be released on providing the sum of recognizance required (para 2(1)(b)(ii)).

[42]   FLA 1996, s 63K(5).

7.63 The court shall not remand a person on bail for a period exceeding 8 clear days except if the arrested person and the other party consent.[43]

7.64 Where a person is before the court following a remand on bail, the court may further remand him or her.[44]

7.65 Practitioners should again be mindful of FPR 1991, r 3.9A(4) requiring that if the proceedings are adjourned and the arrested person is released, he or she should be dealt with within 14 days of the day on which he or she was arrested, unless the court directs otherwise. Should the court not give such a direction, and the proceedings extend beyond 14 days, a notice to commit will have to be issued.

Remands for medical examinations and reports

7.66 Where a judge has reason to consider that a medical report is required the court may remand an arrested person on bail or in custody for the purpose of enabling a medical examination to take place and a report to be made.[45]

7.67 If a court is to remand an arrested person on bail for the purposes of a medical report then the case must not be adjourned for more than 4 weeks at a time.[46]

7.68 However, if the arrested person is remanded in *custody* the adjournment must be for no more than 3 weeks at a time.[47] The legislation does not provide for a maximum number of remands, nor for a maximum total period of remand.

Remands to hospital

7.69 Where a person has been arrested pursuant to a power of arrest or a warrant of arrest and there is reason to suspect that the person is suffering from mental illness or severe mental impairment, the relevant judge has the power to make an order for remand to hospital for a report to be prepared, but not otherwise, on their mental condition.[48]

7.70 The court may remand the person to a hospital specified by the court.[49]

7.71 The court may exercise this power if:

- it is satisfied, on the written or oral evidence of a registered medical practitioner, that there is reason to suspect that the arrested person is suffering from mental disorder; and

- it is of the opinion that it would be impracticable for a report on the arrested person's mental condition to be made if he or she were remanded on bail.[50]

---

[43] FLA 1996, Sch 5, para 2(5)(a).
[44] FLA 1996, Sch 5, para 2(2).
[45] FLA 1996, s 63L(1).
[46] FLA 1996, s 63L(2).
[47] FLA 1996, s 63L(3).
[48] FLA 1996, s 63L(4) and (5). The relevant judge has the same power to make an order under s 35 of the Mental Health Act 1983 (MHA 1983) as the Crown Court has under s 35 of that Act.
[49] MHA 1983, s 35(1).
[50] MHA 1983, s 35(3).

7.72   The person must not be remanded or further remanded for more than 28 days at a time or for more than 12 weeks in all; and the court may at any time terminate the remand if it appears to the court that it is appropriate to do so.[51]

APPLICATIONS TO COMMIT

7.73   Where a person:

* refuses or fails to comply with a requirement under a FMPO or promised in an undertaking; or

* disobeys an order or undertaking to abstain from an act,

the order or undertaking can be enforced by committal to prison.

7.74   In circumstances where a person is in breach of the terms of a FMPO or undertaking given to the court, an applicant can issue an application notice seeking the committal for contempt of court of the person.

7.75   Such proceedings should be initiated by issue of a Form N78 ('Notice to show good reason why you should not be committed to prison') together with an affidavit in support.

7.76   The application notice must:

* identify the provisions of the FMPO or undertaking which it is alleged have been disobeyed or broken;

* list the ways in which it is alleged that the FMPO has been disobeyed or the undertaking has been broken; and

* be supported by an affidavit stating the grounds on which the application is made.[52]

7.77   Unless a court dispenses with the requirement of service, the application notice and copy of the affidavit must be served on the respondent to the committal proceedings personally.[53]

7.78   The relevant judge (see earlier definition) may exercise the powers of the court in relation to contempt of court arising from a person's failure to comply with a FMPO or otherwise in connection with such an order.[54]

PROOF OF BREACH OF FMPO/UNDERTAKING

7.79   The burden of proving breach of the terms of a FMPO or undertaking is on the person alleging contempt of court.

---

[51]   MHA 1983, s 35(4). A more detailed analysis of the provisions of this section is outside the scope of this Bulletin. Practitioners are referred to s 35 in its entirety.

[52]   CCR Ord 29, r 1(4A).

[53]   CCR Ord 29, r 1(4), (4A). For detailed consideration of the provisions relating to applications to commit (outside the scope of this publication), practitioners are referred to Sch 2 to the Civil Procedure Rules 1998, SI 1998/3132, containing CCR Ord 29, r 1, President's Direction 16 March 2001 'Committal Applications and Proceedings in which a Committal Order may be Made' [2001] 1 FLR 949 and the most recent edition of The Family Court Practice (Jordans Publishing).

[54]   FLA 1996, s 63O.

7.80 The standard of proof is the criminal standard.[55]

7.81 The presumption in CCR Ord 29, r 1 is that an order shall not be enforced by a committal order unless:

- a copy of the order has been served personally on the person required to do or abstain from doing the act in question; and

- in the case of an order requiring a person to do an act, the copy has been served before the expiration of the time within which he or she was required to do the act and was accompanied by a copy of an order fixing the time.[56]

7.82 The exceptions to this rule are where the court has dispensed with the need for service of the order[57] or notwithstanding that service of the order has not been effected, the judge is satisfied that the person against whom it is sought to enforce the order had notice either:

- by being present when the judgment or order was given or made; or

- by being notified of the terms of the judgment or order whether by telephone, fax, e-mail or otherwise.[58]

7.83 The respondent to the committal proceedings must be allowed to cross-examine witnesses and call evidence if they wish.

7.84 Practitioners will be mindful of the need to give careful consideration to requests for security arrangements and special measures for the giving of evidence in committal applications (see commentary in Chapter 6). Remember also that committal hearings are heard in open court.

Proof of breach in the case of persons who are not named respondents

7.85 The provision for orders to be directed against non-respondents, including unnamed individuals, was identified as necessary to close a loophole: namely the potential for a large number of not always identifiable persons to be involved in arrangements for a forced marriage. However, committing such persons to prison for breach of a FMPO which has not been served upon them and the making of which they may or may not be aware of, is likely to be problematic in many cases.

7.86 At the Report stage of the Forced Marriage (Civil Protection) Bill, Baroness Ashton of Upholland (the then Parliamentary Under-Secretary of State, Ministry of Justice) made the following comments in relation to the issue of un-named parties:[59]

'I will say a few words about how orders to un-named parties will work in practice, as I am sure that will interest noble Lords. It will be for the court to decide in each individual case whether it is necessary to extend an order to the third category of un-named persons. That would be likely to be in circumstances where there was evidence that members of the extended family or the wider community might be involved in forcing a marriage, meaning that it was not possible to identify all the possible respondents. Noble Lords will be aware that orders under Part 4 are always made against named parties. Enforcement of those orders relies on the ability to prove that the respondent is aware

---

[55] *Re C (A Minor) (Contempt)* [1986] 1 FLR 578, at 588; *Dean v Dean* [1987] 1 FLR 517.
[56] CCR Ord 29, r 1(2).
[57] CCR Ord 29, r 1(7).
[58] CCR Ord 29, r 1(6). Modern communications by which notification might be given include text message.
[59] *Hansard* HL Report Stage (13 June 2007), www.publications.parliament.uk/pa/ld200607/ldhansrd/text/70613-0008.htm#07061391000002.

of the terms of the order. When it is attached to an order, a power of arrest is delivered to the local police station together with a statement showing that the respondent has been served with the order or informed of its terms. Orders made against named parties under Part 4A will follow that procedure.

The position in the law regarding orders made against un-named respondents will remain that a person may be committed for contempt only if they are aware of the order that they are breaching. As orders made against unnamed respondents cannot be personally served, it will be for the courts to decide, on evidence, whether the person is aware of an order and is in contempt. The mechanics of serving the order will be set out in rules of court, and that could be supported by a practice direction setting out standard terms of an order and practice.

The power of arrest will also be subject to certain safeguards to ensure that it is used appropriately. Once arrested, the person must be brought before the court within 24 hours, and it will be for the court to decide on the evidence available whether it considers that the person was aware of the contents of the order. There will also be a right of appeal. I hope that noble Lords are assured that we have given careful consideration to putting in place the necessary safeguards to ensure that those provisions work in practice.'

7.87 Practitioners acting on behalf of persons to be protected or applicants (if different) must consider the issue of enforcement at the time that the order is made. Should an order be directed, for instance, against any member of 'Y family', consideration could be given to instructing a process server to serve multiple copies of the order on a known member(s) of the family at a known address(es) together with an accompanying letter stressing that the terms of the order must be brought to the attention of all members of the family.

7.88 It will be a matter of fact for the court to determine whether an unnamed individual or third party is in breach of the order. If they are in breach of the order but were unaware of its existence the court may take the view that no further sanction is appropriate so long as that person is prepared then to submit to the order or give an undertaking.

DISPOSAL

7.89 The court has a number of options available on conclusion of committal proceedings:

- release the arrested person if the breach is not proved;

- immediately commit the person to prison for a period of up to 2 years;[60]

- adjourn consideration of the penalty to be imposed for contempts found proved and such consideration may be restored if the arrested person does not comply with any conditions specified by the court;[61]

- remand the person under MHA 1983, s 35 in order that a report be prepared as to their mental condition;[62]

---

[60]   Contempt of Court Act 1981, s 14(1). The committal shall be for a fixed term and that term shall not on any occasion exceed 2 years.
[61]   FPR 1991, r 3.9A(6), modified by r 3.35(8).
[62]   Where there is reason to suspect that the person who could be committed to prison for contempt of court is suffering from mental disorder.

- make a hospital or guardianship order;[63]

- continue the existing FMPO (including extension)/vary the FMPO/terminate the FMPO;

- consider whether a FMPO should be made, and whether a power of arrest should be attached, if the proven breach was in relation to an undertaking;

- order a fine; or

- make an order for costs.

PURGING CONTEMPT

7.90 It is open to the court to permit a contemnor, on his or her application, to purge his or her contempt either at the time that he or she appears before the court or after a period of time in custody.[64]

---

[63] Contempt of Court Act 1981, s 14(4). Power to make a hospital order or guardianship order under MHA 1983, s 37 or an interim hospital order under MHA 1983, s 38 in the case of a person suffering from mental disorder. See Form FL413 (interim/hospital order) and Form FL414 (guardianship order).

[64] RSC Ord 8, r 2(2); CPR 1998, Sch 2; CCR Ord 29, r 3(1). See also *Harris v Harris* [2002] 1 FLR 248.

APPENDICES

* Existing forms which will be used in FMPO proceedings (not contained within this appendix):
    C8 Confidential Address
    FL405 Record of Hearing
    FL408 Warrant of Arrest
    FL409 Order for Remand
    FL410 Form for taking recognizance
    FL411 Form for taking surety
    FL412 Bail Notice
    FL415 Statement of service
    FL417 Transfer of proceedings

---

[1]   Effective 1 November 2009.

APPENDIX A

FORCED MARRIAGE (CIVIL PROTECTION) ACT 2007

CHAPTER 20

A.1

1 Protection against forced marriage: England and Wales

After Part 4 of the Family Law Act 1996 (c. 27) insert –

'PART 4A
FORCED MARRIAGE

Forced marriage protection orders

63A Forced marriage protection orders

(1) The court may make an order for the purposes of protecting –

    (a)   a person from being forced into a marriage or from any attempt to be forced into a marriage; or

    (b)   a person who has been forced into a marriage.

(2) In deciding whether to exercise its powers under this section and, if so, in what manner, the court must have regard to all the circumstances including the need to secure the health, safety and well-being of the person to be protected.

(3) In ascertaining that person's well-being, the court must, in particular, have such regard to the person's wishes and feelings (so far as they are reasonably ascertainable) as the court considers appropriate in the light of the person's age and understanding.

(4) For the purposes of this Part a person ("A") is forced into a marriage if another person ("B") forces A to enter into a marriage (whether with B or another person) without A's free and full consent.

(5) For the purposes of subsection (4) it does not matter whether the conduct of B which forces A to enter into a marriage is directed against A, B or another person.

(6) In this Part –

    "force" includes coerce by threats or other psychological means (and related expressions are to be read accordingly); and
    "forced marriage protection order" means an order under this section.

63B Contents of orders

(1) A forced marriage protection order may contain –

    (a)   such prohibitions, restrictions or requirements; and

    (b)   such other terms;

as the court considers appropriate for the purposes of the order.

(2) The terms of such orders may, in particular, relate to –

    (a)   conduct outside England and Wales as well as (or instead of) conduct within England and Wales;

    (b)   respondents who are, or may become, involved in other respects as well as (or instead of) respondents who force or attempt to force, or may force or attempt to force, a person to enter into a marriage;

    (c)   other persons who are, or may become, involved in other respects as well as respondents of any kind.

(3) For the purposes of subsection (2) examples of involvement in other respects are –

    (a)   aiding, abetting, counselling, procuring, encouraging or assisting another person to force, or to attempt to force, a person to enter into a marriage; or

    (b)   conspiring to force, or to attempt to force, a person to enter into a marriage.

63C Applications and other occasions for making orders

(1) The court may make a forced marriage protection order –

    (a)   on an application being made to it; or

    (b)   without an application being made to it but in the circumstances mentioned in subsection (6).

(2) An application may be made by –

    (a)   the person who is to be protected by the order; or

    (b)   a relevant third party.

(3) An application may be made by any other person with the leave of the court.

(4) In deciding whether to grant leave, the court must have regard to all the circumstances including –

    (a)   the applicant's connection with the person to be protected;

    (b)   the applicant's knowledge of the circumstances of the person to be protected; and

    (c)   the wishes and feelings of the person to be protected so far as they are reasonably ascertainable and so far as the court considers it appropriate, in the light of the person's age and understanding, to have regard to them.

(5) An application under this section may be made in other family proceedings or without any other family proceedings being instituted.

(6) The circumstances in which the court may make an order without an application being made are where –

    (a)   any other family proceedings are before the court ("the current proceedings");

    (b)   the court considers that a forced marriage protection order should be made to protect a person (whether or not a party to the current proceedings); and

    (c)   a person who would be a respondent to any such proceedings for a forced marriage protection order is a party to the current proceedings.

(7) In this section –

    "family proceedings" has the same meaning as in Part 4 (see section 63(1) and (2)) but also includes –

        (a)   proceedings under the inherent jurisdiction of the High Court in relation to adults;

    (b)   proceedings in which the court has made an emergency protection order under section 44 of the Children Act 1989 (c. 41) which includes an exclusion requirement (as defined in section 44A(3) of that Act); and

    (c)   proceedings in which the court has made an order under section 50 of the Act of 1989 (recovery of abducted children etc.); and

"relevant third party" means a person specified, or falling within a description of persons specified, by order of the Lord Chancellor.

(8) An order of the Lord Chancellor under subsection (7) may, in particular, specify the Secretary of State.

Further provision about orders

63D Ex parte orders: Part 4A

(1) The court may, in any case where it considers that it is just and convenient to do so, make a forced marriage protection order even though the respondent has not been given such notice of the proceedings as would otherwise be required by rules of court.

(2) In deciding whether to exercise its powers under subsection (1), the court must have regard to all the circumstances including –

    (a)   any risk of significant harm to the person to be protected or another person if the order is not made immediately;

    (b)   whether it is likely that an applicant will be deterred or prevented from pursuing an application if an order is not made immediately; and

    (c)   whether there is reason to believe that –

        (i)   the respondent is aware of the proceedings but is deliberately evading service; and

        (ii)   the delay involved in effecting substituted service will cause serious prejudice to the person to be protected or (if a different person) an applicant.

(3) The court must give the respondent an opportunity to make representations about any order made by virtue of subsection (1).

(4) The opportunity must be –

    (a)   as soon as just and convenient; and

    (b)   at a hearing of which notice has been given to all the parties in accordance with rules of court.

63E Undertakings instead of orders

(1) The court may, subject to subsection (3), accept an undertaking from the respondent to proceedings for a forced marriage protection order if it has power to make such an order.

(2) No power of arrest may be attached to an undertaking given under subsection (1).

(3) The court may not accept an undertaking under subsection (1) instead of making an order if a power of arrest would otherwise have been attached to the order.

(4) An undertaking given to the court under subsection (1) is enforceable as if the court had made the order in terms corresponding to those of the undertaking.

(5) This section is without prejudice to the powers of the court apart from this section.

63F Duration of orders

A forced marriage protection order may be made for a specified period or until varied or discharged.

63G Variation of orders and their discharge

(1) The court may vary or discharge a forced marriage protection order on an application by –

(a)   any party to the proceedings for the order;
(b)   the person being protected by the order (if not a party to the proceedings for the order); or
(c)   any person affected by the order.

(2) In addition, the court may vary or discharge a forced marriage protection order made by virtue of section 63C(1)(b) even though no application under subsection (1) above has been made to the court.

(3) Section 63D applies to a variation of a forced marriage protection order as it applies to the making of such an order.

(4) Section 63E applies to proceedings for a variation of a forced marriage protection order as it applies to proceedings for the making of such an order.

(5) Accordingly, references in sections 63D and 63E to making a forced marriage protection order are to be read for the purposes of subsections (3) and (4) above as references to varying such an order.

(6) Subsection (7) applies if a power of arrest has been attached to provisions of a forced marriage protection order by virtue of section 63H.

(7) The court may vary or discharge the order under this section so far as it confers a power of arrest (whether or not there is a variation or discharge of any other provision of the order).

Arrest for breach of orders

63H Attachment of powers of arrest to orders

(1) Subsection (2) applies if the court –

(a)   intends to make a forced marriage protection order otherwise than by virtue of section 63D; and
(b)   considers that the respondent has used or threatened violence against the person being protected or otherwise in connection with the matters being dealt with by the order.

(2) The court must attach a power of arrest to one or more provisions of the order unless it considers that, in all the circumstances of the case, there will be adequate protection without such a power.

(3) Subsection (4) applies if the court –

(a)   intends to make a forced marriage protection order by virtue of section 63D; and
(b)   considers that the respondent has used or threatened violence against the person being protected or otherwise in connection with the matters being dealt with by the order.

(4) The court may attach a power of arrest to one or more provisions of the order if it considers that there is a risk of significant harm to a person, attributable to conduct of the respondent, if the power of arrest is not attached to the provisions immediately.

(5) The court may provide for a power of arrest attached to any provisions of an order under subsection (4) to have effect for a shorter period than the other provisions of the order.

(6) Any period specified for the purposes of subsection (5) may be extended by the court (on one or more occasions) on an application to vary or discharge the order.

(7) In this section "respondent" includes any person who is not a respondent but to whom an order is directed.

63I Arrest under attached powers

(1) Subsection (2) applies if a power of arrest is attached to provisions of a forced marriage protection order under section 63H.

(2) A constable may arrest without warrant a person whom the constable has reasonable cause for suspecting to be in breach of any such provision or otherwise in contempt of court in relation to the order.

(3) A person arrested under subsection (2) must be brought before the relevant judge within the period of 24 hours beginning at the time of the person's arrest.

(4) In calculating any period of 24 hours for the purposes of subsection (3), Christmas Day, Good Friday and any Sunday are to be ignored.

63J Arrest under warrant

(1) Subsection (2) applies if the court has made a forced marriage protection order but –

    (a)   no power of arrest is attached to any provision of the order under section 63H;
    (b)   such a power is attached only to certain provisions of the order; or
    (c)   such a power was attached for a shorter period than other provisions of the order and that period has expired.

(2) An interested party may apply to the relevant judge for the issue of a warrant for the arrest of a person if the interested party considers that the person has failed to comply with the order or is otherwise in contempt of court in relation to the order.

(3) The relevant judge must not issue a warrant on an application under subsection (2) unless –

    (a)   the application is substantiated on oath; and
    (b)   the relevant judge has reasonable grounds for believing that the person to be arrested has failed to comply with the order or is otherwise in contempt of court in relation to the order.

(4) In this section "interested party", in relation to a forced marriage protection order, means –

    (a)   the person being protected by the order;
    (b)   (if a different person) the person who applied for the order; or
    (c)   any other person;

but no application may be made under subsection (2) by a person falling within paragraph (c) without the leave of the relevant judge.

63K Remand: general

(1) The court before which an arrested person is brought under section 63I(3) or by virtue of a warrant issued under section 63J may, if the matter is not then disposed of immediately, remand the person concerned.

(2) Schedule 5 has effect in relation to the powers of the court to remand a person by virtue of this section but as if the following modifications were made to the Schedule.

(3) The modifications are that –

(a)   in paragraph 2(1) of Schedule 5, the reference to section 47 is to be read as a reference to this section; and

(b)   in paragraph 2(5)(b) of the Schedule, the reference to section 48(1) is to be read as a reference to section 63L(1).

(4) Subsection (5) applies if a person remanded under this section is granted bail under Schedule 5 as modified above.

(5) The person may be required by the relevant judge to comply, before release on bail or later, with such requirements as appear to the relevant judge to be necessary to secure that the person does not interfere with witnesses or otherwise obstruct the course of justice.

63L Remand: medical examination and report

(1) Any power to remand a person under section 63K(1) may be exercised for the purpose of enabling a medical examination and report to be made if the relevant judge has reason to consider that a medical report will be required.

(2) If such a power is so exercised, the adjournment must not be for more than 4 weeks at a time unless the relevant judge remands the accused in custody.

(3) If the relevant judge remands the accused in custody, the adjournment must not be for more than 3 weeks at a time.

(4) Subsection (5) applies if there is reason to suspect that a person who has been arrested –

(a)   under section 63I(2); or
(b)   under a warrant issued on an application made under section 63J(2);

is suffering from mental illness or severe mental impairment.

(5) The relevant judge has the same power to make an order under section 35 of the Mental Health Act 1983 (c. 20) (remand for report on accused's mental condition) as the Crown Court has under section 35 of that Act in the case of an accused person within the meaning of that section.

Jurisdiction and procedure

63M Jurisdiction of courts: Part 4A

(1) For the purposes of this Part "the court" means the High Court or a county court.

(2) Subsection (1) is subject to any provision made by virtue of subsections (3) and (4).

(3) Section 57(3) to (12) (allocation of proceedings to courts etc.) apply for the purposes of this Part as they apply for the purposes of Part 4 but as if the following modification were made.

(4) The modification is that section 57(8) is to be read as if there were substituted for it –

"(8) For the purposes of subsections (3), (4) and (5), there are two levels of court –

(a)   the High Court; and
(b)   any county court."

63N Power to extend jurisdiction to magistrates' courts

(1) The Lord Chancellor may, after consulting the Lord Chief Justice, by order provide for magistrates' courts to be included among the courts who may hear proceedings under this Part.

(2) An order under subsection (1) may, in particular, make any provision in relation to magistrates' courts which corresponds to provision made in relation to such courts by or under Part 4.

(3) Any power to make an order under this section (including that power as extended by section 65(2)) may, in particular, be exercised by amending, repealing, revoking or otherwise modifying any provision made by or under this Part or any other enactment.

(4) The Lord Chief Justice may nominate a judicial office holder (as defined in section 109(4) of the Constitutional Reform Act 2005 (c. 4)) to exercise the Lord Chief Justice's functions under this section.

63O Contempt proceedings: Part 4A

The powers of the court in relation to contempt of court arising out of a person's failure to comply with a forced marriage protection order or otherwise in connection with such an order may be exercised by the relevant judge.

63P Appeals: Part 4A

(1) The Lord Chancellor may, after consulting the Lord Chief Justice, by order make provision as to the circumstances in which appeals may be made against decisions taken by courts on questions arising in connection with the transfer, or proposed transfer, of proceedings by virtue of an order made under section 57(5) as applied by section 63M(3) and (4).

(2) Except so far as provided for in any order made under subsection (1), no appeal may be made against any decision of a kind mentioned in that subsection.

(3) The Lord Chief Justice may nominate a judicial office holder (as defined in section 109(4) of the Constitutional Reform Act 2005) to exercise the Lord Chief Justice's functions under this section.

Supplementary

63Q Guidance

(1) The Secretary of State may from time to time prepare and publish guidance to such descriptions of persons as the Secretary of State considers appropriate about –

   (a)   the effect of this Part or any provision of this Part; or
   (b)   other matters relating to forced marriages.

(2) A person exercising public functions to whom guidance is given under this section must have regard to it in the exercise of those functions.

(3) Nothing in this section permits the Secretary of State to give guidance to any court or tribunal.

63R Other protection or assistance against forced marriage

(1) This Part does not affect any other protection or assistance available to a person who –

    (a)   is being, or may be, forced into a marriage or subjected to an attempt to be forced into a marriage; or

    (b)   has been forced into a marriage.

(2) In particular, it does not affect –

    (a)   the inherent jurisdiction of the High Court;

    (b)   any criminal liability;

    (c)   any civil remedies under the Protection from Harassment Act 1997 (c. 40);

    (d)   any right to an occupation order or a non-molestation order under Part 4 of this Act;

    (e)   any protection or assistance under the Children Act 1989 (c. 41);

    (f)   any claim in tort; or

    (g)   the law of marriage.

63S Interpretation of Part 4A

In this Part –

"the court" is to be read with section 63M;

"force" (and related expressions), in relation to a marriage, are to be read in accordance with section 63A(4) to (6);

"forced marriage protection order" has the meaning given by section 63A(6);

"marriage" means any religious or civil ceremony of marriage (whether or not legally binding); and

"the relevant judge", in relation to any order under this Part, means –

    (a)   where the order was made by the High Court, a judge of that court; and

    (b)   where the order was made by a county court, a judge or district judge of that or any other county court.'

2 Protection against forced marriage: Northern Ireland

Schedule 1 (protection against forced marriage: Northern Ireland) has effect.

3 Consequential amendments etc.

(1) Schedule 2 (consequential amendments) has effect.

(2) The Lord Chancellor may by order make such supplementary, incidental or consequential provision as the Lord Chancellor considers appropriate for the purposes of section 1 or in consequence of that section.

(3) The Department of Finance and Personnel may by order make such supplementary, incidental or consequential provision as the Department considers appropriate for the purposes of section 2 and Schedule 1 or in consequence of those provisions.

(4) An order under subsection (2) –

    (a)   may contain such transitional, transitory or saving provision as the Lord Chancellor considers appropriate; and

    (b)   is to be made by statutory instrument.

(5) An order under subsection (3) –

    (a)   may contain such transitional, transitory or saving provision as the Department of Finance and Personnel considers appropriate; and

    (b)   is to be made by statutory rule for the purposes of the Statutory Rules (Northern Ireland) Order 1979 (S.I. 1979/1573 (N.I. 12)).

(6) Any power to make an order under this section may, in particular, be exercised by amending, repealing, revoking or otherwise modifying any provision made by or under an enactment (including any Act passed in the same Session as this Act).

(7) No order is to be made under this section –

  (a)   by the Lord Chancellor unless a draft of the order has been laid before, and approved by a resolution of, each House of Parliament;
  (b)   by the Department of Finance and Personnel unless a draft of the order has been laid before, and approved by a resolution of, the Northern Ireland Assembly.

(8) Subsection (7)(a) does not apply to an order which does not amend or repeal any provision of an Act and an order of the Lord Chancellor under this section which does not amend or repeal any provision of an Act is subject to annulment in pursuance of a resolution of either House of Parliament.

(9) Subsection (7)(b) does not apply to an order which does not amend or repeal any provision of an Act or Northern Ireland legislation and an order of the Department of Finance and Personnel under this section which does not amend or repeal any provision of an Act or Northern Ireland legislation is subject to negative resolution (within the meaning of section 41(6) of the Interpretation Act (Northern Ireland) 1954 (c. 33 (N.I.))).

(10) In this section 'enactment' includes Northern Ireland legislation.

4 Short title, commencement and extent

(1) This Act may be cited as the Forced Marriage (Civil Protection) Act 2007.

(2) Section 1, section 3(1) (so far as relating to Part 1 of Schedule 2) and Part 1 of Schedule 2 come into force on such day as the Lord Chancellor may by order appoint; and different days may be appointed for different purposes.

(3) An order under subsection (2) –

  (a)   may contain such transitional, transitory or saving provision as the Lord Chancellor considers appropriate; and
  (b)   is to be made by statutory instrument.

(4) Section 2, section 3(1) (so far as relating to Part 2 of Schedule 2), Schedule 1 and Part 2 of Schedule 2 come into force on such day as the Department of Finance and Personnel may by order appoint; and different days may be appointed for different purposes.

(5) An order under subsection (4) –

  (a)   may contain such transitional, transitory or saving provision as the Department of Finance and Personnel considers appropriate; and
  (b)   is to be made by statutory rule for the purposes of the Statutory Rules (Northern Ireland) Order 1979 (S.I. 1979/1573 (N.I. 12)).

(6) Section 1 and Part 1 of Schedule 2 extend to England and Wales only.

(7) Section 2, Schedule 1 and Part 2 of Schedule 2 extend to Northern Ireland only.

(8) Section 3 and this section extend to England and Wales and Northern Ireland only.

SCHEDULE 1

Section 2

Protection against forced marriage: Northern Ireland

PART 1
FORCED MARRIAGE PROTECTION ORDERS

1 Forced marriage protection orders

(1) The court may make an order for the purposes of protecting –

  (a) a person from being forced into a marriage or from any attempt to be forced into a marriage; or

  (b) a person who has been forced into a marriage.

(2) In deciding whether to exercise its powers under this paragraph and, if so, in what manner, the court must have regard to all the circumstances including the need to secure the health, safety and well-being of the person to be protected.

(3) In ascertaining that person's well-being, the court must, in particular, have such regard to the person's wishes and feelings (so far as they are reasonably ascertainable) as the court considers appropriate in the light of the person's age and understanding.

(4) For the purposes of this Schedule a person ('A') is forced into a marriage if another person ('B') forces A to enter into a marriage (whether with B or another person) without A's free and full consent.

(5) For the purposes of sub-paragraph (4) it does not matter whether the conduct of B which forces A to enter into a marriage is directed against A, B or another person.

(6) In this Schedule –

  'force; includes coerce by threats or other psychological means (and related expressions are to be read accordingly); and

  'forced marriage protection order' means an order under this paragraph.

2 Contents of orders

(1) A forced marriage protection order may contain –

  (a) such prohibitions, restrictions or requirements; and

  (b) such other terms;

as the court considers appropriate for the purposes of the order.

(2) The terms of such orders may, in particular, relate to –

  (a) conduct outside Northern Ireland as well as (or instead of) conduct within Northern Ireland;

  (b) respondents who are, or may become, involved in other respects as well as (or instead of) respondents who force or attempt to force, or may force or attempt to force, a person to enter into a marriage;

(c) other persons who are, or may become, involved in other respects as well as respondents of any kind.

(3) For the purposes of sub-paragraph (2) examples of involvement in other respects are –

(a) aiding, abetting, counselling, procuring, encouraging or assisting another person to force, or to attempt to force, a person to enter into a marriage; or
(b) conspiring to force, or to attempt to force, a person to enter into a marriage.

3 Applications and other occasions for making orders

(1) The court may make a forced marriage protection order –

(a) on an application being made to it; or
(b) without an application being made to it but in the circumstances mentioned in sub-paragraph (6).

(2) An application may be made by –

(a) the person who is to be protected by the order; or
(b) a relevant third party.

(3) An application may be made by any other person with the leave of the court.

(4) In deciding whether to grant leave, the court must have regard to all the circumstances including –

(a) the applicant's connection with the person to be protected;
(b) the applicant's knowledge of the circumstances of the person to be protected; and
(c) the wishes and feelings of the person to be protected so far as they are reasonably ascertainable and so far as the court considers it appropriate, in the light of the person's age and understanding, to have regard to them.

(5) An application under this paragraph may be made in other family proceedings or without any other family proceedings being instituted.

(6) The circumstances in which the court may make an order without an application being made are where –

(a) any other family proceedings are before the court ('the current proceedings');
(b) the court considers that a forced marriage protection order should be made to protect a person (whether or not a party to the current proceedings); and
(c) a person who would be a respondent to any such proceedings for a forced marriage protection order is a party to the current proceedings.

(7) In this paragraph –

'family proceedings' has the same meaning as in the Family Homes and Domestic Violence (Northern Ireland) Order 1998 (S.I. 1998/1071 (N.I. 6)) (see Article 2(2) and (3)) but also includes –

(a) proceedings under the inherent jurisdiction of the High Court in relation to adults;
(b) proceedings in which the court has made an emergency protection order under Article 63 of the Children (Northern Ireland) Order 1995 (S.I. 1995/755 (N.I. 2)) which includes an exclusion requirement (as defined in Article 63A(3) of that Order); and
(c) proceedings in which the court has made an order under Article 69 of the Order of 1995 (recovery of abducted children etc.); and

'relevant third party' means a person specified, or falling within a description of persons specified, by order of the Department of Finance and Personnel.

(8) An order of the Department of Finance and Personnel under sub-paragraph (7) may, in particular, specify that Department.

4 Ex parte orders

(1) The court may, in any case where it considers that it is just and convenient to do so, make a forced marriage protection order even though the respondent has not been given such notice of the proceedings as would otherwise be required by rules of court.

(2) In deciding whether to exercise its powers under sub-paragraph (1), the court must have regard to all the circumstances including –

(a) any risk of significant harm to the person to be protected or another person if the order is not made immediately;
(b) whether it is likely that an applicant will be deterred or prevented from pursuing an application if an order is not made immediately; and
(c) whether there is reason to believe that –

(i) the respondent is aware of the proceedings but is deliberately evading service; and
(ii) the delay involved in effecting substituted service will cause serious prejudice to the person to be protected or (if a different person) an applicant.

(3) If the court makes an order by virtue of sub-paragraph (1), it must specify a date for a full hearing.

(4) In sub-paragraph (3), "full hearing" means a hearing of which notice has been given to all the parties in accordance with rules of court.

5 Duration of orders

A forced marriage protection order may be made for a specified period or until varied or discharged.

6 Variation of orders and their discharge

(1) The court may vary or discharge a forced marriage protection order on an application by –

(a) any party to the proceedings for the order;
(b) the person being protected by the order (if not a party to the proceedings for the order); or
(c) any person affected by the order.

(2) In addition, the court may vary or discharge a forced marriage protection order made by virtue of paragraph 3(1)(b) even though no application under sub-paragraph (1) above has been made to the court.

(3) Paragraph 4 applies to a variation of a forced marriage protection order as it applies to the making of such an order; and, accordingly, references in that paragraph to making a forced marriage protection order are to be read as references to varying such an order.

PART 2

ENFORCEMENT

7 Offence of contravening an order

Any person who, without reasonable excuse, contravenes a forced marriage protection order, commits an offence and is liable on summary conviction –

    (a)   to a fine not exceeding level 5 on the standard scale;
    (b)   to imprisonment for a term not exceeding 6 months; or
    (c)   to both.

PART 3

JURISDICTION AND PROCEDURE

8 Jurisdiction of courts

(1) For the purposes of this Schedule 'the court' means the High Court or a county court.

(2) Sub-paragraph (1) is subject to any provision made by virtue of sub-paragraphs (3) and (4).

(3) Article 34(3) to (10) of the Family Homes and Domestic Violence (Northern Ireland) Order 1998 (S.I. 1998/1071 (N.I. 6)) (allocation of proceedings to courts etc.) apply for the purposes of this Schedule as they apply for the purposes of that Order but as if the following modification were made.

(4) The modification is that Article 34(8) is to be read as if there were substituted for it –

    '(8) For the purposes of paragraphs (3), (4) and (5), there are two levels of court –

        (a)   the High Court; and
        (b)   a county court.'

9 Power to extend jurisdiction to courts of summary jurisdiction

(1) The Lord Chancellor may, after consulting the Lord Chief Justice, by order provide for courts of summary jurisdiction to be included among the courts who may hear proceedings under this Schedule.

(2) An order under sub-paragraph (1) may, in particular, make any provision in relation to courts of summary jurisdiction which corresponds to provision made in relation to such courts by or under the Family Homes and Domestic Violence (Northern Ireland) Order 1998 (S.I. 1998/1071 (N.I. 6)).

(3) Any power to make an order under this paragraph (including that power as extended by paragraph 14(3)) may, in particular, be exercised by amending, repealing, revoking or otherwise modifying any provision made by or under this Schedule or any other enactment.

(4) In sub-paragraph (3) 'enactment' includes Northern Ireland legislation.

(5) The Lord Chief Justice may nominate any of the following to exercise the Lord Chief Justice's functions under this paragraph –

(a) the holder of one of the offices listed in Schedule 1 to the Justice (Northern Ireland) Act 2002 (c. 26);

(b) a Lord Justice of Appeal (as defined in section 88 of that Act).

10 Contempt proceedings

The powers of the court in relation to contempt of court arising out of a person's failure to comply with a forced marriage protection order or otherwise in connection with such an order may be exercised by the relevant judge.

11 Appeals from county courts

(1) An appeal lies to the High Court against –

(a) the making by a county court of any order under this Schedule; or
(b) any refusal by a county court to make such an order;

as if the decision had been made in the exercise of the jurisdiction conferred by Part 3 of the County Courts (Northern Ireland) Order 1980 (S.I. 1980/397 (N.I. 3)) (original civil jurisdiction) and the appeal were brought under Article 60 of that Order (ordinary appeals in civil cases).

(2) But an appeal does not lie to the High Court under sub-paragraph (1) where the county court is a divorce county court exercising jurisdiction under the Matrimonial Causes (Northern Ireland) Order 1978 (S.I. 1978/1045 (N.I. 15)) in the same proceedings.

(3) Provision must be made by rules of court for an appeal to lie (upon a point of law, a question of fact or the admission or rejection of any evidence) to the Court of Appeal against –

(a) the making of any order under this Schedule; or
(b) any refusal to make such an order;

by a county court of the type referred to in sub-paragraph (2).

(4) Sub-paragraph (3) is without prejudice to Article 61 of the County Courts (Northern Ireland) Order 1980 (S.I. 1980/397 (N.I. 3)) (cases stated).

(5) On an appeal under sub-paragraph (1), the High Court may make such orders as may be necessary to give effect to its determination of the appeal.

(6) Where an order is made under sub-paragraph (5), the High Court may also make such incidental or consequential orders as appear to it to be just.

(7) Any order of the High Court made on an appeal under sub-paragraph (1) (other than one directing that an application be re-heard by the county court) is to be treated, for the purposes of –

(a) the enforcement of the order; and
(b) any power to vary, revive or discharge orders;

as if it were an order of the county court from which the appeal was brought and not an order of the High Court.

(8) This paragraph is subject to paragraph 12.

12 Appeals: transfers and proposed transfers

(1) The Lord Chancellor may, after consulting the Lord Chief Justice, by order make provision as to the circumstances in which appeals may be made against decisions taken by courts on questions arising in connection with the transfer, or proposed transfer, of proceedings by virtue of an order made under Article 34(5) of the Family Homes and Domestic Violence (Northern Ireland) Order 1998 (S.I. 1998/1071 (N.I. 6)) as applied by paragraph 8(3) and (4) above.

(2) Except so far as provided for in any order made under sub-paragraph (1), no appeal may be made against any decision of a kind mentioned in that sub-paragraph.

(3) The Lord Chief Justice may nominate any of the following to exercise the Lord Chief Justice's functions under this paragraph –

(a) the holder of one of the offices listed in Schedule 1 to the Justice (Northern Ireland) Act 2002 (c. 26);

(b) a Lord Justice of Appeal (as defined in section 88 of that Act).

PART 4

SUPPLEMENTARY

13 Guidance

(1) The Department of Finance and Personnel may from time to time prepare and publish guidance to such descriptions of persons as the Department of Finance and Personnel considers appropriate about –

(a) the effect of this Schedule or any provision of this Schedule; or

(b) other matters relating to forced marriages.

(2) A person exercising public functions to whom guidance is given under this paragraph must have regard to it in the exercise of those functions.

(3) Nothing in this paragraph permits the Department of Finance and Personnel to give guidance to any court or tribunal.

14 Orders

(1) An order made by the Department of Finance and Personnel under paragraph 3(7) –

(a) may make different provision for different purposes;

(b) may contain such incidental, supplemental, consequential, transitional, transitory or saving provision as the Department of Finance and Personnel considers appropriate;

(c) is to be made by statutory rule for the purposes of the Statutory Rules (Northern Ireland) Order 1979 (S.I. 1979/1573 (N.I. 12)); and

(d) is subject to negative resolution (within the meaning of section 41(6) of the Interpretation Act (Northern Ireland) 1954 (c. 33 (N.I.))).

(2) An order made by the Lord Chancellor by virtue of paragraph 8(3) and (4) or under paragraph 12(1) –

(a) may make different provision for different purposes;

(b) may contain such incidental, supplemental, consequential, transitional, transitory or saving provision as the Lord Chancellor considers appropriate;

(c)   is to be made by statutory rule for the purposes of the Statutory Rules (Northern Ireland) Order 1979 (S.I. 1979/1573 (N.I. 12)); and

(d)   is subject to annulment in pursuance of a resolution of either House of Parliament in the same manner as a statutory instrument (and section 5 of the Statutory Instruments Act 1946 (c. 36) applies accordingly).

(3)   An order made by the Lord Chancellor under paragraph 9 –

(a)   may make different provision for different purposes;

(b)   may contain such incidental, supplemental, consequential, transitional, transitory or saving provision as the Lord Chancellor considers appropriate;

(c)   is to be made by statutory rule for the purposes of the Statutory Rules (Northern Ireland) Order 1979 (S.I. 1979/1573 (N.I. 12)); and

(d)   is not to be made unless a draft of the order has been laid before, and approved by a resolution of, each House of Parliament.

15 Other protection or assistance against forced marriage

(1)   This Schedule does not affect any other protection or assistance available to a person who –

(a)   is being, or may be, forced into a marriage or subjected to an attempt to be forced into a marriage; or

(b)   has been forced into a marriage.

(2)   In particular, it does not affect –

(a)   the inherent jurisdiction of the High Court;

(b)   any criminal liability;

(c)   any right to an occupation order or a non-molestation order under the Family Homes and Domestic Violence (Northern Ireland) Order 1998 (S.I. 1998/1071 (N.I. 6));

(d)   any civil remedies under the Protection from Harassment (Northern Ireland) Order 1997 (S.I. 1997/1180 (N.I. 9));

(e)   any protection or assistance under the Children (Northern Ireland) Order 1995 (S.I. 1995/755 (N.I. 2));

(f)   any claim in tort; or

(g)   the law of marriage.

16 Interpretation

In this Schedule –

'the court' is to be read with paragraph 8(1);

'force' (and related expressions), in relation to a marriage, are to be read in accordance with paragraph 1(4) to (6);

'forced marriage protection order' has the meaning given by paragraph 1(6);

'marriage' means any religious or civil ceremony of marriage (whether or not legally binding); and

'the relevant judge', in relation to any order under this Schedule, means –

(a)   where the order was made by the High Court, a judge of that court; and

(b)   where the order was made by a county court, a judge or district judge of that or any other county court.

SCHEDULE 2

Consequential amendments

PART 1

ENGLAND AND WALES

1

In paragraph 3(f)(i) of Schedule 1 to the Supreme Court Act 1981 (c. 54) (distribution of business in High Court: family division) after 'Part IV' insert 'or 4A'.

2

In section 58A(2)(f) of the Courts and Legal Services Act 1990 (c. 41) (conditional fee agreements: supplementary) for 'Part IV' substitute 'Parts 4 and 4A'.

3

(1) The Family Law Act 1996 (c. 27) is amended as follows.

(2) In section 63(2) (interpretation of Part 4: family proceedings), after paragraph (b), insert –

'(ba) Part 4A;'.

(3) In section 65 (rules, regulations and orders) –

   (a)   in subsection (3) after '5(8)' insert ', 63N'; and
   (b)   in subsection (4) after '5(8)' insert 'or 63N'.

PART 2

NORTHERN IRELAND

4

In Article 2(3) of the Family Homes and Domestic Violence (Northern Ireland) Order 1998 (S.I. 1998/1071 (N.I. 6)) (interpretation: family proceedings), after sub-paragraph (h), insert –

'(i) Schedule 1 to the Forced Marriage (Civil Protection) Act 2007.'

5

In Article 39(2) of the Access to Justice (Northern Ireland) Order 2003 (S.I. 2003/435 (N.I. 10)) (conditional fee agreements: supplementary), after sub-paragraph (g), insert –

'(h) Schedule 1 to the Forced Marriage (Civil Protection) Act 2007,'.

APPENDIX B

THE FAMILY PROCEEDINGS (AMENDMENT) RULES 2008

(SI 2008/2446)

B.1

1 Citation and commencement

(1) These Rules may be cited as the Family Proceedings (Amendment) Rules 2008.

(2) These rules shall come into force as follows

  (a)   this rule and rules 2, 3(a), 5, 6, 10 and 12 shall come into force on 3rd November 2008; and
  (b)   the remaining rules shall come into force on 25th November 2008.

2 Amendments to the Family Proceedings Rules 1991

The Family Proceedings Rules 1991 shall be amended in accordance with the provisions of rules 3 to 13.

3   In the Arrangement of Rules

  (a)   in the entry for rule 3.23, for 'Child Support Commissioner', substitute 'Upper Tribunal';
  (b)   after the entry for rule 3.24, insert –

'3.25 Proceedings under Part 4A of the Family Law Act 1996: interpretation of rules and forms

3.26 Applications under Part 4A of the Family Law Act 1996 for forced marriage protection orders

3.27 Leave stage for forced marriage protection orders

3.28 Service of the application for a forced marriage protection order

3.29 Transfer of proceedings

3.30 Parties to proceedings for a forced marriage protection order

3.31 Orders for disclosure against a person not a party

3.32 Claim to withhold inspection or disclosure of a document

3.33 Hearing of applications for forced marriage protection orders

3.34 Forced marriage protection orders made by the court of its own motion

3.35 Enforcement of forced marriage protection orders

3.36 Applications under Part 4A of the Family Law Act 1996: bail'; and

(c)   after the entry for rule 8.1A, insert –

'8.1B Appeals from orders made under Part 4A of the Family Law Act 1996'.

4   In rule 3.8, for paragraph (9) substitute –

'(9) Subject to any enactment, where an application for an occupation order or a nonmolestation order is pending, the court may transfer the proceedings to another court of its own motion or on the application of either party; and any order for transfer shall be made in Form FL417.'

5 In rule 3.22(1) for 'appeal tribunals' substitute 'First-tier Tribunal'.

6 In rule 3.23 –

(a)   in the heading for 'Child Support Commissioner' substitute 'Upper Tribunal';
(b)   in paragraph (1) for the words '25 of the Act of 1991' to the end, substitute '13 of the Tribunals, Courts and Enforcement Act 2007(a) (right to appeal to Court of Appeal etc)';
(c)   in paragraph (2) for 'Commissioner' substitute ' Upper Tribunal'; and
(d)   in paragraph (3) for 'Commissioner's' substitute 'Upper Tribunal's'.

7   After rule 3.24, insert –

3.25 Proceedings under Part 4A of the Family Law Act 1996: interpretation of rules and forms

(1) In rules 3.26 to 3.36 –

'a forced marriage protection order' means an order under section 63A of the Family Law Act 1996(b);
'the person who is the subject of the proceedings' means the person who will be protected by the forced marriage protection order applied for or being considered by the court of its own motion, if that order is made, or who is being protected by such an order.

(2) In connection with proceedings under Part 4A of the Family Law Act 1996, references in the forms mentioned below to 'respondent' are to be read –

(a)   in Forms FL408, FL413 and FL414, as references to the respondent or other person who has failed to comply with the forced marriage protection order or is otherwise in contempt of court in relation to the order;
(b)   in Forms FL409, FL410, FL411 and FL412, as references to the respondent or other person arrested under section 63I or 63J of the Family Law Act 1996.

3.26 Applications under Part 4A of the Family Law Act 1996 for forced marriage protection orders

(1) An application for a forced marriage protection order, including an application for a forced marriage protection order which is made in other proceedings which are pending, shall be made in Form FL401A.

(2) An application for a forced marriage protection order made by an organisation shall state –

(a)   the name and address of the person submitting the application; and
(b)   the position which that person holds in the organisation.

(3) Where an application is made without notice, it shall be supported by a sworn statement explaining why notice has not been given.

3.27 Leave stage for forced marriage protection orders

(1) Where the leave of the court is required to apply for a forced marriage protection order, the person seeking leave shall file –

(a)   a written request for leave in Form FL430 setting out –

   (i)   the reasons for the application;
   (ii)   the applicant's connection with the person to be protected;
   (iii)   the applicant's knowledge of the circumstances of the person to be protected; and
   (iv)   the applicant's knowledge of the wishes and feelings of the person to be protected; and

(b)   a draft of the application for the making of which leave is sought, together with sufficient copies for one to be served on each respondent and the person to be protected.

(2) As soon as practicable after receiving a request under paragraph (1), the court shall –

(a)   grant the request, or
(b)   direct that a date be fixed for the hearing of the request and fix the date,

and the proper officer shall inform the following persons of the court's action under this paragraph –

   (i)   the person making the request,
   (ii)   the respondent,
   (iii)   (if different) the person to be protected, and
   (iv)   any other person directed by the court.

(3) Where leave is granted to bring proceedings, the application shall proceed in accordance with rule 3.26.

3.28 Service of the application for a forced marriage protection order

(1) Subject to paragraph (3), in every application made on notice the applicant shall serve a copy of the application, together with the notice of proceedings in Form FL402A, on –

(a)   the respondent,
(b)   the person who is the subject of the proceedings (if not the applicant), and
(c)   any other person directed by the court, personally not less than 2 days before the date on which the application will be heard.

(2) The court may abridge the period specified in paragraph (1).

(3) Service of the application shall be effected by the court if the applicant so requests.

This does not affect the court's power to order substituted service.

(4) The applicant shall file a statement in Form FL415 after the application has been served.

3.29 Transfer of proceedings

(1) Subject to any enactment, where proceedings under Part 4A of the Family Law Act 1996 are pending, the court may transfer the proceedings to another court of its own motion or on the application of a party or (if not a party) the person who is the subject of the proceedings.

(2) The order for transfer shall be in Form FL417.

3.30 Parties to proceedings for a forced marriage protection order

(1) In proceedings under Part 4A of the Family Law Act 1996, a person may file a request in Form FL431 for that person or another person to –

(a)   be joined as a party, or

(b)   cease to be a party.

(2) As soon as practicable after receiving a request under paragraph (1), the court shall do one of the following –

(a)   in the case only of a request under paragraph (1)(a), grant the request;

(b)   order that the request be considered at a hearing, and fix a date for the hearing; or

(c)   invite written representations as to whether the request should be granted, to be filed within a specified period, and upon expiry of that period act under subparagraph (a) or (b) as it sees fit;

and the proper officer shall inform the following persons of the court's action under this paragraph –

(i)   the person making the request,

(ii)   the applicant and the respondent,

(iii)   (if different) the person who is the subject of the proceedings, and

(iv)   any other person directed by the court.

(3) The court may direct –

(a)   that a person who would not otherwise be a respondent under these rules be joined as a party to the proceedings; or

(b)   that a party to the proceedings cease to be a party; and such a direction may be made by the court of its own motion as well as upon a request under paragraph (1).

3.31 Orders for disclosure against a person not a party

(1) This rule applies where an application is made to the court under any Act for disclosure by a person who is not a party to the proceedings.

(2) The application must be supported by evidence.

(3) The court may make an order under this rule only where –

(a)   the documents of which disclosure is sought are likely to support the case of the applicant or adversely affect the case of one of the other parties to the proceedings; and

(b)   disclosure is necessary in order to dispose fairly of the proceedings or to save costs.

(4) An order under this rule shall –

(a)   specify the documents or the classes of documents which the non-party must disclose; and

(b)   require the non-party, when making disclosure, to specify any of those documents –

(i)   which are no longer in his control; or

(ii)   in respect of which he claims a right or duty to withhold inspection.

(5) Such an order may –

(a)   require the non-party to indicate what has happened to any documents which are no longer in his control; and

(b)   specify the time and place for disclosure and inspection.

3.32 Claim to withhold inspection or disclosure of a document

(1) A person may apply, without notice, for an order permitting him to withhold disclosure of a document on the ground that disclosure would damage the public interest.

(2) Unless the court orders otherwise, an order of the court under paragraph (1) –

    (a)   must not be served on any other person; and

    (b)   must not be open to inspection by any person.

(3) A person who wishes to claim that he has a right or duty to withhold inspection of a document, or part of a document, must state in writing –

    (a)   that he has such a right or duty; and

    (b)   the grounds on which he claims that right or duty.

(4) The statement referred to in paragraph (3) must be made to the person wishing to inspect the document.

(5) A party or (if different) the person who is the subject of the proceedings may apply to the court to decide whether a claim made under paragraph (3) should be upheld.

(6) For the purpose of deciding an application under paragraph (1) (application to withhold disclosure) or paragraph (3) (claim to withhold inspection), the court may –

    (a)   require the person seeking to withhold disclosure or inspection of a document to produce that document to the court; and

    (b)   invite any person, whether or not a party, to make representations.

(7) An application under paragraph (1) or paragraph (3) shall be supported by evidence.

(8) This rule does not affect any rule of law which permits or requires a document to be withheld from disclosure or inspection on the ground that its disclosure or inspection would damage the public interest.

3.33 Hearing of applications for forced marriage protection orders

(1) The hearing of an application for a forced marriage protection order shall be in chambers unless the court otherwise directs.

(2) A record of the hearing shall be made in Form FL405.

(3) The order made on the hearing shall be issued in Form FL404B.

(4) The court may direct the withholding of any submissions made, or any evidence adduced, for or at the hearing –

    (a)   in order to protect the person who is the subject of the proceedings or any other person, or

    (b)   for any other good reason.

(5) The applicant shall serve –

    (a)   a copy of the order;

    (b)   a copy of the record of the hearing; and

    (c)   where the order is made without notice, a copy of the application together with any statement supporting it; on the respondent, the person being protected by the order (if neither the applicant nor a respondent) and any other person named in the order, personally as soon as reasonably practical.

(6) Service of the documents mentioned in paragraph (5) shall be effected by the court if the applicant so requests or where the court made the order of its own motion.

(7) The court may direct that a further hearing be held to consider any representations made by the respondent, the person being protected by the order (if neither the applicant nor a respondent) and any other person named in the order.

(8) An application to vary, extend or discharge a forced marriage protection order shall be made in Form FL403A and this rule shall apply to the hearing of such an application.

3.34 Forced marriage protection orders made by the court of its own motion

(1) Where the court makes a forced marriage protection order of its own motion under section 63C of the Family Law Act 1996(a), it shall set out in the order –

    (a)   a summary of its reasons for making the order; and
    (b)   the names of the persons who are to be served with the order.

(2) The court may order service of the order on –

    (a)   any of the parties to the current proceedings;
    (b)   (if different) the person being protected by the order; and
    (c)   any other persons whom the court considers should be served.

(3) The court will give directions as to how the order is to be served.

(4) The court may direct that a further hearing be held to consider any representations made by any of the persons named in the order.

(5) Rule 3.33(8) applies to an order made under this rule as it applies to an order made under rule 3.33.

3.35 Enforcement of forced marriage protection orders

(1) Subject to the following modifications, rule 3.9A shall apply to a forced marriage protection order as it applies to an order made under Part IV of the Family Law Act 1996.

(2) In paragraph (1) –

    (a)   for 'an occupation order', substitute 'a forced marriage protection order'; and
    (b)   for 'FL406', substitute 'FL406A'.

(3) For paragraph (1A), substitute –

    '(1A) Where paragraph (1) applies, the following documents shall be delivered to the officer for the time being in charge of any police station for the address of the person being protected by the order or of such other police station as the court may specify –

        (a)   Form FL406A, and
        (b)   a statement showing that the respondents and any other persons directed by the court to be served with the order have been so served or informed of its terms (whether by being present when the order was made or by telephone or otherwise).'

(4) In paragraph (1B) –

    (a)   delete the words 'on the respondent' in both places where they occur;
    (b)   in sub-paragraph (a), for '3.9(2) or (4)', substitute '3.33(5)'; and
    (c)   in sub-paragraph (b), for '3.9(5)', substitute '3.33(6) or 3.34(3)'.

(5) In paragraph (2) –

(a) for 'an occupation order or, as the case may be, any provisions of a nonmolestation order', substitute 'a forced marriage protection order'; and

(b) for 'the applicant's address', substitute 'the address of the person being protected by the order'.

(6) For paragraph (3), substitute –

'(3) An application for the issue of a warrant for the arrest of a person under section 63J(2) of the Family Law Act 1996 shall be –

(a) made in Form FL407A; and
(b) accompanied by a sworn statement.

(3A) An application for the issue of a warrant of arrest made by a person who is neither the person being protected by the order nor (if different) the person who applied for the order shall be treated, in the first instance, as an application for leave and the court shall either –

(a) grant the application; or
(b) direct that a date be fixed for the hearing of the application and fix a date,

and shall in either case inform the following persons of the court's action –

(i) the person applying for the issue of the warrant;
(ii) the person being protected by the order;
(iii) any other person directed by the court.

(3B) The warrant shall be issued in Form FL408.'

(7) In paragraph (5) –

(a) for 'IV', substitute '4A'; and
(b) for the words from 'and CCR Order 29' to the end, substitute 'and CCR Order 29, rule 1 shall have effect, as if for paragraph (3) there was substituted the following –

'(3) At the time when the order is drawn up, the proper officer shall, where the order made is (or includes) a forced marriage protection order, issue a copy of the order, indorsed with or incorporating a notice as to the consequences of disobedience, for service in accordance with paragraph (2).'

(8) In paragraph (6), for 'respondent', substitute 'arrested person'.

(9) In paragraph (7)(b) –

(a) after 'applicant', insert 'and (if different) the person being protected by the order'; and
(b) for 'respondent', substitute 'person who has failed to comply with the order or is otherwise in contempt of court in relation to the order'.

(10) In paragraph (9), for 'respondent', substitute 'arrested person'.

(11) In paragraph (10) –

(a) for 'an occupation order', substitute 'a forced marriage protection order';
(b) for '47(2) or (3)', substitute '63H(2) or (4)'; and
(c) for '47(8)', substitute '63J(2)'.

3.36 Applications under Part 4A of the Family Law Act 1996: bail

(1) Subject to the following modifications, rule 3.10 shall apply to a forced marriage protection order as it applies to an order made under Part IV of the Family Law Act 1996.

(2) In paragraph (1) –

(a)   for 'an occupation order', substitute 'a forced marriage protection order';

(b)   for '47(2) or (3)', substitute '63H(2) or (4)';

(c)   for '47(8)', substitute '63J(2)'.

(3) In paragraph (3), for 'the applicant for the Part IV order', substitute –

' –

(a)   the applicant for the forced marriage protection order;

(b)   the (or any other) respondent to the application for the order;

(c)   (if different) the person being protected by the order; and

(d)   any other person named in the order.'

(4) In paragraph (4), omit sub-paragraphs (b) and (c).'.

8   After rule 8.1A, insert –

'8.1B Appeals from orders made under Part 4A of the Family Law Act 1996

(1) This rule applies to all appeals from orders made under Part 4A of the Family Law Act 1996 and on such an appeal –

(a)   paragraphs (2), (3), (4) and (5) of rule 4.22;

(b)   paragraphs (5) and (6) of rule 8.1; and

(c)   paragraphs (4)(e) and (6) of rule 8.2;

shall apply to the following provisions of this rule and with the necessary modifications.

(2) A district judge may dismiss an appeal to which this rule applies for want of prosecution and may deal with any question of costs arising out of the dismissal or withdrawal of an appeal.

(3) Any order or decision granting or varying an order (or refusing to do so) in proceedings under Part 4A of the Family Law Act 1996 shall be treated as a final order for the purposes of CCR Order 37, rule 6 and, on an appeal from such an order, the judge may exercise his own discretion in substitution for that of the district judge and the provisions of CCR Order 37, rule 6 shall apply.'

9   In rule 9.1(3), after 'the Act of 1989', insert ', Part 4A of the Family Law Act 1996'.

10   In rule 10.20A(3), in the fourth entry in the second column, for 'an appeal tribunal' substitute 'the First-tier Tribunal'.

11   In rule 10.21 –

(a)   after paragraph (1), insert –

'(1A) In proceedings under Part 4A of the Family Law Act 1996, a party is also not required to reveal the address of –

(a)   the person who is the subject of the proceedings; or

(b)   any witness;

unless the court directs otherwise.'; and

(b)   in paragraph (2), for 'paragraph (1) above', substitute 'this rule'.

12

In rule 10.21A(2)(c) for 'an appeal tribunal' substitute 'the First-tier Tribunal'.

13

In Appendix 1 –

    (a)   in the list of forms, at the end, insert the list of forms set out in Schedule 1;

    (b)   for Forms FL413 and FL414, substitute the Forms set out in Schedule 2; and

    (c)   at the end of Appendix 1, insert the forms set out in Schedule 3.

14 Transitional provision

Where proceedings have been commenced before rule 4 comes into force, the Family Proceedings Rules 1991 shall apply to those proceedings as if rule 4 had not been made.

****

APPENDIX C

THE FAMILY PROCEEDINGS (AMENDMENT) RULES 2009

SI 2009/636

C.1

The Family Proceedings Rule Committee makes the following Rules in exercise of the powers conferred by section 40(1) of the Matrimonial and Family Proceedings Act 1984(1):

1 Citation and commencement

These Rules may be cited as the Family Proceedings (Amendment) Rules 2009 and come into force on 6th April 2009.

2 Amendments to the Family Proceedings Rules 1991

The Family Proceedings Rules 1991(2) are amended in accordance with rules 3 to 16.

3   In the Arrangement of Rules –

    (a)   in the heading to Part IV, after 'Children Act 1989' insert ', etc.';
    (b)   omit the entries for rules 4.22, 7.28, 8.1A and 8.1B;
    (c)   before the entry for rule 8.1 insert –

    "8.A1 Interpretation";

        (d)   in the entry for rule 8.2, for 'Appeals under Domestic Proceedings and Magistrates' Courts Act 1978' substitute 'Appeals from magistrates' courts and appeals from district judges under the Act of 1989 and Parts 4 and 4A of the Family Law Act 1996';
    (e)   after the entry for rule 8.2, insert –

    "8.2A Notice of Appeal;

    8.2B Respondents;

    8.2C Stay;

    8.2D Amendment of appeal notice;

    8.2E Powers of a district judge;

    8.2F Appeal court's powers;

    8.2G Hearing of appeals;

    8.2H Appeals from orders made under Parts 4 and 4A of the Family Law Act 1996".

4 In rule 1.2 –

   (a)   in paragraph (1), in the definition of district registry, omit ', except in rule 4.22(2A),'; and

   (b)   in paragraph (9)(b), omit 'and 8.1A'.

5 In rule 3.13(1), for paragraph (e) substitute –

   '(e)   where the mother, or alleged mother, of the person whose parentage is in issue has previously been known by different names, if known –

      (i)   each full name by which she has previously been known; and

      (ii)   the dates between which she was known by each name;".

6 In the heading to Part IV, after "Children Act 1989" insert ", etc.".

7 In rule 4.1(2) –

   (a)   at the end of sub-paragraph (h), omit 'or';

   (b)   at the end of sub-paragraph (i), insert 'or'; and

   (c)   after sub-paragraph (i), insert –

      '(j)   on an application for a warrant under section 79 of the Childcare Act 2006(3).'.

8 In rule 4.4(4) –

   (a)   at the end of sub-paragraph (d), omit 'or';

   (b)   at the end of sub-paragraph (e), insert 'or'; and

   (c)   after sub-paragraph (e), insert –

      '(f)   a warrant under section 79 of the Childcare Act 2006,'.

9 Omit rules 4.22, 7.28, 8.1A and 8.1B.

10 Before rule 8.1, insert –

8.A1 "Interpretation

References to –

   (a)   'the court below' in rules 8.2A to 8.2G are references to the court from which, or the person from whom, the appeal lies; and

   (b)   'the appeal court' in rules 8.2F and 8.2G are to the court to which an appeal is made.'.

11 In rule 8.1, for paragraph (7) substitute –

"(7) This rule does not apply to –

   (a)   the proceedings referred to in rule 8.2; and

   (b)   any appeal by a party to proceedings for the assessment of costs against a decision in those proceedings.'.

12 For rule 8.2 substitute –

8.2 "Appeals from magistrates' courts and appeals from district judges under the Act of 1989 and Parts 4 and 4A of the Family Law Act 1996

(1) Rules 8.2A to 8.2H apply where –

(a)   there is an appeal under –

      (i)   section 4(7) of the Maintenance Orders Act 1958(4);
      (ii)   section 29 of the Domestic Proceedings and Magistrates' Courts Act 1978(5);
      (iii) section 60(5) of the Act of 1986(6);
      (iv) section 94(1) to (9) of the Act of 1989(7);
      (v)   section 61 of the Family Law Act 1996(8); or
      (vii) any other enactment giving a person a right of appeal against a decision of a magistrates' court; or

(b)   an appeal lies from any decision of a district judge to the judge of the court in which the decision was made in proceedings –

      (i)   listed in rule 4.1(2); or
      (ii)   to which Parts 4 and 4A of the Family Law Act 1996 apply.

(2) In proceedings referred to in paragraph (1)(b)(i) and (ii), any party may appeal from an order or decision made or given by the district judge in a county court to a judge on notice and CCR Order 13, rule 1(10) and Order 37, rule 6 shall not apply.

(3) Appeals under paragraph (1)(b) shall be heard in chambers unless the judge directs otherwise.

(4) Rules 8.2A to 8.2H are subject to any enactment.

8.2A Notice of appeal

(1) The appellant shall file and serve on –

(a)   the parties to the proceedings in the court below;
(b)   any children's guardian; and
(c)   where applicable, the local authority that prepared a report under section 14A(8) or (9) of the Act of 1989,

the documents set out in paragraph (2).

(2) The documents referred to in paragraph (1) are –

(a)   notice in writing of the appeal, setting out the grounds of the appeal;
(b)   a certified copy of the summons or application and of the order appealed against, and of any order staying its execution;
(c)   a copy of any notes of the evidence; and
(d)   a copy of any reasons given for the decision.

(3) The appellant shall file and serve the notice of appeal in accordance with paragraph (1) –

(a)   within 14 days after the determination against which the appeal is brought;
(b)   in the case of an appeal against an order under section 38(1) of the Act of 1989, within 7 days after the making of the order;
(c)   in the case of an appeal against an order under section 29 of the Domestic Proceedings and Magistrates' Courts Act 1978, within 21 days after the making of the order; or
(d)   with the leave of the court to which, or judge to whom, the appeal is brought, within such other time as that court or judge may direct.

(4) Subject to any direction of the court to which, or judge to whom, the appeal is brought, the appellant shall file and serve the documents mentioned in paragraph (2)(b) to (d) as soon as practicable after filing and service of the notice of appeal under paragraph (1).

(5) Where the magistrates' court is the court below, the appellant shall serve the documents mentioned in paragraph (2)(a) and (b) on the designated officer for that court.

8.2B Respondents

(1) Subject to paragraph (2), a respondent who wishes to contend –

    (a)   on the appeal that the decision of the court below should be varied, either in any event or in the event of the appeal being allowed in whole or in part;

    (b)   that the decision of the court below should be affirmed on grounds other than those relied upon by that court; or

    (c)   by way of cross-appeal that the decision of the court below was wrong in whole or in part, shall, within 14 days of receipt of notice of the appeal, file and serve on all other parties to the appeal a notice in writing, setting out the grounds upon which the respondent relies.

(2) No notice under paragraph (1) may be filed or served in an appeal against an order under section 38 of the Act of 1989.

8.2C Stay

Unless the court orders otherwise, an appeal under rule 8.2 (1) shall not operate as a stay of proceedings on the order or decision appealed against.

8.2D Amendment of appeal notice

(1) The appellant may amend the appeal notice, without leave, by serving a supplementary notice not less than 7 days before the date of the hearing of the appeal, on each of the persons on whom the notice to be amended was served.

(2) Within 2 days after service of a supplementary notice under paragraph (1) the appellant must file two copies of the notice in the court in which the appeal notice was filed.

(3) Except with the leave of the court hearing the appeal, the appellant may not rely on grounds other than those stated in the notice of appeal or any supplementary notice under paragraph (1).

(4) The court may amend the grounds of appeal or make any other order, on such terms as it thinks just, to ensure the determination on the merits of the real question in controversy between the parties.

8.2E Powers of a district judge

(1) A district judge may –

    (a)   dismiss an appeal to which this rule applies –

        (i)   for want of prosecution; or
        (ii)   with the consent of the parties; or

    (b)   give leave for the appeal to be withdrawn,

and may deal with any question of costs arising out of the dismissal or withdrawal.

(2) Unless the court directs otherwise, any interlocutory application in an appeal under rule 8.2 (1)(a) may be made to a district judge.

8.2F Appeal court's powers

(1) In relation to an appeal the appeal court has all the powers of the court below.

(2) The appeal court has power to –

    (a)   affirm, set aside or vary any order or judgment made or given by the court below;

> (b) refer any application or issue for determination by the court below;
> (c) order a new hearing;
> (d) make orders for the payment of interest;
> (e) make a costs order.

(3) The appeal court may exercise its powers in relation to the whole or part of an order of the lower court.

8.2G Hearing of appeals

(1) Every appeal will be limited to a review of the decision of the court below unless –

> (a) an enactment makes different provision for a particular category of appeal; or
> (b) the court considers that in the circumstances of an individual appeal it would be in the interests of justice to hold a re-hearing.

(2) Unless it orders otherwise, the appeal court will not receive –

> (a) oral evidence; or
> (b) evidence which was not before the court below.

(3) The appeal court will allow an appeal where the decision of the court below was –

> (a) wrong; or
> (b) unjust because of a serious procedural or other irregularity in the proceedings in the court below.

(4) The appeal court may draw any inference of fact which it considers justified on the evidence.

8.2H Appeals from orders made under Parts 4 and 4A of the Family Law Act 1996

Where an appeal is brought against the making of a hospital order or a guardianship order under the Mental Health Act 1983(9) a copy of any written evidence considered by the magistrates' court under section 37(1)(10) of the 1983 Act shall be sent by the designated officer to the county court in which the documents relating to the appeal are filed.".

13   In rule 8.3 –

> (a) renumber the existing text as paragraph (1);
> (b) in paragraph (1), omit 'and rule 8.2(4) shall apply, with the necessary modifications, to such proceedings'; and
> (c) after paragraph (1), insert

"(2) On entering the appeal, or as soon as practicable thereafter, the appellant shall, unless otherwise directed, lodge in the principal registry –

> (a) three certified copies of the summons and of the order appealed against, and of any order staying its execution;
> (b) three copies of the clerk's notes of the evidence;
> (c) three copies of the justices' reasons for their decision;
> (d) a certificate that notice of motion has been duly served on the clerk and on every party affected by the appeal; and
> (e) where the notice of motion includes an application to extend the time for bringing the appeal, a certificate (and a copy) by the appellant's solicitor, or the appellant if he is acting in person, setting out the reasons for the delay and the relevant dates.'.

14   In rule 9.3(1)(a), for "father", wherever it occurs, substitute "parent".

15 In Appendix 1, for Forms C19 and C23, substitute the forms set out in the Schedule.

16 In Appendix 3 –

(a) at the end of column (i), insert 'Section 79 of the Childcare Act 2006';

(b) in the corresponding entry in column (ii), insert '1 day'; and

(c) in the corresponding entry in column (iii), insert 'Any person preventing or likely to prevent Her Majesty's Chief Inspector of Education, Children's Services and Skills from exercising a power conferred on him by section 77'.

17 Transitional provision

Where a person has filed a notice of appeal or lodged a notice of motion before these rules come into force, the Family Proceedings Rules 1991 shall apply to those proceedings as if rules 3(b) to (e), 4 and 9 to 13 had not been made.

Schedule

Rule 15

Application for a warrant of assistance	Form C19

Section 102 Children Act 1989
Section 33 Adoption Act 1976
Section 79 Childcare Act 2006

The court	To be completed by the court
	Date issued
The full name(s) of the child(ren) (if known)	Case number
	Child(ren)'s number(s)

---

1   About you (the applicant)

State • *your title, full name, address, telephone number and relationship to the child(ren) (if any)*
      • *your solicitor's name, address, reference, telephone, FAX and DX numbers*
      • *whether you are:*

☐ a person authorised by the local authority

☐ a person authorised by the Welsh Ministers

☐ a person authorised by the Secretary of State

☐ a supervisor acting under a supervision order

☐ Her Majesty's Chief Inspector of Education, Children's Services and Skills

2   Description of the child(ren) (if applicable)

If a child's identity is not known, state details which will identify the child.
You may enclose a recent photograph of the child, which should be dated.

3   The grounds for the application

☐   I am attempting to exercise powers under an enactment within Section 102(6) Children Act 1989 or under section 77(1) or (2) of the Childcare Act 2006 at the following premises *(give full address)*:

and

☐ **I have been** prevented from exercising those powers by

☐ **I am likely to be** prevented from exercising those powers by

PERSON AUTHORISED BY THE LOCAL AUTHORITY	*s62(6)*	☐	[being, or likely to be, refused entry to accommodation provided by a voluntary organisation] [being, or likely to be, refused access to a child in accommodation provided by a voluntary organisation]
	s64(4)	☐	[being, or likely to be, refused entry to a children's home] [being, or likely to be, refused access to a child in a children's home]
	s67(3)	☐	[being, or likely to be, refused entry to a private foster home] [being, or likely to be, refused access to a child in a private foster home]
	s86(5)	☐	[being, or likely to be, refused entry to a residential care, nursing or mental nursing home] [being, or likely to be, refused access to a child in a residential care, nursing or mental nursing home]
	s87(5)	☐	[being, or likely to be, refused entry to an independent school] [being, or likely to be, refused access to a child in an independent school]
	Section 33 Adoption Act 1976	☐	[being, or likely to be, refused entry to premises on which a protected child is, or is likely to be, kept] [being, or likely to be prevented from visiting a protected child]
PERSON AUTHORISED BY THE WELSH MINISTERS	*s79U*	☐	[being, or likely to be, refused entry to domestic premises where child-minding is carried on] [being, or likely to be, refused access to a child on domestic premises where child-minding is carried on]
		☐	[being, or likely to be, refused entry to premises on which day care for children under the age of 8 is provided] [being, or likely to be, refused access to a child in premises on which day care for children under the age of 8 is provided]
PERSON AUTHORISED BY THE SECRETARY OF STATE	*s80(8)*	☐	[being, or likely to be, refused entry to any of the premises specified by Section 80(1) Children Act 1989] [being, or likely to be, refused access to a child in any of the premises specified by Section 80(1) Children Act 1989]
SUPERVISOR UNDER THE SUPERVISION ORDER	*Paragraph 8(1)(b) Schedule 3*	☐	[being, or likely to be, refused entry to accommodation where a supervised child is living]
	Paragraph 8(2)(b) Schedule 3	☐	[being, or likely to be, refused contact with a supervised child by a responsible person]
HER MAJESTY'S CHIEF INSPECTOR OF EDUCATION, CHILDREN'S SERVICES AND SKILLS	*Section 77(1) Childcare Act 2006*	☐	[being, or likely to be, refused entry to premises on which I have reasonable cause to believe early years provision or later years provision is being provided in breach of section 33(1), 34(1), 52(1) or 53(1) of the Childcare Act 2006]
	Section 77(2) Childcare Act 2006	☐	[being, or likely to be, refused entry for a purpose in section 77(2)(a) or (b) to premises on which early years provision or later years provision is being provided]

4   The respondent(s)

For each respondent state the title, full name, address, telephone number and relationship (if any) to each child.

5   The reason(s) for the application

If you are relying on a report or other documentary evidence, state the date(s) and author(s) and enclose a copy.

6   The direction(s) sought

State   •   *whether you wish to accompany the constable, if the warrant is granted*
       •   *whether you wish the constable to be accompanied by a registered medical practitioner, registered nurse or registered midwife, if he so wishes.*

Signed
(Applicant)   Date

In the

Case Number:

Child(ren)'s Number(s):

Order	Emergency Protection Order
	Section 44 Children Act 1989

	The full name(s) of the child(ren)	Boy or Girl	Date(s) of birth

[described as

Warning | **It is an offence intentionally to obstruct any person exercising the power under Section 44(4)(b) Children Act 1989 to remove, or prevent the removal, of a child (Section 44(15) Children Act 1989).**

The Court grants | an Emergency Protection Order to the applicant who is

The order gives the applicant parental responsibility for the child[ren].

The Court authorises | [the applicant to remove the child[ren] to accommodation provided by or on behalf of the applicant]
[the applicant to prevent the child[ren] being removed from

[This order directs that | any person who can produce the child[ren] to the applicant must do so.]

The Court directs that | [[a named person] be excluded from [a named address] [forthwith] [from [date]] so that the child may continue to live there, consent to the exclusion requirement having been given by [a named person]]

[a power of arrest be attached to the exclusion requirement for a period of   ]

This order ends on | at | [am] [pm]

Ordered by | [Mr][Mrs] Justice
[His][Her] Honour Judge
District Judge [of Family Division]
Justice[s] of the Peace

on | at | [am] [pm]

C23 (01.09)

Notes about the Emergency Protection Order

About this order

This is an Emergency Protection Order.
This order states what has been authorised in respect of the child[ren] and when the order will end.
The court can extend this order for up to 7 days but it can only do this once.

Warning

If you are shown this order, you must comply with it. If you do not, you may commit an offence. Read the order now.

What you may do

You may apply to the court at any time
      to **change the directions**
or   to **end the order.**

If you would like to ask the court to change the directions, or end the order, you must fill in a form. You can obtain the form from a court office.

If the court has directed that the child[ren] should have a medical, psychiatric or another kind of examination, you may ask the court to allow a doctor of your choice to be at the examination.

What you should do

Go to a solicitor as soon as you can.

Some solicitors specialise in court proceedings which involve children. You can obtain the address of a solicitor or advice agency from the Yellow Pages or the Solicitors' Regional Directory.
You will find these books at
• a Citizens Advice Bureau
• a Law Centre
• a local library

A solicitor or an advice agency will be able to tell you whether you may be eligible for legal aid.

EXPLANATORY NOTE

(This note is not part of the Rules)

These Rules amend the Family Proceedings Rules 1991 ("the 1991 Rules").

Rules 3 and 4 and 9 to 12 amend the rules relating to the process for—

(a) statutory rights of appeal from decisions of a magistrates' court; and

(b) internal appeals in a county court from a decision of a district judge to a judge in proceedings which are listed in rule 4.1(2) of the 1991 Rules and to which Parts 4 and 4A of the Family Law Act 1996 (c.27) apply.

Rules 8.A1 and 8.2 to 8.H ("the new rules") which are inserted into the 1991 Rules by these Rules, replace rules 4.22, 7.28, 8.1A and 8.1B of the 1991 Rules and are modelled on those rules, Order 55 of the Rules of the Supreme Court 1965 (S.I. 1965/1776) and rules 180 and 181 of the Family Procedure (Adoption) Rules 2005 (S.I. 2005/2795). The new rules are freestanding and rationalise and modernise the existing rules. A notice of appeal is the common way of commencing the appeals within the scope of the new rules.

In addition, the new rules will be able to accommodate the appeals which are proposed to come to a county court from decisions of a magistrates' court under the Access to Justice Act 1999 (Destination of Appeals) (Family Proceedings) Order 2009 ("the draft order") which has been laid in draft before Parliament. New rule 8.2A(3)(c) changes the time limit for appealing against an order under section 29 of the Domestic Proceedings and Magistrates' Courts Act 1978 (c.22) from 6 weeks to 21 days so that the time will be in line with the time for appealing against decisions of the magistrates' court under the proposed new section 111A of the Magistrates' Courts Act 1980 (c.43) (in article 4(3) of the draft order) on the ground that the decision is wrong in law and in excess of jurisdiction.

In consequence of the new rules, rule 13 adds a new paragraph to rule 8.3 of the 1991 Rules which relates to appeals under section 13 of the Administration of Justice Act 1960 (c.65).

By virtue of rule 17, the new rules will not apply to any appeal in which the appeal notice is filed or notice of motion is lodged before these Rules come into force.

Rule 5 amends rule 3.13(1)(e) of the 1991 Rules to require, on an application for a declaration of parentage, information to be given about any change of name of the mother or alleged mother and not just changes made on marriage. This would include change of name on entry into a civil partnership. This takes account of the fact that, on the coming into force of section 42 of the Human Fertilisation and Embryology Act 2008 (c.22), the existence of a civil partnership entered into by the mother may be a relevant consideration. Rule 14 amends rule 9.3 of the 1991 Rules to provide that where service on a child (who is not also a protected party) could previously be effected on a father it may now be effected on either parent.

Rules 6 to 8 and 16 are consequential on the coming into force of the Childcare Act 2006 (c.21) ("the 2006 Act"). The amendments insert provision to ensure that an application for a warrant by Her Majesty's Chief Inspector of Education, Children's Services and Skills under section 79 (power of constable to assist in exercise of powers of entry) of the 2006 Act may be made ex parte, and to specify for such an application the appropriate form, periods of notice and respondents. Rule 15 substitutes a new Form C19 (Warrant of Assistance) which form now refers to an application under section 79 and makes provision for an application under section 102 of the Children Act 1989 (c.41) in relation to the exercise of powers, in Wales, under section 79U of that Act.

Rule 15 also substitutes a new Form C23 (Emergency Protection Order) in consequence of the repeal of section 45(9) of the Children Act 1989 by section 30 of the Children and Young Persons Act 2008 (c.23).

APPENDIX D

THE RIGHT TO CHOOSE: MULTI-AGENCY STATUTORY GUIDANCE FOR DEALING WITH FORCED MARRIAGE

D.1

Foreign and Commonwealth Office
Home Office
Department for Children Schools and Families
Department of Health
Department for Communities and Local Government
Department for Innovation, Universities and Skills
Welsh Assembly Government
Association of Chief Police Officers

CONTENTS

PART ONE
CONTEXT

Chapter 1
BACKGROUND

1   There is a clear distinction between a forced marriage and an arranged marriage. In arranged marriages, the families of both spouses take a leading role in arranging the marriage but the choice whether or not to accept the arrangement remains with the prospective spouses. In forced marriages, one or both spouses do not (or, in the case of some vulnerable adults, cannot) consent to the marriage and duress is involved. Duress can include physical, psychological, financial, sexual and emotional pressure.

2   All Chief Executives, directors and senior managers providing services to victims of forced marriage and honour-based violence need to be aware of the 'one chance' rule. That is, their staff may only have one chance to speak to a potential victim and thus their staff may only have one chance to save a life. This means that all professionals working within statutory agencies need to be aware of their responsibilities and obligations when they come across forced marriage cases. If the victim is allowed to walk out of the door without support, that one chance might be wasted.

3   The government regards forced marriage as an abuse of human rights and a form of domestic abuse and, where it affects children and young people, child abuse. It can happen

to both men and women although most cases involve young women and girls aged between 13 and 30. There is no 'typical' victim of forced marriage. Some may be under 18 years old, some may be over 18 years old, some may have a disability, some may have young children and some may be spouses from overseas.

4   The majority of cases of forced marriage reported to date in the UK involve South Asian families. This is partly a reflection of the fact that there is a large, established South Asian population in the UK. However, it is clear that forced marriage is not solely a South Asian problem and there have been cases involving families from the Middle East, Europe and Africa. Some forced marriages take place in the UK with no overseas element, while others involve a partner coming from overseas or a British citizen being sent abroad.

5   In August 1999, Home Office Minister for Community Relations, Mike O'Brien MP established a Forced Marriage Working Group to undertake an investigation into the scale and extent of forced marriage across the UK. The Working Group's findings were published in 'A Choice by Right'[1] in 2000.

6   The Foreign & Commonwealth Office responded to the recommendations in 'A Choice by Right' by setting up the Community Liaison Unit in 2000. In 2005, the Unit developed into a joint Home Office and Foreign & Commonwealth Office Unit known as the Forced Marriage Unit (FMU). The role of the Unit is to provide information and support to the victims of forced marriage and to provide advice to professionals handling cases. The Unit, together with relevant government departments and agencies, has also published practice guidelines for police officers, health professionals, social workers and education professionals on dealing with cases[2] – these are to be updated following the publication of the statutory guidance.

7   In the first nine months of 2008 alone, over 1,300 incidences of suspected forced marriage have been reported to the Forced Marriage Unit. Cases also come to the attention of the police, social care services, health, education and voluntary organisations. Many others go unreported.[3] With greater awareness of the help available, the number of cases reported is likely to increase.

8   As part of the Forced Marriage Unit's continuing work to tackle the issue, a consultation paper, 'Forced Marriage, A Wrong Not a Right', was published in 2005 to establish whether or not forced marriage should become a criminal offence. Agencies, professionals and individuals were invited to respond to the paper.

9   While there was no clear majority among respondents about whether or not a specific criminal offence should be created, the majority felt that the disadvantages of creating new legislation would outweigh the advantages and potentially drive forced marriage underground by preventing victims from coming forward. As a consequence of the consultation paper, the Forced Marriage (Civil Protection) Act was enacted in 2007 and came into force on 25 November 2008. The Act forms part of the Family Law Act 1996 and makes provision for protecting children, young people and adults from being forced into marriage without their free and full consent. Part Two of this guidance is issued under s.63Q(1) of the 2007 Act.

---

[1]   www.fco.gov.uk/resources/en/pdf/a-choice-by-right.

[2]   www.fco.gov.uk/en/fco-in-action/nationals/forced-marriage-unit/info-forprofessionals.

[3]   Information provided by victims at seminars 2000 – 2008.

Chapter 2
THE STATUS AND PURPOSE OF THIS GUIDANCE

THE STATUS OF THIS DOCUMENT AS STATUTORY GUIDANCE

10 Part Two of this guidance is issued as statutory guidance under section 63Q(1) of the Forced Marriage (Civil Protection) Act 2007 (2007 c.20). Section 63Q of the Act states:

    1 The Secretary of State may from time to time prepare and publish guidance to such descriptions of person as the Secretary of State considers appropriate about –

        a The effect of this Part or any provision of this Part;
        or
        b Other matters relating to forced marriages.

    2 A person exercising public functions to whom guidance is given under this section must have regard to it in the exercise of those functions.

    3 Nothing in this section permits the Secretary of State to give guidance to any court or tribunal.

11 As statutory guidance issued under section 63Q of the Act, a person exercising public functions to whom the guidance is given must have regard to it in the exercise of those functions. This means that a person to whom the guidance is given must take the guidance into account and, if they decide to depart from it, have clear reasons for doing so.

12 Front-line staff dealing with cases of forced marriage are strongly recommended to consult the practice guidelines issued by the Forced Marriage Unit.[4]

AUDIENCE

13 This guidance is given to all persons and bodies in England and Wales who exercise public functions in relation to safeguarding and promoting the welfare of children as listed in section 11(1) or section 28(1) of the Children Act 2004 or under section 175 of the Education Act 2002. Such persons and bodies include schools, local authorities, police authorities and chief officers of police and youth offending teams. This guidance is also given to the Children and Family Court Advisory and Support Service (established under section 11 of the Criminal Justice and Courts Services Act 2000) and Local Safeguarding Children Boards (established under section 13 or section 31 of the Children Act 2004).

14 This guidance is also given to all persons and bodies in England and Wales who exercise public functions to protect vulnerable adults from abuse. Examples of these bodies may include but are not limited to police authorities and chief officers of police, and NHS trusts. Also key elements of local authorities and/or district councils in particular adult social care services, strategic health authorities, primary care trusts, local health boards.

15 This guidance is also given to any third party who is exercising public functions on behalf of a person or body mentioned in paragraphs 13 and 14.

THE PURPOSE OF THIS GUIDANCE

16 This guidance is targeted at Chief Executives, directors and senior managers of persons and bodies mentioned in paragraph 13 or 14 of third parties mentioned in paragraph 15. It outlines their responsibilities concerning developing and maintaining local procedures and practice arrangements to enable their front-line practitioners to handle cases of forced

---

4   www.fco.gov.uk/en/fco-in-action/nationals/forced-marriage-unit/info-forprofessionals.

marriage effectively. It sets out how cases of forced marriage should be responded to using existing frameworks for safeguarding children, protecting vulnerable adults and victims of domestic abuse.

17   This document is not intended to be used by frontline practitioners as practice guidelines. Front-line practitioners handling cases of forced marriage are strongly recommended to consult the practice guidelines issued by the Forced Marriage Unit.[5]

AIMS

18   This document sets out the duties and responsibilities of agencies with the aim of protecting children, young people and adults facing forced marriage. It does not attempt to replicate existing guidance.

19   As forced marriage is a form of child/adult/domestic abuse, it should form part of existing child and adult protection structures, policies and procedures.

20   The document highlights specific arrangements that may inadvertently place a victim at risk of harm. These include failure to share information appropriately between agencies, the danger of involving families, breaches of confidentiality and all forms of family counselling, mediation, arbitration and reconciliation.

DEFINITIONS

Adult

21   In this guidance 'adult' means a person aged 18 years or over.

Child abuse and neglect

22   Throughout this document the recognised categories of maltreatment as set out in Working Together to Safeguard Children[6&7] have been used. These are:
- Physical abuse
- Sexual abuse
- Emotional abuse
- Neglect

Child, children and young people

23   As defined in the Children Act 1989 and 2004, child means a person who has not reached their 18th birthday. This includes young people aged 16 and 17 who are living independently; their status and entitlement to services and protection under the Children Act 1989 is not altered by the fact they are living independently.

Child in need

24   Children who are defined as being 'in need' under section 17 of the Children Act 1989, are those whose vulnerability is such that they are unlikely to reach or maintain a satisfactory level of health or development, or their health or development will be significantly

---

[5]   www.fco.gov.uk/en/fco-in-action/nationals/forced-marriage-unit/info-forprofessionals.
[6]   *Working Together to Safeguard Children* 2006.
[7]   *Working Together to Safeguard Children* under the Children Act 2004 (Welsh Assembly Government).

impaired, without the provision of services (section 17 (10) Children Act 1989), plus those who are disabled. Local authorities have a duty to safeguard and promote the welfare of children in need.

Domestic abuse

25   The government defines domestic abuse as: 'any incident of threatening behaviour, violence or abuse (psychological, physical, sexual, financial or emotional) between adults who are or have been intimate partners or family members, regardless of gender or sexuality.'

Forced marriage

26   A forced marriage is a marriage in which one or both spouses do not (or, in the case of some vulnerable adults, cannot) consent to the marriage and duress is involved. Duress can include physical, psychological, financial, sexual and emotional pressure.

Honour-based violence

27   The term 'honour crime' or 'honour-based violence' embraces a variety of crimes of violence (mainly but not exclusively against women), including assault, imprisonment and murder where the person is being punished by their family or their community. They are being punished for actually, or allegedly, undermining what the family or community believes to be the correct code of behaviour. In transgressing against this correct code of behaviour, the person shows that they have not been properly controlled to conform by their family and this is to the 'shame' or 'dishonour' of the family.

28   Welshman and Hossain state 'The term crimes of honour encompasses a variety of manifestations of violence against women; including murder termed 'honour killings', assault, confinement or imprisonment and interference with choice in marriage where the publicly articulated justification is attributed to a social order claimed to require the preservation of a concept of honour vested in male family and or conjugal control over women and specifically women's sexual conduct – actual, suspected or potential.'[8]

Relevant third party

29   The Forced Marriage (Civil Protection) Act 2007 provides for three types of applicant who may apply for a Forced Marriage Protection Order. They are the victim, anyone on their behalf with the permission of the court and a relevant third party. A relevant third party may apply on behalf of a victim and does not require the leave of the court. The Lord Chancellor has specified that, once designated, local authorities will be able to act as a relevant third party.

The concept of significant harm

30   The Children Act 1989[9] introduced the concept of significant harm as the threshold that justifies compulsory intervention in family life in the best interests of children and young people. Under section 47 of the Act, local authorities have a duty to make enquiries to decide whether they should take action to safeguard or promote the welfare of a child who is suffering, or likely to suffer, significant harm.[10]

---

[8]   Welchman, Lynn and Hossain, Sara, eds. (2005) *Honour: Crimes, Paradigms and Violence against Women* (Zed Books, London).

[9]   Section 31(9) The Children Act 1989 – www.opsi.gov.uk/acts/acts1989/ukpga_19890041_en_6#pt4-pb1-l1g31.

[10]   Section 1.23 *Working Together to Safeguard Children* 2006.

Vulnerable adult

31   *No Secrets*[11] defines a 'vulnerable adult' as a person over the age of 18 years 'who is, or may be, in need of community care services by reason of mental or other disability, age or illness and who is, or may be, unable to take care of him or herself, or unable to protect him or herself against significant harm or exploitation.'

32   In line with *No Secrets* and *In Safe Hands*[12] – Welsh Assembly Government (WAG), 'community care services' includes all care services provided in any setting or context.

Chapter 3
UNDERSTANDING THE ISSUES AROUND FORCED MARRIAGE

MOTIVES PROMPTING FORCED MARRIAGE

33   Parents who force their children to marry often justify their behaviour as protecting their children, building stronger families and preserving cultural or religious traditions. They often do not see anything wrong in their actions. Forced marriage cannot be justified on religious grounds; every major faith condemns it and freely given consent is a prerequisite of Christian, Jewish, Hindu, Muslim and Sikh marriages.

34   Often parents believe that they are upholding the cultural traditions of their home country, when in fact practices and values there may have changed. Some parents come under significant pressure from their extended families to get their children married. In some instances, an agreement may have been made about marriage when a child is in their infancy. Many young people live their entire childhoods with the expectation that they will marry someone their parents select – some may be unaware that they have a fundamental human right to choose their spouse.

35   While it is important to have an understanding of the motives that drive parents to force their children to marry, these motives should not be accepted as justification for denying them the right to choose a marriage partner and enter freely into marriage. Forced marriage is a breach of children's rights under the UN Convention on the Rights of the Child (UNCRC) as well as an abuse of human rights.

36   Some of the key motives that have been identified[13] are:
- Controlling unwanted sexuality (including perceived promiscuity, or being lesbian, gay, bisexual or transgender) – particularly the behaviour and sexuality of women.
- Controlling unwanted behaviour, for example, alcohol and drug use, wearing make-up or behaving in a 'westernised manner'.
- Preventing 'unsuitable' relationships, e.g. outside the ethnic, cultural, religious or caste group.
- Protecting 'family honour' or 'izzat'.
- Responding to peer group or family pressure.
- Attempting to strengthen family links.
- Achieving financial gain.
- Ensuring land, property and wealth remain within the family.
- Protecting perceived cultural ideals.
- Protecting perceived religious ideals which are misguided.

---

[11]   *No Secrets: Guidance on developing and implementing multi-agency policies and procedures to protect vulnerable adults from abuse*, HO & DH, 2000.

[12]   *In Safe Hands: Implementing Adult Protection Procedures in Wales*, July 2000 Welsh Assembly Government (WAG).

[13]   By practitioners working with victims of forced marriage.

- Ensuring care for a child or vulnerable adult with special needs when parents or existing carers are unable to fulfil that role.
- Assisting claims for UK residence and citizenship.
- Long-standing family commitments.

FORCED MARRIAGE IS AN ABUSE OF HUMAN RIGHTS

37 Forced marriage is an abuse of human rights and an abuse of the rights of the child.

'Marriage shall be entered into only with the free and full consent of the intending spouses.'

Universal Declaration of Human Rights, Article 16(2)

'No marriage shall be legally entered into without the full and free consent of both parties.'

UN Convention on consent to marriage, minimum age for marriage and registration of marriages, Article 1

'In all actions concerning children, whether undertaken by public or private social welfare institutions, courts of law, administrative authorities or legislative bodies, the best interests of the child shall be a primary consideration.'

United Nations Convention on the Rights of the Child, Article 3

'States Parties undertake to protect the child from all forms of sexual exploitation and sexual abuse. For these purposes, States Parties shall in particular take all appropriate national, bilateral and multilateral measures to prevent:
(a) The inducement or coercion of a child to engage in any unlawful sexual activity'

(United Nations Convention on the Rights of the Child, Article 34a)

'A woman's right to choose a spouse and enter freely into marriage is central to her life and her dignity and equality as a human being.'

(General Recommendation No.21, Comment Article 16 (1) (b), UN Convention on the Elimination of All Forms of Discrimination Against Women)[14]

THE VICTIM

38 Isolation is one of the biggest problems facing those trapped in, or under threat of, a forced marriage. They may feel they have no one to speak to about their situation – some may not be able to speak English. These feelings of isolation are very similar to those experienced by victims of other forms of domestic abuse and child abuse. Only rarely will an individual disclose fear of forced marriage. Therefore, someone who fears they may be forced to marry will often come to the attention of health professionals, police, social care services, education services or other professionals for various behaviours consistent with distress.

39 Young people forced to marry, or those who fear they may be forced to marry, are frequently withdrawn from education, restricting their educational and personal development. They may feel unable to go against the wishes of their parents and be threatened with disownment if they do – consequently they may suffer emotionally, often leading to depression and self-harm. These factors can contribute to impaired social development, limited career and educational opportunities, financial dependence and lifestyle restrictions. Studies have shown that self-harm and suicide are significantly higher

---

[14] www.un.org/womenwatch/daw/cedaw/recommendations/recomm.htm#recom21.

among Asian women than other groups[15] and contributory factors include lack of self-determination, excessive control, weight of expectations of the role of women and concerns about their marriages.

40 A mental or physical disability or illness adds to a young person's, or an adult's, vulnerability and may make it more difficult for them to report abuse or to extricate themselves from an abusive situation. Their care needs may make them dependent on their carers.

POSSIBLE CONSEQUENCES OF FORCED MARRIAGE

41 Women forced to marry may find it very difficult to initiate any action to end the marriage and may be subjected to repeated rape (sometimes until they become pregnant) and ongoing domestic abuse within the marriage. In some cases, they suffer violence and abuse from the extended family often being forced to undertake all the household chores for the family. Victims frequently end up trapped in a relationship marked by physical and sexual abuse. The impact this has on children within the marriage is immense. Children may learn that it is acceptable to be abusive and that violence is an effective way to get what you want. They may learn that violence is justified, particularly when you are angry with someone. Children witnessing abuse can be traumatised because witnessing persistent violence undermines children's emotional security and capacity to meet the demands of everyday life. Children's academic abilities can be affected. Witnessing violence as a child is associated with depression, trauma-related symptoms and low self-esteem in adulthood.

42 Both male and female victims of forced marriage may feel that running away is their only option. For many young people, especially women from minority ethnic communities, leaving their family can be especially hard. They may have no experience of life outside the family – leaving may mean they lose their children and friends. For many, finding accommodation for themselves and their children can be very difficult – especially for those who do not have leave to remain and therefore do not have recourse to public funds.[16] Living away from home with little support can make a victim more isolated, thus making it more likely that they will return to the abusive situation. In addition, leaving their family (or accusing them of a crime or simply approaching statutory agencies for help) may be seen as bringing shame on their honour and on the honour of their family in the eyes of the community. This may lead to social ostracism and harassment from the family and community. For many, this is simply not a price they are prepared to pay.

43 Those who do leave often live in fear of their own families, who will go to considerable lengths to find them and ensure their return. Families may solicit the help of others to find their runaways, or involve the police by reporting them missing or falsely accusing the young person of a crime (for example theft). Some families have traced individuals through medical and dental records, bounty hunters, private investigators, local taxi drivers, members of the community and shopkeepers or through National Insurance numbers, benefit records, school and college records. Sometimes having traced them, the family may murder them (so called 'honour killing').

44 Women trapped in a forced marriage often experience violence, rape, forced pregnancy and forced childbearing. Many girls and young women are withdrawn from education early. Some are taken and left abroad for extended periods, which isolates them from help and

---

15 See, for example, *Self harm in British South Asian Women: psychosocial correlates and strategies for prevention* – Husain M, Waheed W, Husain N: Annals of General Psychiatry 2006.

16 If a person does not have indefinite leave to remain, some form of discretionary leave or a right of abode in the UK, then they are likely to have a restriction on receiving public funds (no recourse to public funds). Public funds include income support and housing benefit.

support – this limits their choices so that often they go through with the marriage as the only option. Their interrupted education limits their career choices. Even if the woman manages to find work, however basic, they may prevented from taking the job or their earnings may be taken from them. This leads to economic dependence, which makes the possibility of leaving the situation even more difficult. Some may be unable to leave the house unescorted – living virtually under house arrest.

DIFFICULTIES FACED WHEN A FORCED MARRIAGE TAKES PLACE OVERSEAS

45   For many it may be their first experience of travelling overseas. If they are being held against their will and forced to marry there are various difficulties they may encounter if they want to return to the UK. They may find it impossible to communicate by telephone, letter and e-mail. They may not have access to their passport and money. Women may not be allowed to leave the house unescorted. They may be unable to speak the local language. Often individuals find themselves in remote areas where even getting to the nearest road can be hazardous. They may not receive the assistance they expect from the local police, neighbours, family, friends or taxi-drivers. Some individuals may find themselves subjected to violence or threats of violence.

THE LEGAL POSITION

46   Although there is no specific criminal offence of 'forcing someone to marry' within England and Wales, criminal offences may nevertheless be committed. Perpetrators – usually parents or family members – could be prosecuted for offences including conspiracy, threatening behaviour, assault, kidnap, abduction, theft (of passport), threats to kill, imprisonment and murder. Sexual intercourse without consent is rape, regardless of whether this occurs within a marriage or not. A woman who is forced into marriage is likely to be raped and may be raped until she becomes pregnant.

47   There are a number of civil and family orders that can be made to protect those threatened with, or already in, a forced marriage. For children, an application for a care or supervision order can be made under the Children Act 1989 or wardship proceedings may be issued in the High Court. Adults can seek an order for protection from harassment or non-molestation.

48   A Forced Marriage Protection Order can be sought under the Forced Marriage (Civil Protection) Act 2007 to protect both adults and children at risk of being forced into marriage and to offer protection for those who have already been forced into marriage. This Act is designed to enable the courts to tailor the terms of an order to protect and meet the specific needs of victims of forced marriage or potential forced marriage.

49   Some forced marriages will be legally valid until they are annulled or a divorce is granted by the court. Others will not be legally valid but may also need to be annulled. There are strict legal requirements that govern whether a marriage is valid under UK law and the rules for recognising a marriage vary depending in which country the marriage took place. When considering the validity of a marriage, particularly a marriage that took place overseas, specialist legal advice should be sought. However, agencies should not assume that a marriage is invalid because it was forced, this will most often not be the case.

POTENTIAL WARNING SIGNS OR INDICATORS

50   Individuals facing forced marriage may appear anxious, depressed and emotionally withdrawn with low selfesteem. They may come to the attention of professionals for a variety of reasons, some of which are described in the diagram opposite. Whilst the factors set out in this diagram may be, collectively or individually, an indication that someone is

facing forced marriage, it should not be assumed that it is forced marriage simply on the basis that someone presents with one or more of these warning signs. These warning signs may indicate other types of abuse that will also require a multi-agency response. These indicators are not intended to be exhaustive.

51   There have been occasions when women have presented with less common warning signs, such as cutting or shaving of a woman's hair as a form of punishment for disobeying or perhaps 'dishonouring' her family. In some cases, a girl may report that she has been taken to the doctors to be examined to see if she is a virgin. There have been reports of women presenting with symptoms associated with poisoning. In certain communities, it is important that women undergo female genital mutilation (FGM) before being able to marry – usually this will be performed during childhood but there have been reports of young girls or young women undergoing FGM just before a forced marriage. FGM is illegal in the UK and it is also a criminal offence to take someone overseas for the purposes of FGM.

WARNING SIGNS OF A VICTIM OF FORCED MARRIAGE

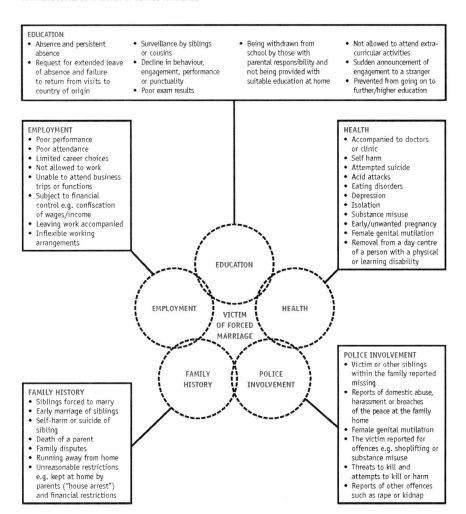

EDUCATION
- Absence and persistent absence
- Request for extended leave of absence and failure to return from visits to country of origin
- Surveillance by siblings or cousins
- Decline in behaviour, engagement, performance or punctuality
- Poor exam results
- Being withdrawn from school by those with parental responsibility and not being provided with suitable education at home
- Not allowed to attend extra-curricular activities
- Sudden announcement of engagement to a stranger
- Prevented from going on to further/higher education

EMPLOYMENT
- Poor performance
- Poor attendance
- Limited career choices
- Not allowed to work
- Unable to attend business trips or functions
- Subject to financial control e.g. confiscation of wages/income
- Leaving work accompanied
- Inflexible working arrangements

HEALTH
- Accompanied to doctors or clinic
- Self harm
- Attempted suicide
- Acid attacks
- Eating disorders
- Depression
- Isolation
- Substance misuse
- Early/unwanted pregnancy
- Female genital mutilation
- Removal from a day centre of a person with a physical or learning disability

FAMILY HISTORY
- Siblings forced to marry
- Early marriage of siblings
- Self-harm or suicide of sibling
- Death of a parent
- Family disputes
- Running away from home
- Unreasonable restrictions e.g. kept at home by parents ("house arrest") and financial restrictions

POLICE INVOLVEMENT
- Victim or other siblings within the family reported missing
- Reports of domestic abuse, harassment or breaches of the peace at the family home
- Female genital mutilation
- The victim reported for offences e.g. shoplifting or substance misuse
- Threats to kill and attempts to kill or harm
- Reports of other offences such as rape or kidnap

EDUCATION

EMPLOYMENT   VICTIM OF FORCED MARRIAGE   HEALTH

FAMILY HISTORY   POLICE INVOLVEMENT

PART TWO
STATUTORY GUIDANCE

Chapter 4
ACTIONS FOR CHIEF EXECUTIVES, DIRECTORS AND SENIOR MANAGERS TO WHOM THIS GUIDANCE IS ADDRESSED

52 Forced marriage is a violation of human rights and a form of child/adult/domestic abuse and should be treated as such. Therefore, ignoring the needs of victims is not an option. Cases should be tackled regardless of cultural sensitivities using **existing structures, policies and procedures** designed to safeguard children, vulnerable adults and victims of domestic violence.

53 Existing strategic bodies should ensure that their member agencies work effectively using agreed policies and procedures to tackle this issue. This includes Local Councils, Local Strategic Partnerships, Local Safeguarding Children Boards, Children's Trusts, Multi-agency Risk Assessment Conferences, Learning Disability Partnership Boards, Local Criminal Justice Boards, Local Family Justice Councils and Multi-Agency Adult Protection Management Committees.

SENIOR MANAGEMENT COMMITMENT

54 Chief Executives, directors and senior managers should ensure that their organisation has:
- A lead person with overall responsibility for safeguarding children, protecting vulnerable adults or victims of domestic abuse – the same person should lead on forced marriage.[17]
- Policies and procedures in place to protect those facing forced marriage. The policies and procedures should be in line with existing statutory and nonstatutory guidance on safeguarding children[18,19,20,21,22 &23] protecting vulnerable adults[24,25 &26] and protecting victims of domestic abuse[27,28,29,30,31,32,33,34 &35]. These policies and procedures should form part of an overall child/adult protection strategy.

---

[17] In schools, this would be the designated person for child protection.
[18] Statutory guidance on making arrangements to safeguard and promote the welfare of children under section 11 of the Children Act 2004.
[19] *Working Together to Safeguard Children* 2006.
[20] Education – Safeguarding Children and Safer Recruitment in Education 2006.
[21] Home Office (2008) *Gang's: You and Your Child* London: Home Office.
[22] Safeguarding Children – Working Together Under the Children Act 2004 (Welsh Assembly Government).
[23] What to do if you are worried a child is being abused, DCSF 2006.
[24] Mental Capacity Act 2005.
[25] *In Safe Hands: Implementing Adult Protection Procedures in Wales*, July 2000.
[26] *No Secrets: Guidance on developing and implementing multi-agency policies and procedures to protect vulnerable adults from abuse*, HO & DH, 2000.
[27] Responding to domestic abuse: A handbook for health professionals, DH 2006.
[28] The National Domestic Violence Delivery Plan: Progress Report 2007/08 www.crimereduction.homeoffice.gov.uk/dv/dv017.htm.
[29] Home Office (2005) Domestic Violence and Children: Good practice guidelines www.crimereduction.homeoffice.gov.uk/dv/dv08e.htm.
[30] Home Office (2007) Co-ordinated Community Response to Domestic Violence Model www.crimereduction.homeoffice.gov.uk/dv/dv014.htm.
[31] Association of Chief Police Officers (2008) Honour-based Violence Strategy www.acpo.police.uk.
[32] Tackling Domestic Abuse: The All Wales National Strategy – A Joint Agency Approach, 2005.
[33] Domestic Violence: A resource manual for Health Care Professionals in Wales. Welsh Assembly Government 2003.
[34] Home Office 'Safety and Justice: sharing personal information in the context of domestic violence.
[35] National Policing Improvement Agency guidelines on Investigating Domestic Abuse, 2008.

- Policies and procedures that are updated regularly to reflect any structural, departmental and legal changes.
- A named person whose responsibility it is to ensure that cases of forced marriage are handled, monitored and recorded properly.

ROLES AND RESPONSIBILITIES

55   Chief Executives, directors and senior managers should ensure that:
- Their staff understand their role in protecting people under threat of, or already trapped in, a forced marriage.
- Through policies and procedures, their staff are familiar with their duties and responsibilities when protecting individuals threatened with, or already in, a forced marriage.
- Their staff know to whom they should refer cases within their organisation and when to refer cases to other agencies.
- Front-line staff dealing with cases of forced marriage have access to, and are strongly recommended to consult, the practice guidelines issued by the Forced Marriage Unit.

CLEAR LINES OF ACCOUNTABILITY

56   Chief Executives, directors, lead members for adult services, lead members for children's services and senior managers should ensure that:
- There is a designated person within the organisation who is accountable for promoting awareness of forced marriage and a designated individual responsible for developing and updating all policies and procedures associated with forced marriage. This is likely to be the person with overall responsibility for promoting awareness of, and updating policies and procedures concerning the protection of children/adults/vulnerable adults or victims of domestic abuse.
- The designated person is a specialist in domestic abuse, adult protection or child protection with existing experience, expertise and knowledge.
- There is a senior specialist who has undertaken additional training who can be approached to discuss and direct difficult cases.
- There are clear lines of accountability from the front-line staff to senior management.

VICTIM-CENTRED APPROACH

57   Chief Executives, directors and senior managers should ensure that:
- Victims are listened to and they are able to communicate their needs and wishes.
- Victims are given accurate information about their rights and choices.
- Victims wishes are respected about the level of intervention they require.
- Staff are aware that relatives, friends, community leaders and neighbours should not be used as interpreters or advocates – despite any reassurances from this known person. If it is appropriate to use an advocate then an independent advocate would be advised.

EFFECTIVE INTER-AGENCY WORKING AND INFORMATION SHARING

58   Chief Executives, directors and senior managers should ensure that:
- There are policies and procedures in place so organisations can work effectively together to protect people facing forced marriage. These procedures are set out in existing guidance on safeguarding children and vulnerable adults.
- These procedures include arrangements for sharing information and arrangements for making referrals including, where appropriate, with police, social care services, health and the Forced Marriage Unit.

- Staff understand the importance of sharing information with other agencies at the earliest opportunity.
- Staff understand the difference between breaking confidence (involving the family without the individual's consent) and sharing information with other professionals to protect the individual from significant harm.

59 Local Safeguarding Children Boards and Multi-Agency Adult Protection Management Committees are likely to take a lead role in developing policies and procedures for inter-agency working and information sharing to protect adults and children from harm.

CONFIDENTIALITY

60 A dilemma may occur because an individual facing forced marriage may be concerned that if confidentiality is breached and their family finds out that they have sought help they will be in serious danger. On the other hand, those facing forced marriage are often already facing serious danger because of domestic abuse, 'honour-based' violence, rape, imprisonment etc. Therefore, in order to protect the individual, it is appropriate to share information with other agencies such as the police.

61 Consequently, confidentiality and information sharing are going to be extremely important for anyone threatened with, or already in, a forced marriage. Professionals need to be clear about when confidentiality can be offered and when information given in confidence should be shared.

62 **Chief Executives, directors and senior managers should ensure that:**
- Staff understand that the individual's confidence should be respected at all times and that they should not approach family, friends or members of the community without the express permission of the individual as this may place the individual at risk of harm.
- All records belonging to individuals facing forced marriage should be kept secure to prevent unauthorised access by those within the broader community who may potentially pass on confidential information to a victim's family. Records should only be available to those directly dealing with the case.

STAFF TRAINING AND AWARENESS RAISING

63 **Chief Executives, directors and senior managers should ensure that:**
- Suitable training and awareness raising is incorporated into existing training within agencies to ensure front-line staff are aware of the issue and know how to respond quickly and appropriately to individuals threatened with, or already in, a forced marriage.
- Staff receive updates on the issues surrounding forced marriage and honour-based violence within their existing training on child/adult protection.
- Existing work on social cohesion, equality and community outreach programmes should be used to raise general awareness of forced marriage and the help and support available within the local community.

SIGNPOSTING EXISTING PRACTICE GUIDELINES ON FORCED MARRIAGE

64 **Chief Executives, directors and senior managers should ensure that:**
- All front-line professionals have access to, and are strongly recommended to consult, the practice guidelines issued by the Forced Marriage Unit.

MONITORING AND EVALUATION

65 **Chief Executives, directors and senior managers should ensure that:**
- In line with existing guidance concerning safeguarding children, protecting adults and vulnerable adults, the effectiveness of their organisation's response to forced marriage is monitored and evaluated. This might include collecting information about the number of cases, the source of referrals, information about the individual such as age and gender, together with information about the outcome of the case.

RECORD KEEPING

66 **Chief Executives, directors and senior managers should ensure that:**
- Staff keep clear, concise records of all actions taken and the reasons why particular actions were taken. There should be a recorded agreement of which agency is to undertake each proposed action together with the outcomes of each action.
- If no further action is to be taken this should be clearly documented together with the reasons.

RISK ASSESSMENT

67 **Chief Executives, directors and senior managers should ensure that:**
- Staff within their organisation understand the risks facing victims of forced marriage, their siblings and other family members – including the possibility of 'honour-based' violence, threats to kill, murder, kidnap, rape, imprisonment and being abducted overseas.
- Staff alleviate these risks by undertaking ongoing risk assessments on a case-by-case basis and then manage any risks identified appropriately.
- Their organisational risk assessments are evaluated to ensure that they are appropriate for handling cases of forced marriage – and recognise the potential risk of harm to victims and practitioners.

68 Multi Agency Public Protection Arrangements (MAPPA)[36] and Multi-Agency Risk Assessment Conferences[37] play a role in managing the significant risk to individuals facing forced marriage.

69 For children, the Assessment Framework should be used to assess the risks. (See paragraphs 84–87).

THE DANGER OF FAMILY COUNSELLING, MEDIATION, ARBITRATION AND RECONCILIATION

70 Due to the nature of forced marriage and honourbased violence, some of the underlying principles and themes within existing guidance may inadvertently place young people and vulnerable adults at greater risk of harm. This includes the belief that the best place for them is with their family and the practice of attempting to resolve cases through family counselling, mediation, arbitration and reconciliation.

71 **Chief Executives, directors and senior managers should ensure that:**
- Staff have adequate training to understand the danger of family counselling, mediation, arbitration and reconciliation.

---

[36] www.homeoffice.gov.uk/rds/pdfs05/dpr45.pdf.
[37] www.caada.org.uk.

- Staff understand that in cases of forced marriage, it is important that agencies do not initiate, encourage or facilitate family counselling, mediation, arbitration or reconciliation. Mediation can also place the individual at risk of further emotional and physical abuse.
- Staff are aware that on occasions when an individual insists on meeting with their parents, it should only take place in a safe location, supervised by a trained/specialist professional with an authorised accredited interpreter present (not from the same local community), as parents will sometimes threaten the individual in their other language.
- Staff are aware that allowing a victim to have unsupervised contact with their family is normally extremely risky. Families may use the opportunity to subject the victim to extreme physical or mental duress or take them overseas regardless of any protective measures that may be in place.

PROTECTING CHILDREN AND ADULTS WITH DISABILITIES

72 There have been reports of children and vulnerable adults with mental health needs, learning and physical disabilities being forced to marry. Some vulnerable adults do not have the capacity to consent to the marriage. Some children and vulnerable adults may be unable to consent to consummate the marriage – sexual intercourse without consent is rape. There are various offences under the Sexual Offences Act 2003 that can be committed relating to a person with a mental disorder.

73 Disabled children and vulnerable adults are particularly vulnerable to forced marriage and its consequences because they are often reliant on their families for care, they may have communication difficulties and they may have fewer opportunities to tell anyone outside the family about what is happening to them.

74 Many of the measures for protecting disabled children and vulnerable adults from forced marriage are the same as those for children and adults without disabilities. However, disabled children and vulnerable adults may have particular needs and face challenges which may be substantially different from those encountered by other people facing forced marriage.

75 **Chief Executives, directors and senior managers should ensure that** disabled children and vulnerable adults receive whatever additional assistance and support they require. Good practice in relation to this assistance and support includes:
- Listening to disabled children/vulnerable adults and making sure they know how to raise concerns.
- Meeting the disabled child/vulnerable adult's care and support needs.
- Ensuring disabled children/vulnerable adults have access to adults outside the family to whom they can turn for help.
- Providing speech and language therapists to facilitate communication.
- Providing training and raising awareness about forced marriage amongst staff who care for disabled children or vulnerable adults.
- Providing an Independent Mental Capacity Advocate (IMCA) in cases where the victim lacks mental capacity – so their needs and wishes are understood and communicated.

Chapter 5
SPECIFIC ISSUES TO BE CONSIDERED BY AGENCIES WORKING WITH, OR PROVIDING SERVICES TO, CHILDREN AND YOUNG PEOPLE FACING FORCED MARRIAGE

EXISTING MULTI-AGENCY GUIDANCE CONCERNING CHILDREN AND YOUNG PEOPLE

76   There exists multi-agency statutory and non-statutory guidance on the subject of safeguarding children. This includes:

- *Working Together to Safeguard Children* (HM Government 2006).
- Safeguarding Children *Working Together* under the Children Act 2004 (WAG).
- What To Do If You're Worried A Child Is Being Abused (HM Government 2006).
- Statutory guidance on making arrangements to safeguard and promote the welfare of children under section 11 of the Children Act (HM Government 2004).
- Safeguarding Disabled Children: A Resource for Local Safeguarding Children Boards (Council for Disabled Children 2006).
- Information Sharing: Practitioner's Guide (DCSF, April 2006).[38]
- Statutory Guidance regarding the duty on local authorities in England to identify children not receiving education (DCSF, February 2007, revised version expected December 2008).
- Children Act 1989 Guidance and Regulations Volume 1 Court Orders (2008).

77   Existing guidance sets out the roles and responsibilities of all agencies involved in safeguarding children and the procedures that should be adhered to by all agencies. Existing guidance includes information about identifying children and young people at risk of harm, discussing concerns, making referrals, undertaking initial assessments and the next steps.

78   The guidance in this chapter does not attempt to replicate the guidance set out in *Working Together*[39] but seeks to address some of the particular issues concerning children and young people threatened with, or already in, a forced marriage.

THE DANGER OF INVOLVING THE FAMILY AND THE COMMUNITY

79   One of the underpinning principles of *Working Together*[40] is the involvement of the child's or young person's family. In cases of forced marriage this may increase the risk of significant harm to the child or young person. The family may deny that the child or young person is being forced to marry and they may expedite any travel arrangements and bring forward the marriage.

80   However, the primary principle of *Working Together*[41] is safeguarding children, and section 5.16[42] states that discussion with family and the family's agreement to refer to Local

---

[38]   www.everychildmatters.gov.uk/deliveringservices/informationsharing/.

[39]   *Working Together to Safeguard Children* (HM Government 2006) and Safeguarding Children *Working Together* under the Children Act 2004 (Welsh Assembly Government).

[40]   *Working Together to Safeguard Children* (HM Government 2006) and Safeguarding Children *Working Together* under the Children Act 2004 (Welsh Assembly Government).

[41]   *Working Together to Safeguard Children* (HM Government 2006) and Safeguarding Children *Working Together* under the Children Act 2004 (Welsh Assembly Government).

[42]   S.8.27 *Working Together* under the Children Act 2004 (Welsh Assembly Government) states 'While professionals should seek, in general, to discuss any concerns with the family and, where possible, seek their agreement to making referrals to local authority children's social services this should only be done where such discussion and agreement-seeking will not place a child at increased risk of significant harm'.

Authority children's social care should only be done where such discussion and agreement-seeking will not place a child at increased risk of significant harm. **In cases of forced marriage discussion with the family or any involvement of the family or local community members will often place the child or young person at greater risk of harm.**

81   In care proceedings, local authorities are required to demonstrate to the court that they have considered family members and friends as potential carers at each stage of their decision-making. However, in cases of forced marriage, professionals should exercise extreme caution around how they evidence this, and consider carefully whether, for example, family group conferences are appropriate in these cases (see paragraph 70–71 – The danger of family counselling, mediation, arbitration and reconciliation). Ideally, family group conferences should not be used in cases where a young person is at risk of forced marriage because of the physical danger and potential emotional manipulation they may experience during this type of session with their parents and other members of their family or community.

82   There must not be any burden on the child or young person to agree to a family conference.

83   **Chief Executives, directors and senior managers should ensure that staff have appropriate training in order to:**
    •   Understand the danger of involving the family and the community in cases of forced marriage.
    •   Recognise that they should not approach or involve families if forced marriage is suspected.
    •   Understand that family group conferences are not normally appropriate in cases of forced marriage because it will often place the child or young person at greater risk of harm.

THE ASSESSMENT FRAMEWORK

84   The Framework for the Assessment of Children in Need and their Families[43] [&44] provides a systematic way of analysing, understanding and recording what is happening to children and young people within their families and the wider context of the community in which they live. This framework assists professionals to decide what support a child and family may need.

85   The assessment has three main parts:
    i.   Child's developmental needs
    ii.   Parenting capacity
    iii.   Family and environmental factors

86   The Assessment Framework may not highlight any problems concerning children and young people facing forced marriage. They often come from very loving families where the parents capacity to provide safety, emotional warmth and stability is excellent. The children are often high achievers at school, their health is good, they are well integrated into the local community and have good relations with the wider family – they may not necessarily exhibit the warning signs described on page 15.

87   Therefore, professionals working with children and young people facing forced marriage require additional training in assessing families to identify those where forced marriage

---

[43]   The Framework for the Assessment of Children in Need and their Families: Department of Health, Department for Education and Employment, Home Office, 2000 www.dh.gov.uk/en/Publicationsandstatistics/Publications/ PublicationsPolicyAndGuidance/DH_4003256.
[44]   Framework for the Assessment of Children in Need and Their Families (National Assembly for Wales, June 2001).

may be an issue. *Working Together*[45] section 10.9[46] states, 'In order to make sensitive and informed professional judgements about the child's needs, it is important that professionals are sensitive to differing family patterns and lifestyles and to child-rearing patterns that vary across different racial, ethnic and cultural groups. At the same time they must be clear that child abuse cannot be condoned for religious or cultural reasons' – therefore, forced marriage must be responded to as a protection and safeguarding issue.

88   **Chief Executives, directors and senior managers should ensure that:**
   • Staff have appropriate training in order to enable them to effectively assess children and young people facing forced marriage using the Assessment Framework.

SAFEGUARDING CHILDREN AND YOUNG PEOPLE FROM HARM BY SHARING INFORMATION OR TO PREVENT A CRIME BEING COMMITTED

89   Although there is no specific offence of 'forcing someone to marry', criminal offences may nevertheless be committed. Perpetrators – usually parents or family members – could be prosecuted for offences including threatening behaviour, assault, kidnap, abduction, threats to kill, imprisonment and murder. Sexual intercourse without consent is rape, regardless of whether this occurs within a marriage or not.

90   Section 5.17[47] of Working Together[48] states that 'Whenever LA children's social care has a case referred to it that constitutes, or may constitute, a criminal offence against a child, social workers or their managers should always discuss the case with the police at the earliest opportunity'.

91   Section 5.18 states that 'Whenever other agencies encounter concerns about a child's welfare that constitute, or may constitute, a criminal offence against a child they must consider sharing that information with Local Authority children's social care or the police in order to protect the child or other children from the risk of significant harm. If a decision is reached not to share information, the reasons must be recorded'.

92   **Chief Executives, directors and senior managers should ensure that:**
   • Forced marriage is automatically handled as a child protection issue.
   • Staff have appropriate training in order to understand the importance of sharing information with other agencies at the earliest opportunity to safeguard children and young people from significant harm or to prevent a crime being committed.
   • Staff share information promptly when a child or young person is at risk of forced marriage.
   • Staff provide information to the Forced Marriage Unit.

---

[45]   *Working Together to Safeguard Children* (HM Government 2006) and Safeguarding Children *Working Together under the Children Act 2004* (Welsh Assembly Government).

[46]   S.7.29 *Working Together under the Children Act 2004* (Welsh Assembly Government) states 'The assessment process should always include consideration of the way religious beliefs and cultural traditions in different racial, ethnic and cultural groups influence their values, attitudes and behaviour, and the way in which family and community life is structured and organised. Cultural factors neither explain nor condone acts of omission or commission which place a child at risk of significant harm.

[47]   S. 8.29 *Working Together under the Children Act 2004* (Welsh Assembly Government) states 'Whenever local authorities children's social services have a case referred to them because of concerns about a child's welfare, which constitutes, or may constitute, a criminal offence against a child, they should always discuss the case with the police. Similarly, whenever other agencies, including other local authority departments, encounter concerns about a child's welfare which constitutes or may constitute a criminal offence against a child, they should refer the case to the police without delay in order to protect the child or other children from the risk of serious harm'.

[48]   *Working Together to Safeguard Children* (HM Government 2006) and *Safeguarding Children Working Together under the Children Act 2004* (Welsh Assembly Government).

- Staff understand the difference between breaking confidence (involving the child or young person's family without consent) and sharing information with consent with other appropriate professionals to prevent the child or young person being at risk of significant harm.

IMMEDIATE PROTECTION

93   Ideally, professionals should discuss cases of forced marriage with, and seek advice from, a designated professional or another statutory agency; however, there may be occasions when immediate emergency action is necessary to protect a child or young person from being forced to marry or abducted e.g. police protection or emergency protection orders. In this case, a strategy discussion should take place as soon as possible after the immediate protection to plan the next steps (section 5.50[49] *Working Together*).

94   **Chief Executives, directors and senior managers should ensure that staff have appropriate training in order to:**
- Recognise the importance and relevance of immediate protection.
- Recognise the risk to other siblings in the household who might also be threatened with, or already in, a forced marriage.
- Understand that in almost no circumstances will it be sufficient to protect a child or young person by removing the alleged perpetrator from the household (as in the significant majority of cases the extended family and wider community are also involved).
- Recognise that placing the child or young person with a family member or member of the same community may place them at risk of significant harm from other family members or individuals acting on the family's behalf.

Chapter 6
SPECIFIC ISSUES TO BE CONSIDERED BY AGENCIES WORKING WITH, OR PROVIDING SERVICES TO, VULNERABLE ADULTS

EXISTING MULTI-AGENCY GUIDANCE CONCERNING ADULTS
95
- *No secrets*: guidance on developing and implementing multi-agency policies and procedures to protect vulnerable adults from abuse.
- *In Safe Hands*: Implementing Adult Protection Procedures in Wales, July 2000.
- Responding to domestic abuse: A handbook for health professionals DH 2006.
- Mental Capacity Act 2005.

96   The arrangements described in *No Secrets* and *In Safe Hands* are aimed at protecting vulnerable adults from all forms of abuse including forced marriage. *No Secrets* and *In Safe Hands* set out the roles and responsibilities of all agencies involved in protecting vulnerable adults and the procedures that should be adhered to by all agencies. The guidance in *No Secrets* and *In Safe Hands* is not statutory although it should be complied with unless there are good reasons locally that justify a variation.

97   Section 2.5 of *No Secrets* defines abuse as 'a violation of an individual's human and civil rights by any other person or persons'. It can be physical, psychological, verbal or an act of neglect or omission – 'it may occur when a vulnerable person is persuaded to enter into a

---

[49]   S.8.73 *Working Together under the Children Act 2004* (Welsh Assembly Government) states 'Where an agency with statutory child protection powers has to act immediately to protect a child, a strategy discussion should take place as soon as possible after such action to plan next steps'.

financial or sexual transaction to which he or she has not consented, or cannot consent. Abuse can occur in any relationship and may result in significant harm to, or exploitation of, the person subjected to it'.

98   Section 7.4 of *In Safe Hands* defines abuse as 'a violation of an individual's human and civil rights by any other person or persons'. It can be physical, psychological, financial, verbal or an act of neglect or omission – it may occur when a vulnerable person is persuaded to enter into a financial or sexual transaction to which he or she has not consented, or cannot consent. Abuse can occur in any relationship and may result in significant harm to, or exploitation of, the person subjected to it.

99   Forced marriage should be seen in the context of domestic abuse and, in the case of vulnerable adults, adult abuse. Agencies should adhere to the good practice set out in the policies and procedures concerned with domestic abuse and adult abuse as the most effective way to tackle forced marriage.

100   The guidance in this section is not intended to replace existing guidance but instead it seeks to address some of the particular issues concerning adults and vulnerable adults threatened with, or already in, a forced marriage.

THE DANGER OF INVOLVING THE FAMILY AND THE COMMUNITY

101   Involving families in cases of forced marriage may increase the risk of serious harm to an individual. The family may deny that the individual is being forced to marry and they may expedite any travel arrangements and bring forward the wedding.

102   **Chief Executives, directors and senior managers should ensure that staff receive the appropriate training in order to:**
   - Understand the danger of involving the family and the community in cases of forced marriage.
   - Recognise that discussion with the family or any type of family involvement will often place the vulnerable adult at greater risk of harm.

SAFEGUARDING ADULTS AND VULNERABLE ADULTS BY SHARING INFORMATION WHEN A CRIME MAY HAVE BEEN, OR MAY BE, COMMITTED

103   Although there is no specific offence of 'forcing someone to marry', criminal offences may nevertheless be committed. Perpetrators – usually parents or family members – could be prosecuted for offences including threatening behaviour, assault, kidnap, abduction, threats to kill, imprisonment and murder. Sexual intercourse without consent is rape, regardless of whether this occurs within a marriage or not.

104   Section 6.25 of *No Secrets* states, 'As a matter of course allegations of criminal behaviour should be reported to the police'.

105   Section 7.8 of *In Safe Hands* states, 'When complaints about alleged abuse suggest that a criminal offence has been committed it is imperative that reference should be made to the police as a matter of urgency'.

106   **Chief Executives, directors and senior managers should ensure that staff receive the appropriate training in order to:**
   - Recognise the importance of sharing information with other agencies at the earliest opportunity.

- Understand the difference between breaking confidence (involving a vulnerable adult's family without consent) and sharing information with other professionals to prevent a vulnerable adult being at risk of significant harm.

For further information and advice please contact the Forced Marriage Unit

Forced Marriage Unit
G/58 Old Admiralty Building
London
SW1A 2PA
Tel: 020 7008 0151
(9–5 Monday to Friday, for out of hours emergency support please contact the FCO Response Centre on 020 7008 1500)
Email: fmu@fco.gov.uk

You can download this publication online at:

www.fco.gov.uk/forcedmarriage

Copies of this publication can also be obtained from:

Forced Marriage Unit
G/58 Old Admiralty Building
London
SW1A 2PA
Tel: 020 7008 0151
email: fmu@fco.gov.uk

Extracts from this document may be reproduced for non-commercial education or training purposes on the condition that the source is acknowledged.

APPENDIX E

COURT FORMS

FL401A APPLICATION FORM FOR A FORCED MARRIAGE PROTECTION ORDER

E.1

SCHEDULE 2 Rule 19

Application for a Forced Marriage Protection Order

Part 4A Family Law Act 1996

To be completed by the court	
Date issued	
Case number	
Name of court	

Please read the accompanying notes on page 6 as you complete this form

---

1   About you (the applicant)

Are you (tick only one box)

☐ the person who is to be protected by this order (see page 6)

☐ a relevant third party (see page 6)

☐ any other person (see page 6)

☐ Mr.   ☐ Mrs.   ☐ Ms.   ☐ Miss   ☐ Other _____

Full name

_____

If you do not wish your address to be made known to the respondent, leave this space blank and complete Confidential Address Form C8 (if you have not already done so). See notes for guidance on page 6.

Address

Postcode ☐☐☐☐ ☐☐☐

Telephone no. (optional)

_____

Date of birth (if under 18)

☐☐ / ☐☐ / ☐☐☐☐

For relevant third parties and any other person

Name of organisation (if applicable)

_____

Position held in the organisation

_____

Your solicitor's details (leave blank if you are representing yourself)

Full name

Name of firm

Address

Reference no.

Telephone no.

Postcode

Fax no.

DX no.

2 About the person to be protected (see notes on page 6)

☐ Mr.　　☐ Mrs.　　☐ Ms.　　☐ Miss　　☐ Other _____

Full name

If you do not wish the following address to be made known to the respondent, leave this space blank and complete Confidential Address Form C8 (if you have not already done so). See notes for guidance on page 6.

Address

Postcode

Date of birth (if known)

☐☐ / ☐☐ / ☐☐☐☐

☐ Tick this box if you do not know the date of birth but believe the person to be protected is under 18 years.

3 Your reasons for applying on behalf of the person to be protected
(for Relevant Third Party applications only e.g. local authority applicants)

State briefly your reasons including:

- what you know of the circumstances of the person to be protected;
- the wishes and feelings of the person to be protected so far as you know them.

4 About the respondent(s)

If there are more than two respondents please continue on a separate sheet of paper.

☐ Mr.   ☐ Mrs.   ☐ Ms.   ☐ Miss   ☐ Other _____

Full name

Address   Date of birth (if known)

Postcode

☐ Mr.   ☐ Mrs.   ☐ Ms.   ☐ Miss   ☐ Other _____

Full name

Address   Date of birth (if known)

Postcode

3

5   The Order(s) for which you are applying

State what you want the order to say (for examples see page 6). Give full details in support of your
application below (continue on a separate sheet if necessary) or in a separate statement. Include details of
any violence that the respondent has used or threatened.

☐ Tick this box if you wish the court to hear your application without notice being given to the
respondent. The reasons relied on for an application being heard without notice must be
stated in the sworn statement in support. (See notes for guidance on page 6.)

4

6   At the court

If you or the person to be protected requires an interpreter, you must notify the court now so that one can be arranged.

Will you or the person to be protected need an interpreter at court?

☐ Yes   ☐ No

If Yes, specify the language and dialect:

If you or the person to be protected has a disability for which you require special assistance or special facilities, please state what is needed. The court staff will then get in touch with you.

Please say whether the court needs to make any special arrangements for you or the person to be protected, to attend court (e.g. providing you with a separate waiting room from the respondent or other security provisions).

7   Other information

This could include name and address of any other persons who may become involved as a respondent.

8   Other Proceedings and Orders

If there are any other current family proceedings or orders in force involving you, the respondent(s) or the person to be protected, then where known, state the type of proceedings or orders, the court and the case number. Please attach a copy of the order if available.

This application is to be served upon the respondent and the person to be protected by the order

Signed: Date:

5

Application for a Forced Marriage Protection Order

Notes for guidance

Please read these notes with the leaflet FL701 'Forced Marriage Protection Orders'

Section 1 - Applicants

There are three types of applicant. The person to be protected, someone on their behalf and a relevant third party.

If you are the person to be protected and are applying yourself for an order, with or without legal representation, you are also the applicant. Fill in section 1 only, and then go to section 4.

A relevant third party applicant is a person or organisation that is allowed to make an application on behalf of another without the leave of the court. Only the Lord Chancellor can make a person or organisation a relevant third party. Local authorities, for example, have been specified as relevant third parties.

If you are not a relevant third party and you are not the person who is to be protected by the order you can still make the application, but you need the court's permission. The court can give you the form (FL430) to apply for permission.

Address details

If you **do not** wish your address, or the address of any person named in the application form to be made known to the respondent, leave the space(s) on the form blank and complete Confidential Address Form C8. The court can give you this form.

Section 2 - Person to be protected

This section only needs to be completed if you are applying on behalf of someone. If you are the person to be protected by the order, leave this section blank.

Address details

If you do not wish the address of the person to be protected to be made known to the respondent, leave the space blank and complete Confidential Address form C8. The court can give you this form.

Section 4 - Respondents

A person who you want the court to make an order against is called the respondent. There may be more than one respondent.

If you know of other people who may become involved as a respondent include their details in section 6.

Section 5 - The Order

A forced marriage protection order protects a person from being forced into marriage or a person who has been forced into marriage. Each Forced Marriage Protection Order is specific to each case and contains terms that change the behaviour of the respondent and other people.

Examples of what you might want the court to order are:

- that the respondent does not take you abroad to be forced into marriage
- that the respondent behave in a different way
- that the respondent hands over your passport and travel documents to the court.

In section 5 or in a separate statement say why you are applying and give full details. Include details of violence the respondent has used or threatened, so the court can consider a power of arrest.

Urgent orders

An urgent order made by the court before the notice of the application is served on the respondent is called a without notice order. In deciding whether to make a without notice order the court will consider all the circumstances of the case, including:

- any risk of significant harm to the person to be protected or another person, if the order is not made immediately
- whether it is likely that the applicant will be deterred or prevented from pursuing the application if an order is not made immediately
- whether there is reason to believe that the respondent is aware of the proceedings but is deliberately evading service and the person to be protected or the applicant will be seriously prejudiced by the delay.

If you are applying for a 'without notice' order you must include the reasons why the court should deal with the application without notifying the respondent first. You must make a sworn statement. The court can tell you how to do this.

continued over the page ▯⟩

If the court makes a 'without notice' order, it must give the respondent or other person an opportunity to make representations about the order as soon as just and convenient at a full hearing.

Further details

Further information on making an application is contained in the leaflet FL701 'Forced Marriage Protection Orders'. The leaflet contains information on coming to court, the power of arrest and what happens if a respondent or other person fails to obey a court order.

You can download this leaflet and details of your local court from our website www.hmcourts-service.gov.uk

FL402A NOTICE OF PROCEEDINGS FOR A FORCED MARRIAGE PROTECTION ORDER

E.2

In

Telephone Number

FAX Number

Case Number

Notice of Proceedings
[Hearing] [Directions Appointment]

has applied to the court for an order.

About the [Hearing][Directions Appointment]

You should attend when the Court hears the application at

on

at   [am]   [pm]

What to do next

There is a copy of the application with this Notice. Read the application now, and the notes overleaf.

When you go to court

Please take this Notice with you and show it to a court official.

FL402A Notice of Proceedings for Forced Marriage Protection Order (11.08)   © Crown copyright 2008

About this Notice

If you are named as a respondent in the application form   It is in your own interest to attend the court on the date shown on this form. You should be ready to give any evidence which you think will help you to put your side of the case.

For legal advice go to a solicitor or an advice agency.

You can obtain the address of a solicitor or an advice agency from the Yellow Pages or the Solicitors' Regional Directory.

You will find these books at:

    a Citizens' Advice Bureau

    a Law Centre

    a local library

A solicitor or an advice agency will be able to tell you whether you may be eligible for legal aid.

If you require an interpreter because you do not speak English, please notify the court now so that one can be arranged.

If you have a disability for which you require assistance or special facilities, please contact the court to ask what help is available.

If you need the court to make any special arrangements for you to attend court (e.g. providing you with a separate waiting room from the other respondents or other security provisions) please contact the court.

If you are named as the person to be protected or anyone else   It may be in your interest to attend court on the date shown.

For legal advice go to a solicitor or an advice agency.

You can obtain the address of a solicitor or an advice agency from the Yellow Pages or the Solicitors' Regional Directory.

You will find these books at:

    a Citizens' Advice Bureau

    a Law Centre

    a local library

A solicitor or an advice agency will be able to tell you whether you may be eligible for legal aid.

If you want to become a party to these proceedings, you need to apply to the court. The court can give you the form FL431.

If you require an interpreter because you do not speak English, please notify the court now so that one can be arranged.

If you have a disability for which you require assistance or special facilities, please contact the court to ask what help is available.

If you need the court to make any special arrangements for you to attend court (e.g. providing you with a separate waiting room from the respondent or other security provisions) please contact the court.

FL403A APPLICATION TO VARY, EXTEND OR DISCHARGE A FORCED MARRIAGE PROTECTION ORDER

E.3

Application to vary, extend or discharge a forced marriage protection order	To be completed by the court
Part 4A Family Law Act 1996	Date issued
	Case number

The court to which you are applying:

Note: the application should be made to the court currently dealing with the forced marriage proceedings (whether or not this is the court which made the order you wish to vary).

1 About you (the applicant)

State your title, full name, address, telephone number and date of birth (if under 18).

If you do not wish your address to be made known to the respondent or other persons, leave this space blank and complete Confidential Address Form C8 (if you have not already done so). The court can give you this form.

State your solicitor's name, address, reference, telephone, FAX and DX numbers.

If you are already a party to the case, give your description (for example, applicant, respondent or other).

2 The order(s) for which you are applying *Please attach a copy of the order if possible.*

I am applying to   vary   ☐

extend   ☐

discharge ☐

the order dated:

If you are applying for an order to be varied or extended please give details of the order which you would like the court to make:

3 Your reason(s) for applying

State briefly your reasons for applying.

4 Person(s) to be served with this application

State the title, full name and address (where known) of all
respondents, the person protected by the order
and any other person named in the order.

Signed   **Date**
(Applicant)

FL404B FORCED MARRIAGE PROTECTION ORDER

E.4

In the

Case number

Forced Marriage Protection Order
Part 4A Family Law Act 1996

Notice
(Insert name and address of respondent or other person(s) to whom this order is directed)

To

Address

Warning

You must obey this order. You should read this order carefully. If you do not understand anything in this order you should go to a solicitor, Legal Advice Centre or Citizens Advice Bureau. You have a right to apply to the court to change or cancel the order.

If you do not obey this order, you will be guilty of contempt of court and may be sent to prison.

Terms of the Order
(Attach a separate page for the order if required)

Date of hearing _____

Name of person to be protected

_____

The court makes a Forced Marriage Protection Order in the following terms:

[A power of arrest is attached to [some] [all] of these terms]

Power of Arrest

See separate form FL406A (if attached).

Duration of Order

This order is made until

☐ (The following date and time) _____

☐ Further notice

Notice of further hearing

The court will reconsider the application and whether the order should continue at a further hearing

Place _____

Date _____ Time _____

If you do not attend at the time shown the court may make an order in your absence.

This order is made

☐ without notice

☐ with notice

to the respondent.

Important notice

Where attached to a Forced Marriage Protection Order the power of arrest (see attached form FL406A) also applies to any third party who frustrates the terms of the order or otherwise acts in contempt of court in relation to this order, even where they are not a respondent to the original proceedings.

Ordered by

[Mr] [Mrs] Justice

[His] [Her] Honour Judge

[Deputy] District Judge [of the Family Division]

Recorder

on

FL406A POWER OF ARREST: FORCED MARRIAGE PROTECTION ORDER

E.5

In the

Case number

Click to reset

Power of Arrest
Forced Marriage Protection Order
Part 4A Family Law Act 1996

Applicant
Ref.

Respondent
Ref.

The Court orders that

(Set out those provisions of the order to which this power of arrest is attached and no others)

a power of arrest applies to the following paragraph(s) of an order made under Part 4A of the Family Law Act 1996 on

Power of Arrest
(Delete the part that does not apply)

[Orders with notice]

[Orders without notice]

The court considers that the respondent or other person to whom an order is directed has used or threatened violence against the person being protected or otherwise in connection with the matters being dealt with by the order and

[in all the circumstances, there will not be adequate protection without a power of arrest being attached to the provision(s) of that order.]

or

[that there is a risk of significant harm to a person, attributable to the conduct of the respondent or other person to whom an order is directed, if a power of arrest is not attached to the provision(s) of the order immediately.]

A power of arrest is attached to the order whereby any constable may (under the power given by section 63I of the Family Law Act 1996) arrest without warrant a person if the constable has reasonable cause for suspecting that the person may be in breach of any provision to which the power of arrest is attached or is otherwise in contempt of court in relation to this order.

This Power of Arrest expires on

Note to the Arresting Officer	Where a person is arrested under the power given by section 63I of the Family Law Act 1996, that section requires that the person must be brought before the court within 24 hours beginning at the time of arrest.
	If the matter is not then disposed of forthwith, the court may remand the person arrested.
	Nothing in section 63I authorises the detention of the person arrested after the expiry of the period of 24 hours beginning at the time of arrest, unless remanded by the court.
	The period of 24 hours shall not include Christmas Day, Good Friday or any Sunday.

Ordered by	[Mr] [Mrs] Justice
	[His] [Her] Honour Judge
	[Deputy]District Judge [of the Family Division]
	Recorder
on	

FL407A APPLICATION FOR WARRANT OF ARREST: FORCED MARRIAGE PROTECTION ORDER

E.6

In the

Case Number

Application for a Warrant of Arrest
Forced Marriage Protection Order
Part 4A Family Law Act 1996

Applicant
Ref.
Respondent
Ref.

On the   day of   20   , the Court made an order

(1) Set out the precise parts of the order or undertaking relevant to this application

[*or* the respondent gave an undertaking] as follows:(1)

(2) Insert name of applicant

I,(2)   apply for an order that a warrant should be issued for the arrest of the person who has failed to comply with the order (or broken the undertaking) or is otherwise in contempt of court in relation to the order (or the undertaking).

(3) List the ways in which it is alleged that the person has disobeyed the order or broken the undertaking. If necessary continue on a separate sheet.

The person has disobeyed the order [or broken the undertaking] or is otherwise in contempt of court in relation to the order [or the undertaking] by (3)

Signed   Date

FL430 APPLICATION FOR LEAVE TO APPLY FOR A FORCED MARRIAGE PROTECTION ORDER

E.7

Application for leave to apply for a Forced Marriage Protection Order	**To be completed by the court**
	Date issued
	Case number
Part 4A Family Law Act 1996	Name of court

Complete this form if you are asking for the court's permission to make an application on behalf of the person to be protected. You **must** also complete application form FL401A. The court can give you this form.

1   About you (the applicant)

☐ Mr.   ☐ Mrs.   ☐ Ms.   ☐ Miss   ☐ Other _____

Full name

2   About the person to be protected

☐ Mr.   ☐ Mrs.   ☐ Ms.   ☐ Miss   ☐ Other _____

Full name

3   Your reasons for applying on behalf of the person to be protected

State briefly your reasons including:

- your connection with the person to be protected;
- what you know of the circumstances of the person to be protected;
- the wishes and feelings of the person to be protected so far as you know them.

continue over the page ⇨

FL430 Application for leave to apply for a Forced Marriage Protection Order (11.08)

© Crown copyright 2008

3 continued from over the page

Continue on a separate sheet if needed.

Signed: Date:

FL431 APPLICATION TO BE JOINED AS, OR CEASE TO BE, A PARTY TO FORCED MARRIAGE PROTECTION PROCEEDINGS

E.8

Application to be joined as, or cease to be, a party to Forced Marriage Protection Proceedings

Part 4A Family Law Act 1996

To be completed by the court	
Date issued	
Case number	
Name of court	

For further information please read the leaflet FL701 Forced Marriage Protection Orders.

1   About you (the applicant)

☐ Mr.   ☐ Mrs.   ☐ Ms.   ☐ Miss   ☐ Other _____

Full name

Date of birth (if under 18)

☐☐ / ☐☐ / ☐☐☐☐

If you do not wish your address to be made known to the respondent or other persons, leave this space blank and complete Confidential Address Form C8 (if you have not already done so).

Address

Postcode ☐☐☐☐ ☐☐☐☐

Telephone no. (optional)

Your solicitor's details (leave blank if you are representing yourself)

Full name

Address

Postcode ☐☐☐☐ ☐☐☐☐

DX no.

Reference no.

Telephone no.

Fax no.

2 Your reasons for applying

State briefly your reasons:

3 The persons to be served with this application (The respondent(s))

If there are more than two respondents please continue on a separate sheet of paper.

☐ Mr.   ☐ Mrs.   ☐ Ms.   ☐ Miss   ☐ Other _____

Full name

Address

Postcode

Date of birth (if known)

☐ Mr.   ☐ Mrs.   ☐ Ms.   ☐ Miss   ☐ Other _____

Full name

Address

Postcode

Date of birth (if known)

4   At the court

If you require an interpreter, you must notify the court now so that one can be arranged.

Will you need an interpreter at court?   ☐ Yes   ☐ No

If Yes, specify the language and dialect:

If you have a disability for which you require special assistance or special facilities, please state what your needs are. The court staff will get in touch with you about your requirements.

Please say whether the court needs to make any special arrangements for you to attend court (e.g. providing you with a separate waiting room from the respondent or other security provisions).

Signed: Date:

FL413 HOSPITAL ORDER

E.9

In the

Case Number

[Interim] Hospital Order
Family Law Act 1996

	Applicant Ref. Respondent Ref.

The Court orders that	the respondent whose address is
	be admitted to and detained in the following hospital
	[*(name and address)*
	]
	[and that the respondent be conveyed there by]
[The Court directs that]	[pending admission to that hospital within the period of 28 days the respondent shall be detained at a place of safety, namely:
	]
	[and shall be conveyed there by]
The Court found that	the respondent had breached one or more of the following:

- an occupation order
- a non-molestation order
- a forced marriage protection order
- an exclusion requirement included by virtue of section 38A of the Children Act 1989 in an interim care order made under section 38 of that Act
- an exclusion requirement included by virtue of section 44A of the Children Act 1989 in an emergency protection order under section 44 of that Act.

The Court [heard] [considered]	the [written] evidence of two medical practitioners, namely
	as required by the provisions of section 37 of the Mental Health Act 1983 that the respondent is suffering from [mental illness] [severe mental impairment] within the meaning of that Act.
The Court was satisfied that	- all other conditions, which under section [37] [38] of the Mental Health Act 1983 are required to be satisfied for the making of [a] [an interim] hospital order, are satisfied in respect of the respondent
	- arrangements have been made for the respondent's admission to the hospital named above within 28 days of the date of this order.

Ordered by	[Mr] [Mrs] Justice
	[His] [Her] Honour Judge
	District Judge [of the Family Division]
	Justice[s] of the Peace
	[Assistant] Recorder
on	

FL414 GUARDIANSHIP ORDER

E.10

In the

Case Number

Guardianship Order
Family Law Act 1996

	Applicant *Ref.* Respondent *Ref.*

The Court orders that	the respondent whose address is be placed under the guardianship of [social services authority] [being a person approved by social services authority]

The Court found that   the respondent had breached one or more of the following:

- an occupation order
- a non-molestation order
- a forced marrage protection order
- an exclusion requirement included by virtue of section 38A of the Children Act 1989 in an interim care order made under section 38 of that Act
- an exclusion requirement included by virtue of section 44A of the Children Act 1989 in an emergency protection order under section 44 of that Act.

The Court [heard] [considered]   the [written] evidence of two medical practitioners, namely

as required by the provisions of section 37 of the Mental Health Act 1983 that the respondent is suffering from [mental illness] [severe mental impairment] within the meaning of that Act.

The Court was satisfied that

- all other conditions, which under section 37 of the Mental Health Act 1983 are required to be satisfied for the making of a guardianship order, are satisfied in respect of the respondent
- the [authority] [person] specified above is willing to receive the respondent into guardianship.

Ordered by   [Mr] [Mrs] Justice

[His] [Her] Honour Judge

District Judge [of the Family Division]

Justice[s] of the Peace

[Assistant] Recorder

on

APPENDIX F

SAMPLE ORDERS AND AFFIDAVITS

SAMPLE ORDERS

F.1

Preamble

(1) It will always be helpful where orders are made against respondents or other persons not present at court for the order to be given a series of preambles setting out on the face of the document the circumstances in which the order came to be made. That should include, for example, what documents were before the court and who, if anyone, gave live evidence.

(2) In circumstances where the person to be protected is outside the jurisdiction, the court should be asked to include a preamble inviting assistance from the judicial and administrative bodies, and police authorities, within the country to which the person to be protected has travelled. A preamble might be drafted in the following terms:

'AND THIS COURT RESPECTFULLY INVITES all judicial and administrative bodies and police authorities in [*state name of country concerned*] to render assistance in establishing the whereabouts of [*person to be protected*] and in arranging for him/her to be placed in contact with the British High Commission in [*name location*].'

(3) It may also be helpful for the court to set out by way of preamble its intentions in the making of the orders. For example, the order may recite:

'And whereas this honourable court is anxious to protect and secure the wellbeing of [*insert name of person to be protected*] and to ensure that she may freely express her wishes concerning her country and place of residence.'

(4) The topics that might be covered by such a preamble include:
- To prevent a forced marriage occurring.
- To stop intimidation and violence.
- To reveal the whereabouts of a person.
- To stop someone from being taken abroad.

General orders

(5) The following comprises a menu of orders from which practitioners may select relevant orders for their particular case. The menu is not intended to be prescriptive, but as basic drafts for the assistance of practitioners. They will need to be amended where necessary to cover situations such as where there is a broad category of persons to whom the order is directed (not simply specified respondents) or where a general order is made prohibiting any person from carrying out the act specified.
Practitioners should be aware that the courts will look favourably upon creative orders directed towards preventing the abuses envisaged by the Act.

General prohibition on marriage ceremony

(a)   [*name of respondent(s)*] [*no person*] shall not cause or permit [*person to be protected*] to undergo any ceremony or purported ceremony of betrothal or marriage, civil or religious whether within this jurisdiction or elsewhere.

General prohibition on removal from the jurisdiction

(b)   [*name of respondent(s)*] [*no person*] by themselves or by encouraging, assisting or agreeing with any other person whatsoever shall be forbidden from removing [*insert name of person to be protected*] from the jurisdiction.

Passport/travel documents

(c)   The Identity and Passport Service is requested not to issue any further passport in the name of [*insert name of person to be protected*].

(d)   The passport of [*insert name of person to be protected*] and any other travel documents [*specify where known*] shall be surrendered by [*insert name of respondent(s)*] to [*insert location: eg to the court/British High Commission/or other appropriate location*] by [*insert date*].

(e)   [*insert name of respondent(s)*] are forbidden from applying for any new passport or travel documents for [*insert name of person to be protected*] from the United Kingdom passport agency or from any other foreign passport agency.

Protection from violence/harassment

(f)   [*name of respondent(s)*] [*and ... insert names of any additional respondents*] are forbidden whether by themselves or by instructing or encouraging any other person from using force or threatening force against [*insert name of person to be protected/third party*] within this jurisdiction or elsewhere.

(g)   [*insert name of first or only respondent*] [*and ... insert names of any additional respondents*] are forbidden whether by themselves or by instructing or encouraging any other person from threatening, intimidating or harassing [*person to be protected*].

Orders to enable person to be protected to have private discussions/attend court

(h)   [*names of respondent(s)*] do assist and allow [*insert name of person to be protected*] to meet [*X person*] and to have private discussions with him/her.

(i)   [*and ... insert names of any additional respondents*] do assist and allow [*insert name of person to be protected*] to attend [*insert name of Court*] on [*insert date and time*].

Order to disclose whereabouts

(j)   [*insert name(s) of respondent(s)*] shall disclose to the court the whereabouts of [*name of person to be protected*].

Service of order/evidence

(k) The Solicitors for the Applicant do have permission to serve only this order upon the Respondents pending [*further order*] [*a redacted record of the evidence given at the hearing on* [*insert date*] *being available*] [*the redacted record of the evidence shall be served by* [*insert date*]].

Permission to disclose to the FCO/FMU/British High Commission/Embassy

(l) There be permission to disclose this Forced Marriage Protection Order and the originating application together with supporting documentation to the [*Foreign and Commonwealth Office and/or Forced Marriage Unit and/or British High Commission/Embassy at* [*insert location*]].

Order for return to the jurisdiction/disclosure of whereabouts

(m) [*name of person to be protected*] is to be returned to the jurisdiction of England and Wales [*forthwith/or by specified date/any arrangements required*].

(n) [*name respondent(s)*] shall forthwith disclose the exact whereabouts of [*insert name of person to be protected*] to [*solicitors acting for person applying on behalf of person to be protected and/or the court*].

Order to enable interview by British High Commission

(o) [*and … insert names of any additional respondents*] do assist and allow [*insert name of person to be protected*] to visit the British High Commission in [*insert location*] for [*person to be protected*] to be interviewed alone by an officer of the said High Commission, on a date and time to be agreed between the parties/or insert specific date.[1]

Protective orders encompassing behaviour of persons outside the jurisdiction

(p) [*insert name of first or only respondent*] [*and … insert names of any additional respondents*] are forbidden whether by themselves or by instructing or encouraging any other person whether in the United Kingdom or in [*insert country*] from using force or threatening force against [*insert name of person to be protected*].

(q) [*insert name of first or only respondent*] [*and … insert names of any additional respondents*] are forbidden whether by themselves or by instructing or encouraging any other person whether in the United Kingdom or [*insert country*] from threatening, intimidating or harassing [*person to be protected*].

Permission to serve outside jurisdiction and faxed/PDF order

(r) Permission is granted to serve these proceedings outside the jurisdiction of England and Wales.

---

[1] United Kingdom embassies and High Commissions can only provide consular assistance to British nationals and in certain circumstances nationals of European Union countries or the Commonwealth whose country does not have a local embassy in the country concerned. Where a person to be protected is not a British national an alternative support mechanism should be identified, such as local non-governmental organisations (NGOs).

(s)   Personal service by way of facsimile copy or PDF copy of this order upon any person is hereby deemed to be good service.

SAMPLE AFFIDAVITS

F.2

Sample affidavit for FMPO, application by person to be protected

Filed on behalf of the Applicant

1st Statement

Dated   **the day of**   **2009**

Sworn Statement

In the matter of Part 4A Family Law Act 1996

<u>**IN THE LEEDS COUNTY COURT**</u>

Case No:

Between

LEYLA KAMRAN   Applicant

And

HARRIS KAMRAN   1st Respondent

And

SARA KAMRAN   2nd Respondent

And

DANIYAAL KAMRAN   3rd Respondent

I, LEYLA KAMRAN (D.O.B. 01/01/1991) of an undisclosed address **MAKE OATH AND SAY AS FOLLOWS:-**

1   I make this statement in support of my application for forced marriage protection orders against the Respondents in this matter: Harris Kamran who is my father; Sara Kamran who is my mother; and Daniyaal Kamran who is my older brother. I believe that arrangements have already been put into place for me to travel to Pakistan and, once there, my marriage is to take place.

2   I left home, the home that I share with all of the Respondents, during the course of the morning on 30th March 2009. Instead of going to college I went to the police station and told them of my worries; it was they who made arrangements for me to go into refuge accommodation. I am now really scared about being located and taken to Pakistan against my will. My fears are intensified by the fact that my passport, I believe, is with the Respondents.

3   I am due to sit my A level final examinations this coming summer. My ambition is to go on to university and do a teaching degree. I have been told by my tutors at college that I have the ability to achieve this ambition.

4   Approximately a year ago my father began to talk about me getting married to his brother's son in Pakistan. At first I thought he was teasing but as time went by I began to realise that he was in fact quite serious about the matter.

5   By summer time, last year, my mum also started to talk about marriage. My usual response was that I was too young to get married, but this resulted in my mum reminding me that

she was sixteen years old when she married my dad. I would also tell her that I did not want to marry at this age and that I wanted to study. She would tell me that it would be perfectly possible for me to continue with my studies after marriage.

6   In the last two months, telephone communications between my dad and his brother, in Pakistan, have increased greatly. There have been many occasions when I have walked into the room whilst my father has been talking on the phone to his brother, but he has gone on to abruptly end the calls. When I have tried to ask what the telephone calls were about and why they ended so quickly, it has resulted in my father raising his voice to me. This is something that has upset me greatly as my father is usually a very mild mannered person and, as far as I can remember, he has never shouted at me in the past.

7   On 23rd March 2009 my mother told me that arrangements were being put into place for us all to go to Pakistan for the purpose of a holiday. When I told her that I was worried about missing college especially with my final exams being so close, she did not comment. When I asked her how long we were going for she would not give me a straight answer.

8   On 28th March 2009 my mother and father went out during the day, they returned home with a large amount of gold that they had purchased together with some clothes for me. I, upon seeing this, felt quite sick. I decided to try and talk to them. I told them that all their actions seemed to suggest that my marriage was going to take place in Pakistan and I did not want to get married and I therefore would not be travelling with them. My father said very little but I could see that he was angry. I started to get upset and I repeated, over and over, that I was not going anywhere.

9   At this stage my mother started to cry. She told me what I had already anticipated and feared. She said that she and my father had agreed for my marriage to take place to my paternal uncle's son in Pakistan some months ago and all the practical arrangements for the wedding celebrations were being put in place in readiness for our arrival in Pakistan. She initially tried to persuade me, she said that in agreeing to this marriage I would remain within the family and that would be a good thing.

10   I was beside myself and I simply refused to listen.

11   My mother then began to tell me that if I was to refuse to go through the arrangement then that would be the end of my education and I could forget about going to college on Monday morning, let alone go to university. I told my mother that I did not care about my education. This was not the truth. I was saying anything I could to try to stop the marriage.

12   My father then spoke up, he said that a promise had been made to his brother and if that promise was to be broken then there would be consequences. My father then said that if I was to refuse to go through the marriage then he would divorce my mother. My father then stormed out of the room. My mother was hysterical; she kept telling me that I was going to be responsible for bringing shame to the family.

13   My brother Daniyaal, aged twenty four years, was present throughout this whole incident. Further to my father threatening to divorce my mother and storming out, Daniyaal began to shout at me. He called me a selfish bitch and told me to get out. I ran up to my bedroom. I remained in there for the rest of the day.

14   The following morning I got up and went into the bathroom for a shower. I switched on the shower but realised that I had left my shampoo in my bedroom. I left the shower running and walked out of the bathroom and towards my bedroom, I saw Daniyaal in my bedroom, he was rummaging in my bedside drawer. Upon seeing me he did not even try to explain or apologise for what he was doing. Instead he told me that if was to do anything other than

the right thing then I would be sorry. He also said that if I was to even think about doing "anything funny" then he would find me and deal with me. He told me that he knew people who could locate me regardless of where I was to hide. As he walked out of the room, he barged past me and pushed me aside in the process. I felt scared but unable to say anything back to him. I felt that I could not even report what he had done to my parents as they were angry with me anyway.

15   Later on in the day I told my parents that I was going to travel to Pakistan and I was also agreeable to the marriage taking place. I was in tears as I told them. My mother hugged me and told me that she was pleased that I had made the right decision. My father however remained cold.

16   I, having told my parents that I would act in accordance with their wishes, believed that there would be some sort of acceptance of the situation in my own head. However this was not the case. I felt so desperately unhappy with the decision that I had been forced to make. The more I thought about it, the more distressed I felt. I was violently sick about an hour after telling my parents that I was agreeable to the marriage. I could not eat nor sleep. I was awake for the entire night thinking about the situation that I was in. Despite telling my parents that I would go ahead with their wishes I realised that I simply could not go ahead. I made the decision to get help. During the early hours of the morning I packed my college rucksack with some clothes and a few essential toiletries. It was my intention to pack my passport, which is ordinarily in my room, but I simply could not find it. I then realised that my address book was also missing. It then occurred to me that Daniyaal more than likely removed the items the previous day, when I found him in my bedroom looking through my things.

17   On Monday 30th March 2009, I got ready for college. My mum told me that it would not be necessary for me to go given the trip, but I told her that I had an important assignment to hand in as well as college library books, which if not handed in on time would lead to a fine. My mum told me that either my father or Daniyaal would come to collect me at the lunch time break.

18   I did not go to college I went to the police station and asked them to help me. I was so upset I kept telling the officer that I did not want any of my family members to get into trouble but I did not know what to do in the circumstances. It is the police who transported me to a refuge and one of the refuge support workers who made an emergency appointment for me to meet a solicitor.

19   Despite being in a place of safety I am very frightened for myself. I have received a number of text messages from Daniyaal and it is clear that he is very angry. He has said that he will not rest until he finds me. I am worried that he will locate me and then I will be taken to Pakistan against my will. I am also worried that Daniyaal may do whatever it takes to take me home in the event that he locates me, that includes the use of force by way of violence.

20   I want my parents to know that I will get married someday, but this is not the way that I want things to happen. I want my parents to understand that in doing what they are doing I am not only unhappy but I am also very frightened. I do not want to upset or hurt my parents I simply want them to understand things from my point of view.

21   In the circumstances I seek a Forced Marriage Protection Order from the court. I respectfully request that this application be considered without any prior notice being provided to all three respondents: my parents and Daniyaal. I am concerned that should they have notice of the application then the notice period will be used to locate me and/or contact me to persuade me against proceeding with the application and that may well be by threats of violence and/or emotional blackmail.

Sworn by the above named Leyla Kamran   )
at Leeds in the County of West Yorkshire   )
This day of   2009   )

Before me   )

A Commissioner of Oaths or an Officer of a Court, appointed by the Circuit Judge to take Affidavits.

Sample affidavit for FMPO, application on behalf of person to be protected

Filed on behalf of the Applicant

1st Statement

Dated **the day of** **2009**

Sworn Statement

In the matter of Part 4A Family Law Act 1996

IN THE LEEDS COUNTY COURT

Case No:

Between

STEPHANIE VICTORIA BELL Applicant

and

HARRIS KAMRAN 1st Respondent

and

SARA KAMRAN 2nd Respondent

and

DANIYAAL KAMRAN 3rd Respondent

I, STEPHANIE VICTORIA BELL (D.O.B. 02/03/1991) of an undisclosed address **MAKE OATH AND SAY AS FOLLOWS:-**

1   I seek permission from the Honourable Court to proceed with an application for orders under the Forced Marriage Protection Act on behalf of my friend Leyla Kamran (D.O.B. 01/01/88). I am of the genuine and firm belief that Leyla has been taken to Pakistan against her will and if she has not already been forced into marriage then it is something that will happen very soon.

2   I have known Leyla for almost seven years now. We met on our first day at high school and we very quickly became good friends. After leaving high school we went on to attend the same college. I can say that Leyla and I are very close, in fact I would say that we are best friends.

3   I believe that it was in the early part of the year when Leyla started to tell me of her concerns about being made to marry in Pakistan. In the beginning she would tell me of how worried she was then she would tell herself off for being silly.

4   In the last few weeks, however, Leyla has become very quiet. After a great deal of badgering by me she told me that she believed that her parents were arranging her marriage to a cousin in Pakistan. Leyla mentioned to me that there was an incident when her dad was talking on the phone to someone and when she walked into the room, her dad ended the call. Leyla told me that this had been happening a lot so on this particular occasion she tried to ask her dad why he kept doing this. Leyla told me that her dad shouted at her. Leyla was very upset as she is very much a daddy's girl and was not used to this type of behaviour.

5   Approximately two weeks ago, Leyla told me that her parents were planning a holiday to Pakistan and she was going also. She had very little information about the trip, for example

the travel dates and duration of the trip. Nonetheless, Leyla presumed that the trip would be over the Easter college break and that she would back for the Spring term to start her final preparation for her A Level final exams.

6   I last saw Leyla in college on Monday 30th March 2009. She looked awful, her eyes were all bloodshot and the moment that I approached her, she burst into tears. I took Leyla to the cafeteria and she told me that she had had a horrendous time at home during the weekend. She was told what she had feared: that she was being taken to Pakistan in order to get married to her first cousin. She was so upset when telling me what happened but I do remember her telling me that her dad said that if she did not do as she was being told then he would divorce her mum. I could not believe what I was hearing. I suggested to Leyla that she get her brother Danny to talk to her parents but Leyla said that Danny had made it clear that if she was to go against her parents' wishes then he would cause her problems. Leyla said that Danny was quite threatening and menacing in his tone and attitude. On the one hand I found this quite difficult to believe as I have met Danny on many occasions and I have always thought that he was a nice guy, but having seen the state that Leyla was in I had no reason to doubt that she was being truthful in what she had told me.

7   I suggested to Leyla the options that were available. I initially suggested the police, but Leyla made it quite clear that she did not want her family members to get into trouble. I then suggested that we speak to the college principal. Leyla was initially agreeable to this but then changed her mind. Leyla said that she did not feel too comfortable about dragging other people into what was personal family business. She said that, having spoken to me, she felt a little calmer and stronger and she was going to sit down with her parents and try and make them see things from her point of view. Leyla said that she felt confident that they would understand. I asked her to think about this very carefully. I then left Leyla in the cafeteria as I had a tutorial to attend.

8   My tutorial finished at lunchtime, I then went looking for Leyla, but she was nowhere to be found. I tried to call her on her mobile but it went straight onto the answer-phone facility. At the end of the college day I went to her tutor who told me that Leyla had not registered herself in after the lunch time break. I told myself that she probably went home early to talk to her parents and that she would be back in college the following day. During the course of the evening I called Leyla on her mobile phone. It went straight through to the answer-phone facility. I also tried texting her. She has not responded to my messages or texts.

9   The following day, 1st April 2009, there was no sign of Leyla at college. I felt uneasy about the situation. I went to Leyla's house after college on 2nd April 2009. Her brother Danny opened the door. Upon seeing me he told me that Leyla was sleeping as she was unwell. He was polite but also very curt with me. He said that it was not a good idea to disturb her.

10   By 2nd April 2009 I gave up trying to contact Leyla on her mobile as it was always going onto the answer-phone facility. I phoned her home landline at approximately 8pm. Danny picked up the phone. He initially told me that Leyla was not available. I was desperate to find out what was going on, so I said that I had been asked to speak to Leyla by a college tutor in relation to an outstanding assignment and in the event that this assignment was not handed in, then Leyla would be personally responsible for her course fees to date. It was a complete lie on my part but it was told with a view to finding out where Leyla was. It was at this stage that Danny told me that Leyla had gone to Pakistan with her parents as a family member there had been taken seriously ill. He told me that she would be back in a couple of weeks.

11   I believe that Leyla has been taken to Pakistan against her will and it is for the purpose of a marriage. From the discussions that I last had with her, she certainly did not want to get

married to her cousin in Pakistan, or anybody for that matter. She spoke about trying to make her parents understand her point of view and I believe that she was not successful in doing this. I know that Leyla had hopes and aspirations of going onto university and doing a teaching degree.

12   Under the circumstances I respectfully ask the court to give me the relevant permission to proceed with an application for orders under the Forced Marriage (Civil Protection) Protection Act so that Leyla can get the assistance she needs in respect of the situation that she is in. I do not know where exactly in Pakistan she is, but I am confident that Danny will know.

13   I also ask that the court make the orders, which will assist Leyla without notice being given to Danny. I am worried that if Danny finds out that I am doing this then there may be problems for me. I do not want any problems, I simply want to help Leyla at this moment in time.

Sworn by the above named Stephanie Victoria Bell   )

at Leeds in the County of West Yorkshire   )

This day of   2009   )

Before me   )

A Commissioner of Oaths or an Officer of a Court, appointed by the Circuit Judge to take Affidavits.

APPENDIX G

FUNDING INFORMATION

FORCED MARRIAGE (CIVIL PROTECTION) ACT 2007

G.1

Funding issues – general

1   Public funding in England and Wales is available in respect of applications for forced marriage protection orders. It is also available for issues surrounding forced marriages including representation on applications under the inherent jurisdiction and proceedings for nullity following a forced marriage.

2   Advice and assistance can be given to clients in the office under Legal Help (Level 1) and an application can then be made for a public funding certificate when representation is required in court proceedings.

3   Forced marriage falls within the family category for funding purposes. Therefore only providers who hold family contracts with the Legal Services Commission may make applications for public funding and be remunerated out of the Community Legal Service Fund.

4   Applications for certificated funding should be forwarded to the regional offices to which the solicitor usually sends applications. Applications will be subject to the usual Funding Code means and merits criteria appropriate to the particular application. However, in many cases an urgent application to the court will be required and in these situations providers should consider exercising their devolved powers to grant funding in the usual way, including having regard to all the issues including the source and detail of instructions, means information and in appropriate cases availability of a litigation friend/guardian.

5   For applications for forced marriage protection orders the Funding Code Criteria to be used when considering applications will be the same as in domestic violence cases (ie Criteria 11.10 of the Funding Code). The Funding Code Guidance on these applications can be found in Volume 3 of the Legal Services Commission Manual (paragraph 3C-197).

6   The solicitor rates at which these matters will be remunerated are contained in Table 9(b) of the Payment Annex to the Unified Contract.

Client eligibility

7   As forced marriage protection orders are to protect the client from harm the income and capital waivers applicable for domestic violence cases will also apply. This means that there is no maximum income or capital limit above which legal aid will not be available although the applicant may still be required to pay a contribution if their income or capital are in excess of a certain amount. Details of the current eligibility limits and contributions can be found on the LSC website at www.legalservices.gov.uk. It should be noted, however, that

the waiver only applies to the application for an order to protect the client from harm. It does not extend to other matters in the family proceedings such as nullity, children matters etc.

8   The applicant for public funding does not have to be British or be living in England and Wales to qualify for legal aid. The issue is whether the case relates to the law of England and Wales. Legal aid is also available regardless of immigration status and even if the client has no recourse to public funds. Legal aid is not classed as a 'public fund' for these purposes.

9   In some cases the victim may be overseas or it may not be immediately possible to provide evidence of means. In accordance with the guidance in relation to the use of devolved powers, provided the solicitor makes a justifiable estimate of whether the client is financially eligible and follows the devolved power guidance then they will, even if it turns out that the client is not eligible, be paid for the work done pursuant to the grant of emergency representation. However, because of the eligibility waiver which is available in these cases, the upper eligibility limit will not in any event apply and any issue will usually relate to the level of contribution payable.

Client instructions

10   It is recognised that this type of work may involve cases where the solicitor will not receive instructions direct from the client. There may be difficulties in receiving full instructions from the client and information may have been received from a third party (for example, the Forced Marriage Unit at the Foreign and Commonwealth Office). Therefore as much detail as possible should be provided on the application to enable the Legal Services Commission to process the application.

11   Some of the applicants may be minors and there may also be issues around the identification and appointment of a litigation friend/guardian ad litem. The applying solicitor should ensure that the position is entirely clear from the forms. In cases where the applicant is overseas and information has been provided to the solicitor by the Foreign and Commonwealth Office it may be that there is no suitable family member or friend who is able to be a litigation friend/guardian. In these exceptional cases it is possible that the solicitor will also act as litigation friend/guardian but this should be apparent from the forms provided by the solicitor. However, any certificate issued will not cover work or expenses incurred only as guardian (rather than as solicitor).

Respondents

12   The guidance and criteria as applies to non-molestation orders will apply to applications for funding from Respondents to defend applications for forced marriage protection orders. However, in many cases prospects of success and costs benefit criteria are unlikely to be satisfied by a respondent to a forced marriage protection order. Further guidance is given in the Family Decision-Making guidance (paragraph 3C-197, see, in particular, sub-paragraphs 11 and 12).

APPENDIX H

USEFUL CONTACTS

H.1 The following contact details are reproduced from the publication *Multi-Agency Practice Guidelines: Handling Cases of Forced Marriage*, with the kind permission of the Forced Marriage Unit.

THE FORCED MARRIAGE UNIT

Call the Forced Marriage Unit on 020 7008 0151 between 9am and 5pm Monday to Friday (UK time).

Outside those hours, call 020 7008 1500 and ask for the Foreign Office Response Centre.

Email: fmu@fco.gov.uk.

For more information go to www.fco.gov.uk/forcedmarriage.

BRITISH HIGH COMMISSIONS AND EMBASSIES

Please contact the Forced Marriage Unit if you require further details of any other British High Commission or Embassy.

Bangladesh: Dhaka

British High Commission
United Nations Road
Baridhara
Dhaka
Postal Address:
PO Box 6079, Dhaka–1212
Telephone: (00) (880) (2) 8822705-9
Facsimile: (00) (880) (2) 8823437
Office Hours (GMT): Sun to Wed 03.00–10.15
Thurs 03.00–09.00
Local Time Sun–Wed 08.00–15.15
Thurs 08.00–14.00

BANGLADESH: Sylhet

British High Commission
House 37A
Kumarpara
Sylhet
Telephone: (00) (880) (821) 724694
Facsimile: (00) (880) (021) 720070
Office Hours (GMT): Sun to Wed 03.00–10.15
Thurs 03.00–09.00
Local Time Sun–Wed 08.00–15.15
Thurs 08.00–14.00

ETHIOPIA: Addis Ababa

British Embassy
Comoros Street
Addis Ababa
Postal address: PO Box 858, Addis Ababa
Telephone:(00) (251) (11) 6610588
Facsimile:(00) (251) (11) 6614154
Consular facsimile: (00) (251) (11) 6414154
Office hours (GMT): Mon–Thurs 05.00–13.00
Fri 05.00–10.00
Local time: Mon–Thurs 08.00–16.30
Fri 08.00–13.00

INDIA: New Delhi

British High Commission
Chanakyapuri
New Delhi 110021
Telephone: (00) (91) (11) 2687 2161
Facsimile: (00) (91) (11) 2 6116094
Email: conqry.newdelhi@fco.gov.uk
Office Hours (GMT) Mon–Fri 03.30–07.30
08.30–11.30
Local Time 09.00–13.00
14.00–17.00

INDIA: Mumbai (Bombay)

Office of the British Deputy High Commissioner
Naman Chambers
C/32 G Block
Bandra Kurla Complex (Opposite Dena Bank)
Bandra East
Mumbai 400051
Telephone: (00) (91) (22) 66502222
Facsimile: (00) (91) (22) 66502324
Offi ce Hours (GMT) Mon–Thurs 02.30–10.30
Fri 02.30–07.30 and 08.30–10.30
Local Time Mon–Thurs 08.00–16.00
Fri 08.00–13.00 and 14.00–16.00

PAKISTAN: Islamabad

British High Commission
Diplomatic Enclave,
Ramna 5
PO Box 1122
Islamabad
Telephone: (00) (92) (51) 2012000
Facsimile: (00) (92) (51) 2012019
Email: cons.islamabad@fco.gov.uk
Office Hours (GMT) Mon–Thurs 03.00–11.15
Fri 03.00–08.00
Local Time Mon–Thurs 08.00–16.15
Friday 08.00–13.00

PAKISTAN: Karachi

British Deputy High Commission
Shahrah-E-Iran
Clifton
Karachi 75600
Telephone: (00) (92) (21) 5827000
Facsimile: (00) (92) (21) 5827012
Email: consularenquiries.karachi@fco.gov.uk
Office Hours (GMT) Mon–Thurs 03.00–11.15
Fri 03.00–08.00
Local Time Mon–Thurs 08.00–16.15
Friday 08.00–13.00

TURKEY: Istanbul

British Consulate General
Mesrutiyet Caddesi No 34
Tepebasi Beyoglu 34435
Istanbul
Telephone: (00) (90) (212) 334 6400
Facsimile: (00) (90) (212) 315 6401
Consular facsimile: (00) (90) (212) 334 6407
Email: Cons-istanbul@fco.gov.uk
Office hours (GMT): Mon–Fri 06.30–11.00
11.45–14.45
Local time: 08.30–13.00
13.45–16.45

YEMEN: Sana'a

British Embassy
938 Thaher Himiyar Street
East Ring Road (opposite
Movenpick Hotel)
PO Box 1287
Sana'a
Telephone: (00) (967) 1308 100
Facsimile: (00) (967) 1302454
Email: Consularenquiries.sanaa@fco.gov.uk
Office hours (GMT): Sat–Wed 04.30–11.30
Local time: 07.30–14.30

NATIONAL SUPPORT AGENCIES

This section gives details of national support agencies including addresses, telephone numbers and an explanation of the service.

The Ann Craft Trust

0115 951 5400
www.anncrafttrust.org

The Ann Craft Trust offers advice to professionals, parents, carers and family members on issues relating to the protection of vulnerable children and adults. You can contact them about general issues but they are also happy to give advice about specific cases. If they are unable to answer your question, they will try to find you the most appropriate person to talk to about your concerns.

If you have been abused and would like to talk to someone contact the Respond Helpline on 0808 808 0700.

The Asian Family Counselling Service

020 85713933
www.asianfamilycounselling.org

This is a national service offering counselling on marital and family issues for Asian men and women. The national helpline is open from 9am to 5pm Monday to Friday. Telephone counselling is also available.

BAWSO Women's Aid – (Wales)

0800 731 8147
www.bawso.org.uk

This is an all Wales, voluntary organisation. It provides a specialist service to Black and Minority Ethnic (BME) women and children made homeless through a threat of domestic abuse or fleeing domestic abuse in Wales. They have purpose built refuges across Wales. They also provide emotional and practical support for BME women living in social housing. The service is accessible 24 hrs a day.

Careline

020 8514 1177

This is a national confidential counselling line for children, young people and adults on any issue including family, marital and relationship problems, child abuse, rape and sexual assault, depression and anxiety.

Child Line

0800 1111
www.childline.org.uk

This service is for any child or young person with a problem.

Citizens advice bureau

www.citizensadvice.org.uk

The Citizens Advice Bureau offers free, confidential and impartial information and advice on a wide range of subjects including consumer rights, debt, benefits, housing, employment, immigration, family and personal matters. For a list of branches, see "Citizens Advice Bureau" in the telephone directory.

CLIC

029 2046 2222
www.cliconline.co.uk

CLIC is the national information and advice service for young people in Wales aged 11–25 to help them make informed decisions in their lives. It is funded by the Welsh Assembly Government.

ForcedMarriage.net

www.forcedmarriage.net

This website is for young people facing forced marriage. It provides advice, information and essential contacts to help young people who fear they may be forced to marry or those who are already in a forced marriage.

FORWARD

020 8960 4000
www.forwarduk.org.uk

This service is an African Diaspora led UK-registered campaign and support charity dedicated to advancing and safeguarding the health and rights of African girls and women, in particular female genital mutilation (FGM) and forced and child marriage.

Gatwick Travel Care

01293 504283
www.gatwick-airport-guide.co.uk/disabled-facilities.html

This service ensures that young people are able to leave the airport and arrive at their destination safely and without delay. Victims of forced marriage may require assistance when they arrive at Gatwick and Travel Care can be contacted for advice. The service is available from 9am to 5pm Monday to Friday and 9am to 4pm Saturday, Sunday and Bank Holidays.

Heathrow Travel Care

020 8745 7495
www.heathrowtravelcare.com

This service ensures that young people are able to leave the airport and arrive at their destination safely and without delay. Victims of forced marriage may require assistance when they arrive at Heathrow and Travel Care can be contacted for advice. The service is available from 9am to 5pm Monday to Friday.

Henna Foundation

02920 498600/496920

Henna Foundation operates a "one stop" service that works to meet and advance the needs, concerns and aspirations of Asian and Muslim children and families. It also assists voluntary, statutory services and Government agencies to improve engagement and delivery of mainstream services. Henna Foundation hosts a National (multi-disciplinary) On-line Forced Marriage & HBV Directory and Knowledge Centre (to go live soon).

Honour Network

0800 5999 247
www.karmanirvana.org.uk

The Honour Network helpline is a confidential helpline providing emotional and practical support and advice for victims and survivors (male & female) of forced marriage and/or honour based violence and abuse. It provides advice and support to potential victims, victims in crisis and professional agencies.

Iranian and Kurdish Women's Rights Organisation

0207 490 0303 (9.30-5.00) or 07862 733511 (24hrs)
www.ikwro.org.uk

IKWRO provides advice, support, advocacy and referral in Arabic, Kurdish, Turkish, Dari and Farsi to women, girls and couples living in Britain, in particular helping women facing domestic violence, forced marriage and 'honour'-based violence. Their mission is to protect Middle Eastern women at risk of 'honour' killings, domestic violence, forced marriages and female genital mutilation, and to support them in upholding their right to live without fear or oppression.

Language line

020 7520 1430
http://www.languageline.co.uk/

This service can provide an interpreter on the telephone immediately in 100 different languages, 24 hours a day. This is not a free service.

Local Women's Aid specialist domestic violence services

www.womensaid.org.uk

There are nearly 370 organisations providing specialist domestic violence support services in England. For information about these go to www.womensaid.org.uk. *The Survivors Handbook* provides information for survivors in many different languages. TheHideout.org.uk provides information for children and young people about domestic violence and it is interactive.

Minority Ethnic Women's Network Wales (MEWN Cymru)

029 2046 4445
www.mewn-cymru.org.uk

MEWN is an umbrella body representing ethnic minority (visible and non visible) women across Wales, regardless of their age, religious observance, ethnicity or life choices.

Men's Advice Line

0808 801 0327
www.mensadviceline.org.uk

This service provides a freephone confidential helpline for all men experiencing domestic violence by a current or ex-partner. This includes all men–in heterosexual or same-sex relationships. The service gives men the chance to talk about what is happening to them and provides them with emotional support and practical advice. The advice line also has information about specialist services that can provide advice on legal, housing, child contact, mental health and other issues. The helpline is open Monday to Friday 10am–1pm and 2pm–5pm. You can also email us: info@mensadviceline.org.uk.

MIND

0845 7660163
0208 5192122 (legal helpline)
www.mind.org.uk

MIND is a mental health charity working for a better life for everyone with experience of mental distress. Their services include a legal helpline.

Free phone 24 Hour National Domestic Violence helpline

Run in partnership between Women's Aid and Refuge

0808 2000 247

All Wales Domestic Abuse Helpline

0808 8010 800

This service provides information, support, and practical help, 24 hours a day, 7 days a week, to women experiencing domestic abuse. It can refer women and their children to refuges throughout the UK. They will discuss the practical and legal options available, and if the young person wishes refer them to a local Women's Aid specialist domestic violence service, or other sources of help. All calls are taken in strictest confidence. Alternatively, you can contact the local Women's Aid service through the local phone book, or access the Women's Aid website (www.womensaid.org.uk).

NSPCC

Asian child protection helpline
Bengali speaking advisor
0800 096 7714
Gujurati speaking advisor
0800 096 7715
Hindi speaking advisor
0800 096 7716
Punjabi speaking advisor
0800 096 7717
Urdu speaking advisor
0800 096 7718
English speaking advisor
0800 096 7719

This free, confidential service for anyone concerned about children at risk of harm offers counselling, information and advice. The service also connects vulnerable young people, particularly runaways, to services that can help. It is open Monday–Friday 11.00–19.00.

NSPCC

0808 800 5000 (helpline)
0800 056 0566 (text phone)
www.nspcc.org.uk

This free, 24-hour helpline provides information, advice and counselling to anyone concerned about a child at risk of abuse.

Paladin Team – Heathrow

07747 055938

Practitioners may refer a child or young person to the Paladin Team at Heathrow for a wide variety of child protection issues. There may be concerns that a child or young person is an unaccompanied minor, an asylum-seeking child, being trafficked or about to be forced to marry. The team can be contacted directly on the above number. The service is available from 9am to 5pm Monday to Friday.

Respond

0808 808 0700 (helpline)
020 7383 0700 (admin line)
020 7387 1222 (fax line)
E-mail: admin@respond.org.uk
www.respond.org.uk

Respond provides a range of services to both victims and perpetrators of sexual abuse who have learning disabilities and those who have been affected by other trauma. They also offer support and training to families, carers and professionals.

reunite International Child Abduction Centre

PO Box 7124
Leicester
LE1 7XX
0116 2555345 (admin line)
0116 2556234 (advice line)
0116 2556370 (fax line)
www.reunite.org

reunite is the leading charity specialising in international parental child abduction. It operates a 24-hour advice line providing advice, support and information to parents, family members and guardians who have had a child abducted or who fear abduction. reunite also supports and informs parents who have abducted their children and assists with international contact issues. reunite's advice is impartial and confidential to one or both parties involved in an international parental child abduction case. reunite also provides information and support on the issue of forced marriage.

Samaritans

08457 90 90 90
www.samaritans.org

This is a 24-hour helpline that provides confidential support to any person in emotional distress.

Shelterline

0808 800 4444
www.shelter.org.uk

This service provides emergency access to refuge services.

Southall Black Sisters

020 8571 9595
www.southallblacksisters.org.uk

This is a resource centre offering information, advice, advocacy, practical help, counselling, and support to black and minority women experiencing domestic abuse. Southall Black Sisters specialise in forced marriage particularly in relation to South Asian women. The office is open weekdays (except Wednesday) 10.00–12.30 and 13.30–16.00.

Victim Support

0845 30 30 900
www.victimsupport.org

Victim Support offers information and support to victims of crime, whether or not they have reported the crime to the police. All help given is free and confidential. You can contact Victim

Support direct, or ask the police to put you in touch with your local group. The national helpline is open from 9am to 9pm Monday to Friday and from 9am to 7pm on Saturdays, Sundays and Bank Holidays.

REGIONAL ADVICE

There are also excellent regional organisations that can help victims of forced marriage and the contact details for many of these can be found on the FMU website at www.fco.gov.uk/forcedmarriage. **The list of organisations detailed below is by no means exhaustive. Some additional contacts are provided to those contained in the Multi-Agency Practice Guidelines.**

Ashiana Project (London)

020 8539 0427

Ashiana Project (Sheffield)

0114 255 5740

Cleveland Choice Line (Cleveland)

0800 599 9365

Domestic Violence Helpline (Greater Manchester)

0161 636 7525

The Doli Project (Birmingham)

0845 658 1057

HALT (Help, Advice & the Law Team) (Leeds)

HALT works in Leeds offering legal advice, support and advocacy to women who have experienced domestic or sexual violence, including forced marriage victims.

0113 243 2632
Email: info@halt.org.uk

Hemat Gryffe Women's Aid (Glasgow)

0141 353 0859

Karma Nirvana Asian Men and Women's Project (Derby)

01332 604098
Also runs the Honour Network helpline: 0800 5999 247 (above)

Newham Asian Women's Project (London)

0208 472 0528

Roshni (Nottingham Asian Women's Aid)

0115 948 3450, 24 hour

INDEX

References are to page numbers.